Lights
TO
GUIDE
ME
HOME

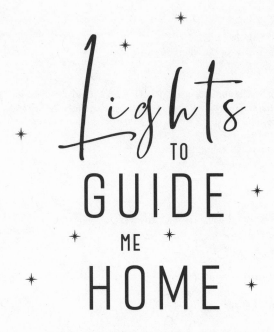

Lights TO GUIDE ME HOME

A Journey Off the Beaten Track in Life,
Love, Adventure and Parenting

MEGHAN J. WARD

FOREWORD BY CAROLINE VAN HEMERT

RMB

For information on purchasing bulk quantities of this book, or to obtain media
excerpts or invite the author to speak at an event, please visit rmbooks.com and
select the "Contact" tab.

RMB | Rocky Mountain Books Ltd.
rmbooks.com
@rmbooks
facebook.com/rmbooks

Cataloguing data available from Library and Archives Canada
ISBN 9781771603591 (hardcover)
ISBN 9781771603607 (electronic)

Design: Lara Minja, Lime Design

Printed and bound in Canada

We would like to also take this opportunity to acknowledge the traditional territories
upon which we live and work. In Calgary, Alberta, we acknowledge the Niitsítapi
(Blackfoot) and the people of the Treaty 7 region in Southern Alberta, which includes
the Siksika, the Piikuni, the Kainai, the Tsuut'ina, and the Stoney Nakoda First
Nations, including Chiniki, Bearpaw, and Wesley First Nations. The City of Calgary
is also home to Métis Nation of Alberta, Region III. In Victoria, British Columbia,
we acknowledge the traditional territories of the Lkwungen (Esquimalt and
Songhees), Malahat, Pacheedaht, Scia'new, T'Sou-ke, and W̱SÁNEĆ (Pauquachin,
Tsartlip, Tsawout, Tseycum) peoples.

We acknowledge the financial support of the Government of Canada through the
Canada Book Fund and the Canada Council for the Arts, and of the province of
British Columbia through the British Columbia Arts Council and the Book Publishing
Tax Credit.

FOR PAUL,

who saw an adventurous spirit in me and pulled it out.

FOR DOUG AND MEREDITH,

who gave me both roots and wings.

Every single choice is a chance to turn towards
the life you really want.

—MARTHA BECK, *The Way of Integrity*

Contents

Map xii–xiii
Foreword by Caroline Van Hemert xv
Author's Note xix

Prologue xxi
New Zealand, February 2014

PART 1 ✳ ONE BECOMES TWO

1 The Journey West **3**
Canada, Spring – Summer 2005

2 Adventure Is a Constant **26**
Caribbean, Fall 2007 – Winter 2008

3 Going Solo **49**
Costa Rica, Spring 2009 – Winter 2010

4 Into the Arctic **67**
Baffin Island, Spring 2011

5 Freedom amongst Giants **86**
Nepal, Fall 2011

PART 2 ✳ TWO BECOME THREE

6 The Next Great Adventure **111**
Canada, Fall 2012 – Summer 2013

7 Where I Begin **130**
New Zealand, Winter 2014

8   A World of Prospects **151**
    Niue and French Polynesia, Spring 2014

9   Growing Pains **172**
    Hawaii and Canada, Fall 2015 – Winter 2016

PART 3 ✦ THREE BECOME FOUR

10 Two Ships in the Night **197**
    Canada, Summer 2017 – Summer 2018

11 My Back to the Sea **214**
    Rapa Nui, Winter 2019

12 Moments of Awe **230**
    Ireland, Fall 2019

13 The Big Picture **249**
    Malta, Fall 2019

14 The Meaning of Home **256**
    Canada, Winter – Summer 2020

    Epilogue **283**
    Canada, July 2021

    Acknowledgements **289**
    Select Reading **293**
    About the Author **294**

MEGHAN'S JOURNEY

Off the Beaten Track

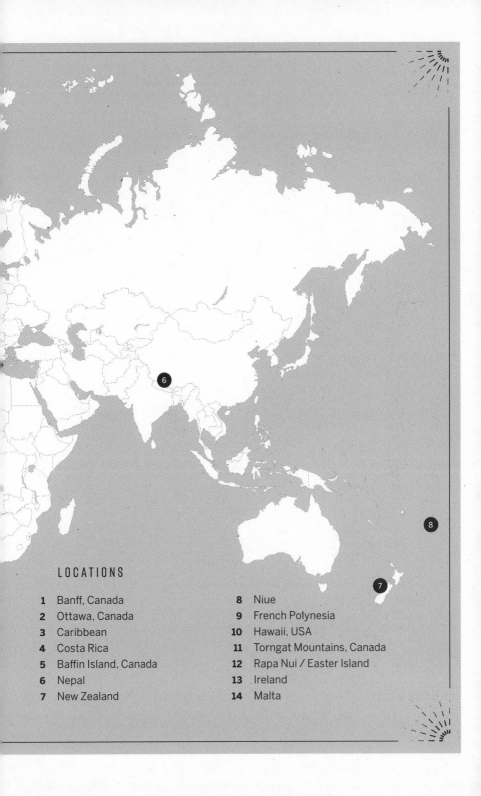

LOCATIONS

1 Banff, Canada
2 Ottawa, Canada
3 Caribbean
4 Costa Rica
5 Baffin Island, Canada
6 Nepal
7 New Zealand

8 Niue
9 French Polynesia
10 Hawaii, USA
11 Torngat Mountains, Canada
12 Rapa Nui / Easter Island
13 Ireland
14 Malta

FOREWORD

I first met Meghan Ward in the small town of Banff, Alberta, home of golden larches, world-class ski terrain and the acclaimed Banff Centre Mountain Film Festival. I had arrived from Alaska to speak at the festival; Meghan was participating as a magazine editor. We'd only been cursorily introduced online, but I immediately felt our connective pulse as fellow writers, travellers and mothers.

We convened on the Banff Centre campus at a cafe with sweeping views of the Bow Valley. Close by, festival banners featured images of climbers traversing steep granite walls and broad glaciers. Despite our shared backgrounds organizing expeditions much like the one featured in the photos, as parents of young children, meeting for coffee presented its own version of logistical gymnastics. Meghan and her husband were juggling two daughters and a busy schedule of travel and festival activities. I was briefly alone after a year of living off-grid and travelling by sailboat with a toddler and a preschooler. Solitude had become precious, to say the least. As a result, our quick coffee date was exactly that – *quick*. Just long enough to know we had lots more to chat about, someday.

I learned later that Meghan's path to the mountains had been a circuitous one, carrying her from a largely scripted existence to one defined by its blurred edges. Transitioning from a traditional lifestyle as a pastor's daughter in suburban Ontario to a freewheeling outdoor community in the Canadian Rockies, her coming of age meant repeatedly pushing against the grain. During her university days, on a whim and her father's recommendation, she set out for a summer job in Banff National Park. She arrived to find her new home, an isolated lodge, flanked by big mountains and even bigger dreams. Chasing opportunities to push deeper and further into her new-found backyard, she faced the parallel thrill and turmoil of venturing beyond familiar boundaries, including her own. Soon after, she met Paul Zizka, budding photographer and mountain aficionado unafraid of bucking convention. Alongside a partner whose passions carried him to stunning but far-flung destinations, Meghan came to crave a lifestyle both unorthodox and wild. Together, she and Paul would travel the world, discovering how discomfort – from scrubbing mould from a sleeping mat to hitchhiking in a downpour – can alternately test and nurture a relationship.

Unlike Meghan, I grew up in Alaska with adventure as part of my family history. As the daughter of parents whose journeys included a dogsled-assisted climb of North America's highest peak and ski-in cabin trips with their three young children in tow, I wasn't naive to backcountry travel. But for much of my childhood I had been a self-proclaimed bookworm, more content to read about others' exploits than chase my own. Only later would I return to my roots, falling back in love with the landscapes of my home and gravitating toward a career in wildlife biology. My own marriage was forged on the side of a remote arctic river, by way of a hand-built bark canoe and a desperately hungry summer. Though the specifics of our experiences differed, Meghan and I shared a desire to follow a less-travelled route, in life, love and, ultimately, parenting. Along the way, we each discovered it's not always easy to meld the elements of life we love most, especially when babies are involved.

At first glance, outdoor adventure and parenthood may not seem like obvious travel companions. But for those who've ventured into both realms, the parallels can be striking. There's an inherent humility required to survive a winter ski trip in the Arctic, just as there is to comfort a wailing child in an airport far from home. There's also much to be learned from our children, who teach us, in tiny increments and soul-shaking leaps, the value of being present. Through adventure and parenthood alike, a partnership demands compassion and balance, the yin and yang that Meghan depicts beautifully in her marriage to Paul.

For many years, my concept of adventure dwelled in the physical world, defined by objectives that were easy to name: from ultramarathons and high peaks to the taste of blood in the back of my throat as I pushed up against the edges of my body's limits. But fast forward to include many thousands of miles of wilderness travel and two young children and my terms have changed. Running a hundred miles in the desert or descending a frozen rope in the darkness still count. But so does carting a baby across seven time zones or surviving on an average of three hours of sleep, for months on end. There's a toughness that motherhood inspires, a kind of grit that at times seems akin to a superpower. Other times, it feels more like running uphill in a snowstorm. Or like chasing an infant through an ant-infested and pesticide-coated shack on Rapa Nui (Easter Island), which is exactly where Meghan and Paul found themselves on what was meant to be a trip of a lifetime. But without ants and jet lag and vomit-inducing heat, there would be no magical nights under the Southern Cross or 6-year-old insights about the fact of being human on Earth. And so the lesson goes – venture far, suffer occasionally and emerge richer for the experience. From trails in the Canadian Rockies to Irish castles and Polynesian beaches, Meghan's family has embraced travel as part of their "norm," combining the perks of Paul's photography career with destinations and cultures that have shaped their relationship to the world, and each other.

At every turn, we're faced with a choice: bend to others' expectations or knit a version of life's mitten that fits – as a traveller, mother, adventurer, scientist, writer or student of the physical and cultural landscapes we inhabit. Or perhaps all of them at once. *Lights to Guide Me Home* shares Meghan's particular journey, while honouring the ways in which we each select the threads of our own story.

—CAROLINE VAN HEMERT,
author of *The Sun Is a Compass:
My 4,000-Mile Journey into the Alaskan Wilds*

AUTHOR'S NOTE

Many of the events recorded in this book occurred at a time when I had no intention of writing a memoir-style book. To string together those memories, I read through my personal journals, consulted photographs, asked questions of people who were with me, conducted research on the destinations I had travelled in and even reviewed some of my previous posts online. All of these gave me the ingredients I needed to fill in the blanks. Any omissions are either intentional (they are not essential) or unintentional (I've forgotten altogether). For privacy, or where requested, I have changed the names of some individuals and places. However, there are no composite "characters" in this book.

Many parts of this book were also being written during the history-making wave of activities that made up the Black Lives Matter/BIPOC movement of May 2020. During that time, and ever since then, acknowledging my privilege as a woman of European descent began to take many new and surprising forms: the privileges of my upbringing, the privilege to go to university, the privilege of travelling, the privilege of having access to my personal history and the privilege to even be writing a book in the first place. This book is about my attempt to navigate the world I inhabit and, in a subtler way, it is also about navigating my privilege. I do this work because I get to, and I am deeply grateful for this.

Finally, this book was written in many places around the world but largely written in my home, which stands on Treaty 7 territory, the traditional lands of the Stoney Nakoda First Nations (Wesley, Chiniki and Bearspaw); the Blackfoot Confederacy (Piikani, Kainai and Siksika); the Tsuut'ina of the Dene People; the Métis Nation of Alberta, Region III; and, prior to the signing of Treaty 7, the Ktunaxa and Maskwacis People. I stand with Indigenous Peoples and strive to better understand what this country we call Canada was really built on.

For all the shoulders I don't even know I'm standing on, *thank you.*

Prologue

NEW ZEALAND, FEBRUARY 2014

The entire mountain filled the windowpane, which reached from floor to ceiling – a transparent wall to the alpine world of New Zealand's Aoraki/Mount Cook. Under different circumstances, I might have been climbing the peak, not sitting at its base staring at it through glass. But I wasn't here for mountaineering pursuits. This was the time for valley-bottom exploration, whatever my husband and I could pull off while we travelled to the other side of the world with a baby in our care. Still, I wondered what the world looked like from that summit, how it felt to crest the highest point.

The summit of Aoraki/Mount Cook doesn't rise sharply from the landscape, like the monolithic apex of the Matterhorn or the steep spire of South America's Cerro Torre. It is only half the size of the highest peaks in the Himalayas. But Aoraki/Mount Cook has an authoritative presence about it, looming over the Tasman and Hooker valleys like an emperor scanning the land. It is beautifully rugged, handsome and strong, enveloped in a robe of snow and ice. The mountain is also cloaked in history, which like that of any prominent peak is filled with stories of attempted climbs, first ascents, new routes and too many tragedies. It is the old stomping grounds of Sir Edmund Hillary, who with Tenzing Norgay so famously made the first ascent of Mount Everest in 1953. At the base of Aoraki/

Mount Cook the Sir Edmund Hillary Alpine Centre in the Hermitage Hotel proudly carries Hillary's name.

It is also where I was served one of the worst cups of drip coffee I've ever consumed, a veritable sin in a nation with as many coffee roasters, baristas and espresso drink varieties as sheep roaming the countryside. After five sleepless nights in a row, I needed coffee. This watered-down cup wasn't cutting it.

We'd set off from Twizel at sunrise for the 50-minute drive to the Hermitage Hotel, figuring we weren't going to sleep more anyway. This was our first hint at caffeine since the day before. The town's name actually means "a fork in the river," but to us it sounded like a chaotic place where nothing goes as planned. We spent the night trying to get a jet-lagged baby to settle down without the confines of a crib or travel bed, hopelessly wrestling her into a sleeping position on a metal-framed bunk bed that hadn't been replaced in 60 years. No one slept. Fortunately, the alpine centre had a highchair, giving us 20 minutes of rest from chasing a toddler who was on the verge of walking. With weak coffee crawling through our veins, Paul and I sat in a sparsely decorated dining room about as charming as an airport gate and stared out the window. Perhaps it felt sparse because we were the only ones sitting there so early in the morning. We took turns breaking off pieces of granola bar for the baby while we waited for the staff to offer a refill. It was a clear day when Aoraki/Mount Cook filled the glass in front of us, towering in the distance against the backdrop of a perfect blue sky.

At least we have a nice view of it, I thought. Deep down I wished we were in a position to at least go hiking in the mountains, to get away from the road and escape into the wilderness. For a moment I wanted to transport myself back to my pre-kid life when adventures were inhibited by only my own apprehensions, not the basic needs of a little human who seemed to be protesting at every opportunity.

"I'm going to go find the washroom," I said, pushing my chair away from the table.

"Sure, Meg," Paul said. "You'll know where to find me." He pointed to his mug and looked up with a sarcastic smile.

Just a few steps away from our table, a museum of old photographs, mountaineering memorabilia and information panels
lined the hallways, documenting the history of the region. I managed to glance at them, bleary-eyed, on my way to the washroom
and lamented the fact I didn't have the energy to take a closer look.
You'd normally be hard-pressed to find a person more satisfied
reading interpretive panels, staring at black and white images and
connecting the dots between her knowledge and learning something new. But without sleep in my body, I was barely functional.
Our baby, Maya, whom we'd hauled here all the way from Canada,
hadn't napped or slept well since we arrived in New Zealand four
days prior.

When I got to the washroom, I closed the door behind me and let
out a sigh of relief I didn't know I'd been holding in. Parents know
the bathroom offers momentary peace, at times immunity from
parental duties for just a few minutes so long as the child is being
supervised by someone else (otherwise they are right in there with
you). I took my time, scanning the fluorescent washroom lights and
surrendering to the quiet.

As I washed my hands, my thoughts wandered into a daydream. I
could hear the clanking of gear against a harness, feel the drag of the
rope behind me, see one foot stepping in front of the other on the
knife-edged ridge of the mountain – the one standing outside that
window of the hotel – as the sun cast the warm glow of sidelight on
our weathered faces.

I splashed my face and retraced my steps past the memorabilia
out into the sun-filled cafe.

* * *

"YOU READY TO GO?" Paul asked, about half an hour later. We'd
moved from the table to taking turns supervising Maya as she scurried around the hotel floor.

"Yes, let's get out of here," I said. I was ready to move on. It was
clear that our encounter with this famed mountain wouldn't get

any better by prolonging our visit. Plus, I was anticipating that the two-and-a-half-hour drive to Wānaka might be like all driving in New Zealand: always longer thanks to corkscrew turns that slow the speed limit every few minutes.

We collected our belongings, and as we left the building I gave a nod to the statue of Hillary that stood outside the alpine centre – his stature and signature tuft of hair forever captured in bronze as he looked up contemplatively at Aoraki/Mount Cook. To people like Paul and me, who revelled in mountaineering history, our visit to Hillary's namesake museum felt a bit like stepping into the Smithsonian Institution, reading nothing but the "Enter" sign on the door, asking for a cup of coffee and walking out again.

I quietly apologized to him. Or maybe it was to me. I felt I'd betrayed his legacy, and mine. That day, motherhood had deflated me beyond recognition – the climber in me was nowhere to be found, the adventurous spirit suppressed under a load of parental duties. Where had it gone?

At least she can't go anywhere, I thought, glancing at Maya in her car seat. She'd probably scream all the way to Wānaka, especially if we ran out of rice cakes, but at least I wasn't chasing her as she dirtied her knees crawling around a hotel floor.

I flopped down in the passenger seat and off we went to the next stop. Lake Pukaki shimmered in sunlight as we drove the length of it, away from its headwaters high up in the Southern Alps. A sense of serenity washed over me. In Wānaka, we had a friend to stay with and I'd track down a travel crib – the one thing I'd contemplated bringing and hadn't, which turned out to be a big mistake. We'd have four days to reset and recalibrate, as well as an internet connection to adjust our plans. It was clear we needed fewer stops and more time in them, and that our camping gear would go unused for the duration of our time in New Zealand.

But nothing could be done until we got to Wānaka. As we twisted our way through the rolling foothills, I soaked in the beauty of the gentle landscape. If the softening landscape was any indication of what our experience would be in this next lakeside town, I was satisfied leaving the height and ruggedness of Aoraki/ Mount Cook behind.

Surely, things would get better.

part one

ONE BECOMES TWO

I may not have gone where I intended to go,
but I think I have ended up
where I needed to be.

—DOUGLAS ADAMS

1
The Journey West

CANADA, SPRING-SUMMER 2005[1]

Darkness concealed the mountains as we approached the shores of Bow Lake, Alberta. The skies had opened a faucet and rain pounded the vehicle, sending water down the windshield while the wipers struggled to keep up. With my new boss at the wheel, I sat with Rachel in the back seat and held my breath in anticipation as we drove a long driveway toward the orange glow of a building: Num-Ti-Jah Lodge. The headlights flickered through a veil of mist and the car teetered side to side as it cautiously rolled through large potholes. I had been dreaming about this place for nearly a year, ever since I first got the idea of working in the mountains. Yet beyond that glow was a black canvas, not the vista I'd been envisioning.

We slowed down to pull in behind the lodge, and the moon glanced out from behind moving clouds to illuminate the sky. I cranked my neck to see out the back seat window and for the first time got a glimpse of the mountains I'd be waking up to every day. There they were, silhouetted against a silver sky, telling me, *you've arrived.*

---

1   All seasonal references are based on seasons in the northern hemisphere.

When I opened the car door, a chill rattled my body and I noticed the air was much colder than in Lake Louise, only 30 minutes away. We had been gaining elevation since we took a turn onto the Icefields Parkway. It was mid-May but felt like the tail end of winter – a far cry from the humidity and tulip-growing temperatures of Ottawa I'd left behind. As I ran from the car toward the warm lights of Num-Ti-Jah, I noticed we were surrounded by piles of snow that had melted into mounds of ice.

I nudged the lodge's back door open and smelled the age of the place wafting out into the cool air. Pine, wood fire smoke, a hint of must – I was instantly enamoured by it. The floors creaked as I tiptoed past the housekeeping area to the front desk, passing through a lounge where several taxidermy mounts looked down on a pool table. Old photographs of explorers, vibrant artwork of mountain landscapes and topographic maps, yellowed with age, piqued my curiosity. The history of the place oozed out of every crevice, every artifact, as I passed them by.

The property beckoned me to explore, but I was overcome by exhaustion. Rachel and I had flown from Ottawa that morning and in Calgary boarded a shuttle bound for Banff National Park. We didn't arrive at our final destination until just before midnight.

Lodge guests had long retired to their rooms, so in hushed voices we asked for some linens and towels that were allocated to staff members. We'd get our job orientations tomorrow. For now, it was time to pile into the beds in a room we were sharing on the backside of the staff laundry building – a pine-coloured A-frame, just a short walk from the lodge.

Our new home away from home.

∗ ∗ ∗

THE DREAM of a mountain adventure, one where we could work and play in the Canadian Rockies for the summer, had started nearly a year prior, in July 2004. Rachel, a childhood friend I knew from church, had recruited me to work with her window washing company, a franchise entrusted mainly to university students wanting to make some money and gain business skills. I had just completed my first year at Queen's University in Kingston, where I was pursuing a bachelor of arts (honours) in drama. I liked the idea of working with friends and being active outdoors as a summer job.

In the mornings our crew gathered at Rachel's house, filled our coffee mugs and hit the road in her red Volkswagen with tall ladders strapped to the roof with bungee cords. The work was routine: we would fill the buckets, add some dish soap, gear up with dry cloths and squeegees and get to washing and wiping. The challenge amidst the monotony of washing 400 houses that summer was to keep the jokes flying and to try to make every job more efficient than the last.

Perhaps all that time spent atop ladders made us eager to reach higher elevations. Or maybe it was spending an entire summer washing windows in the town where I grew up. But when my aunt and uncle came to Ottawa for my sister's wedding, they told me how much my cousin, Jen, was enjoying her time working at Num-Ti-Jah Lodge, on the shores of Bow Lake in Banff National Park – hence her absence from the wedding. I'd been in Banff with my family about five years prior but didn't remember seeing that lodge.

"She's been hiking mountains and backcountry camping almost every week," my aunt told me. From the sounds of it, Jen had fallen in love with the place.

My wheels started to turn. Maybe I could find my own adventure next summer? I wasn't sure why I wanted something different, only that I did.

"What do you think of me working in Kingston next summer?" I asked my dad a short time later. I decided to keep my objective closer to Ottawa, to my university town, so I wouldn't be pushing my luck. I was an adult but also a people pleaser. I still felt compelled to seek my parents' approval.

"I'd like to experience it in the summertime," I explained.

He didn't take long to respond.

"I'd rather you be on the other side of the country than be in Kingston...if you're not going to be home," he said with a wink.

He'd called my bluff. He'd suspected my underlying intentions; that I was really asking to move to the mountains next summer after what I'd heard from my aunt. He understood the call of the west himself, having worked in the mountains with a geologist in his late teens. He often talked about it with fondness. And it was clear: if I wasn't going to be home, he'd rather me be *far* away.

His response had sparked something in me. I could go to the mountains if I wanted to. I was 21 years old and still couldn't stand the idea of doing something that might disappoint my parents. My sisters and I had few consequences or strict rules growing up, yet my parents had achieved compliance by making it clear we should not disappoint them. Their reactions, combined with my own need to please, were enough to keep me in line almost all the time.

Yet my dad gave his approval without blinking an eye. My mother, normally one to support my ambitions, would do the same. Working out west would take me far away, but they had given me wings.

I ran the idea past Rachel. She was a friend but also known as the unofficial fourth sister in my family. If there was someone I was going to board a plane with and fly across the country, with no sense of what was about to unfold, it was her. She was keen to join me and we set our eyes on Num-Ti-Jah. They hired both of us to job share between the gift shop and housekeeping departments. And so our own journey west began.

* * *

MORNING CAME and my empty stomach reminded me of the two-hour time difference. It was a mix of butterflies, hunger, jet lag and adjustments with every step away from the bed. Looking out the window, I saw trees and the adjacent house, where the lodge innkeepers lived with their young daughter. We freshened up and Rachel and I walked across the parking lot to the back door of the kitchen where staff went to get their breakfast. Food soon became an afterthought when I saw a mountain rising like a pyramid in front of me, just beyond the red-roofed lodge. I'd been to the Rockies before and knew them to be impressive. Yet this mountain seemed colossal. Its beauty was overwhelming.

Wetness lingered in the air from the rain the night before, and high up on the mountain it had fallen as snow. Cliff bands had accumulated a powdery layer, like dust on a shelf, revealing depth and detail on the mountain's face. The sun was still low in the sky, casting a gentle sidelight onto the peak's east face.

In search of a better view, we walked around the lodge, past the dining room windows and Adirondack chairs that sat in front of large wooden beams supporting the front entryway. Somehow the mountain looked even taller from this vantage point as a low fog drifted over the still-frozen lake. *This – all of this – is home*, I thought. *The mountains, the lake, the lodge, the forest.*

The panorama of Bow Lake had a wonderful symmetry to it, with a triangular peak anchoring it all in the middle and moraines that fanned out from the bottom like an A-line skirt. I learned later it is Crowfoot Mountain, named after the glacier shaped like a crow's foot that brands the mountain's eastern flanks. That crow's foot has only two toes left – glacial recession has claimed the third – but tourists still stop in throngs at a nearby parking lot to photograph it. The water sources that melt and flow here are the headwaters of the Bow River, which eventually depart the Canadian Rockies and make a cross-country journey to empty into Hudson Bay. The Piikani (Blackfoot) call the river Makhabn, which means "river where bow reeds grow."

Being springtime, it would be a few weeks before we would see these reeds growing, the ones Indigenous Peoples used to make their bows.

Feeling curious, Rachel and I sauntered down to a rock beach by the lake, which was still covered in ice and snow. There, the marks of humanity were behind us, the lodge out of view. It was just us and the mountains, the view I had missed when we arrived in the dark the night before. It was magnificent. I breathed, deeply. Contentment washed over me.

I lingered for the view, but I also lingered to muster up some courage. I come from a family of mostly extroverts, and have learned how to act like one. But meeting new people was not on my list of favourite activities. I didn't know which person to put forward and, these days, "myself" wasn't a simple answer. Perhaps it was because the person many people knew me to be wasn't the person I felt like inside.

* * *

I WAS ONLY FIVE WEEKS OLD when my parents moved our family from Calgary to Kanata, a suburb of Ottawa, Ontario, after my dad took a new posting as the minister of a small Baptist church that was meeting in an elementary school. There were plans to build a new church building. The lot the church had chosen was a largely undeveloped plot of land, yet it wasn't entirely empty. On it stood a dilapidated farmhouse where my family lived before we could move into a home my parents had purchased nearby. For two months, they chased mice out of the kitchen while tending to three children under the age of 5.

Being a baby when we arrived, I never knew life without that church community or the friendly faces that smiled at me there. I also never knew life without a belief system built into my upbringing, as deeply ingrained as my ABC's. The church building felt like another home. We were a Sunday morning, multiple service, after-dinner devotionals, Thursday night youth group, and church choir kind of family.

My mother began a career as a high school music teacher when I entered grade school. She was busy enough as it was, but she was also committed to helping with numerous church activities and music programs. I noticed how often she took meals or muffins over to families who were having a hard time.

Service to others was always front and centre. And as a pastor's kid, I felt personally responsible for the vitality of the congregation.

I have two older sisters and the church felt like an older brother that protected and defended me, as though the building itself shielded me from the nuances and deviations of the real world. I could feel safe in the teachings that, at my young age, could allow

me to define my world in black and white. I believed wholeheartedly in what I was taught and, being a good student, aced every
question in Sunday school, perfected my memorization of Scripture
and marked up my Bible with notes, scribbles and highlighter like
I was studying for law school. We lived by the principles of the
Bible, as did my extended family, on both sides – at least from what
I could tell. I knew, without a shadow of a doubt, that I was expected to eventually marry a Christian man and raise children in the
faith – that to be "unequally yoked" would set me up for a lifetime
of unhappiness.

Beneath it all was an intense desire to please my family and
demonstrate my commitment to my faith in whatever ways I could.
As the pastor's daughter, I felt like all eyes were on me. The shame I
might feel if I didn't adhere to expectations would be unbearable.
I had witnessed church members who stood up in front of the whole
congregation to announce their sins and seek forgiveness from the
community. I would not be that person.

I thought the only thing that mattered was being flawless in the
eyes of God and others, especially my parents, whom I adored and
idolized. This meant both seeking perfection and hiding any wrong-
doing where I could. I drew the same conclusion about school too:
aim for the straight A's, seek perfection.

And then came a time when the foundation of my faith began to
crack. There was no singular, triggering event, no moment I could
pinpoint. But in my black and white world, this crack was a strip of
grey in the middle.

It began as a feeling that I'd lost my connection with God. Rather
oddly, a rift made its appearance during a month-long Leaders
in Training program at a Christian camp. It was nothing I could
explain, but something had shifted. My rational mind suddenly
couldn't make sense of some of the miracles of the Bible. I watched
a worship session as though I was on the outside of a fishbowl –
my fellow leaders waving their arms and belting out their lungs
with songs I knew intimately but suddenly couldn't utter without
feeling like a fake. I questioned some of the teachings that weren't

necessarily Biblical but interpreted the Bible in such a way that elevated those who did Christianity "right" and discredited those who didn't.

Why hadn't I seen all this before? I began to ask questions and wrote in my journal as I searched for answers. The grey expanded, almost imperceptibly, both within and on the exterior. I knew how to play the part, so even while questions swirled underneath, I could keep the status quo. The truth was I felt too ashamed to talk to anyone about it, particularly members of my family. I didn't even know *how* to talk to them about it.

About eight months later, I lost two loved ones in the span of a month – the first deaths I had to wrestle with as a teenager. Though as a pastor's family we had been regularly exposed to the dramas and traumas of others, I didn't feel equipped to deal with them myself. I had more questions, and few answers. One of the deaths had been by suicide. How could I even begin to make sense of that?

Over time, the questions that flooded in brought with them a deluge of doubts. The grey continued to expand. I finally asked myself the pivotal question: What do I *really* believe?

I moved away for university and with that distance I had an opportunity to gain some objectivity. I still went to church, frequently mingled with the Christian community and sought out other believers as housemates. But I also met new people, from all walks of life, who challenged my status quo. My academic interests opened up my eyes to topics and historical occurrences that had been largely left out of my education. I was angered and dismayed by what I learned, from the residential schools built to assimilate Indigenous Peoples into Canadian culture to issues highlighted by feminist perspectives on religion. Growing up, the church, and my parents, had taught me to have compassion for the poor, underprivileged and marginalized. Yet, as deeply as I felt the injustices I had so far been exposed to, I wasn't fully aware of the privilege that my white, middle-class status was affording me. I also hadn't recognized sexism for what it was. I didn't see the inequalities or wonder why I rarely saw a woman preaching. I had never questioned the system behind the roles that women played, and didn't play, within the church – and society. In a more general sense, it hadn't occurred to me to investigate the idea that women's voices had largely been left out of history. That just because it was in a history book didn't mean it was true.

I had swallowed things whole as a child and now I was choking on them.

I sat through university lectures on these topics with my jaw open, utterly dumbfounded. The veil had been lifted and I could no longer ignore the incongruous parts of my own belief system. I loved my community and feared the judgment that would arise if I spoke honestly about my doubts and confusion. I worried that I would break the bonds with my family held together by faith.

So, like an iceberg, the tip of me willingly took comfort in the company of other believers and put forth a "good girl" persona, while a mass of questions drifted under the surface below.

By the time second year was over, I was on my way to Bow Lake, running full throttle into a new experience, unaware I was also tip-toeing away from the life I'd known.

* * *

"READY TO EAT?" I asked Rachel, tearing my gaze from the view of Crowfoot Mountain. I was reluctant to leave but breakfast was waiting. So were the other employees we would be spending our entire summer with.

"Sure thing!" she said as she tied her light-brown hair into a low ponytail. I had always envied her hair, which dried into a natural wave – and her slender figure. She was just slightly shorter than me, but where she was long-waisted and slender I was built with a short torso, long legs and an athletic frame. We both had brown eyes and brown hair, though mine was darker and so fine it hung limply when I didn't take time to style it. People often assumed we were sisters, which had become a running joke between us.

After retrieving our food, Rachel and I carried our plates from the lodge kitchen to a picnic table outside. We were ready to dive into our egg breakfasts but first introduced ourselves to the only other co-worker sitting at the table, a dark-haired, goateed, mid-20s-looking guy wearing the standard lodge dining room uniform: a black button-up shirt, black pants, black shoes and a black apron. Like a dark horse. He seemed uninterested in meeting us, a bit aloof, but I didn't know him or how to read his body language. Maybe his mind was elsewhere?

Then he looked up, dark eyes briefly catching Rachel's, then mine, before he looked back down at his plate, dug his fork into his eggs and said, "Hey, I'm Paul."

* * *

AS SPRINGTIME PROGRESSED, the peaks awoke from their slumber. Snow in the alpine started to loosen, cascading down hundreds of metres in large avalanches that cracked and rumbled like thunder. More heat meant more snowmelt, and soon the creek that meandered near the lodge grew from a trickle to a quick-moving flow. Rabbit tracks imprinted the surface of the hard-packed snow. Birds chirped, welcoming the spring that had been delayed at the high elevations. And soon the tourists arrived and the lodge became animated by people curious about the taxidermy hanging in the dining room, admiring the building's architecture and taking a moment to soak up the jaw-dropping setting before tucking into the gift shop. In contrast with the quiet of housekeeping, the flurry of activity during my gift shop shifts kept me on my toes all day, with a cacophony of *dings* and clanking coming from the cash register while we explained to tourists which peaks outside were which and that the bear bells do not go *on* the bear.

Hiking season kicked off as the earth dried up. I joined staff on some excursions, soaking up each new place and the alpine world opening up around me. We didn't have a car, so each adventure began at the lodge or from a nearby trailhead if we were successful in our hitchhiking efforts. Paul, whom I'd met at breakfast that first day, mostly led the excursions. Standing at five foot ten inches, Paul had broad shoulders and a slight upper body. Yet his power was in his legs, which were strong and nimble, like a mountain goat's. He could move quickly and efficiently, even under a heavy pack. Though he'd been standoffish at first, he seemed happy to find people who wanted to hike. Rachel and I had no idea what we were doing, but we followed with smiles on our faces and that was enough. Along the way, Rachel and I cracked jokes – we had a talent for endless banter – and I was surprised we hadn't scared him off. Paul was quiet and a bit detached as he hiked ahead, guiding us to high points and along glacial moraines, stopping to take photos on his point-and-shoot camera. He lit up when he saw we'd hiked above the treeline.

"There's the Wapta Icefield," he said on an early-season hike to Helen Lake, stopping to point out the enormous white slab of ice that blanketed the mountains across the valley. You could only see a small piece of it, the Bow Glacier, from the lodge itself, but a new world was opening up to me the higher I went.

"And Mount Balfour, Gordon, Saint Nicholas, Rhondda, Baker," he said, pointing to peaks in sequence. His Québécois accent at times emphasized different syllables than I was accustomed to.

"Baker looks like a sleeping giant facing the sky. And that," he pointed again, "is the Waputik Icefield."

After a few weeks at the lodge, I was disappointed to learn that Paul's plan was to stay for the rest of the month before joining his girlfriend in Vancouver. I had developed friendships with other staff members, but I knew Paul was my ticket to getting outdoors and feeling more comfortable in the mountain environment. He had spent three years working seasonally at Bow Lake already and knew the area intimately. It was clear from the way the lodge innkeepers, Lee and Becky, talked about him that he was a respected staff member and that they'd miss him too.

Between micro-adventures with Rachel, Paul and various staff, life at Num-Ti-Jah felt a bit like a summer camp for adults, with late-night campfires after the kitchen closed down and elaborate games of capture the flag in the wooded area that bordered the staff road. This old dirt road spanned from the lodge, past several staff cabins, and down to the old horse corral area comprised of abandoned hitching posts and a few older cabins once used for horse equipment. Paul actually lived in the smaller of two cabins, a red-painted log building called the "Tack Shack." It was a tiny, battered structure heated only by a wood stove and also home to resident mice. Larger residents – a family of grizzlies – made a home out of the horse corral for several weeks of the year, attracted to the robust vegetation that had sprouted from decades of horse manure spread over the area. Parks Canada visited to brief the staff on living with bears and what to do in case of an encounter – a good thing considering how frequently staff encountered them, and how often we walked down that road with nothing but the moon to light the way.

There was a sense of camaraderie with the lodge staff, but also no shortage of dramas. Some of it originated at the lodge itself, some infiltrated from people's lives into the bubble that was life on the Icefields Parkway. Each day invited contrasting forces: the splendour of waking up to mist moving across the mountains, later followed by busloads of tourists we needed to feed in under an hour. The peacefulness of living so far from any other hint of civilization was mixed with the turbulence of having 30-plus "housemates" to deal with, for better or for worse.

The best remedy, I discovered, was to escape into the backcountry, away from the noise, whether an idling bus or the chatter in my head. Wherever my escapades took me, I'd eventually end up back at the lodge, often well after dark, beckoned home by the lamplight spilling out from the lodge's windows.

"Heeeey, bear!!" I'd yell, every few minutes. I wasn't keen on surprising a grizzly.

Otherwise, I'd hike the shoreline in silence, the ever-present Bow Lake breeze kissing my face, and walk in the direction of the glow.

* * *

MY FAMILY didn't hike and camp while I was growing up, but the serendipitous location of my childhood home exposed me to the wonders of nature early on. I also grew up in a time when unstructured, unsupervised outdoor play wasn't a planned event. We were simply outside, all the time. Our home in Kanata, which we moved into when I was 3 years old, backed onto a protected green space, and I made weekly trips into the trees, away from the rows of houses that made up our neighbourhood.

I'd frequently stop at a place in those woods, along the Old Quarry Trail, where the boardwalk provides a path through what becomes waist-high water and mud in springtime. There, the trees lining the trail gave way to marshland and open skies. But even in winter, when the trees were barren, the forest largely blocked the presence of the not-too-distant homes. Standing on that boardwalk one might never know the treed oasis sat just half a kilometre from a major road. As a child, the forest seemed enormous – a Narnia-like land where a matrix of trails beckoned me to explore.

This was not the typical suburban experience. Access to this network of paths – a part of Canada's Capital Greenbelt – sits just metres away from the front stoop where I'd tie my shoelaces before catching the bus to school. The Greenbelt comprises 20,000 hectares of protected green space, but our clan of siblings and neighbourhood kids mostly used the same single square kilometre. And that was all we needed.

In winter, we would strap our cross-country skis on just outside the garage, grab hold of old bamboo poles and ski across the cul-de-sac to reach the Trans Canada Trail. Once there, we'd set our skis in the tracks, if there were any, and swish our way through the woods, gliding under evergreen boughs weighted with snow and whacking them with ski poles as we went by. Whichever unsuspecting soul was skiing behind would be hit with a cascade of snow and pine needles. Other times we set off in our winter boots, skates slung around our necks, in search of the perfect rink. What we'd discover was nothing short of a miracle: smooth ice captured in pools deep in the woods, the marsh frozen solid. Weaving in and out of trees, we'd skate until our toes told us it was time to go home. The sun was often setting by the time we emerged from the woods, soaked through with snowmelt, guided home by the streetlights as they flickered on. My parents didn't need to ask where we'd been.

The transition to spring was never all that immediate. The temperature gradually rose and the snowbanks, once transformed into our elaborate cave system, thawed into slush. Then suddenly you'd hear it: birds chirping gleefully in the trees, the two-tone song of the blue jay heralding a new dawn. From our home we could see one bud in the woods turn to dozens, then hundreds. Simultaneously, Stony Swamp filled with water, the trees mirrored in the small lake forming around their trunks. We watched in anticipation for the water to subside. Its presence meant Old Quarry Trail was a muddy mess, sometimes covered in fallen trees the city had not yet cleared from wintertime. Still, we were often too eager to wait. If the smiles on our faces didn't reveal we'd snuck in an early trip to the woods, the mud caked to our rain boots certainly gave us away.

Summers spent on Old Quarry Trail made us feel like country-living kids. It didn't matter that the city – a planned community and high-tech boomtown – was one of the fastest growing in Canada, or that we were always just minutes away from a road or man-made structure. In the protection of those woods, we could play forever, interrupted only by lunch awaiting us back home or the sun saying farewell for the day. We rode our bikes through the trails, memorizing where the big hills met sharp turns and where rocks and roots jutted out along the path. We often stopped along the way, sidetracked by trails that led to imaginary worlds. Minutes turned to hours spent running, hiding, exploring. And when we weren't building forts, we were stopping halfway along our main trail of choice where there stood a magnificent climbing tree we couldn't say no to. Many years later, its lower branches would be sawed off. Perhaps a few of us had climbed too high.

Fall was unforgettable as the vibrant greens and fullness of summer gradually morphed into a canvas of colour. Maroon, red, orange, yellow — we could see the forest's transformation from our kitchen window. The maple trees kept track of time for us. The changing colours meant a new school year had started. It meant it was time to go for walks in the woods with my family, crunching leaves underfoot as we gazed up at the painted canopy.

In the low sun of autumn, I'd sneak in a few more bike rides through the woods. In the brisk air, I could see my breath and rays of light flickered through the trees, sunbeams suspended on air. I loved the feeling of flying as I rode the downhills, using the momentum to cruise through the flat sections, trying not to use my pedals. It was a game I played even when I was by myself, riding the trails for the sheer fun of it.

No matter if dinner would soon be on the table, in the stretch of trail just after a boardwalk I could never resist hopping off my bike to run my fingers along ripples embedded in the sandstone. The undulations told a story, though my young mind couldn't comprehend why or how they were there. I loved the feeling of the ridges gliding under my fingertips, wrinkled relics of the sea from when it washed over the place 450 million years ago. No matter how different the trail looked from one season to another, no matter if they lay under a metre of snow, the ripples were always there.

Each feature of Old Quarry Trail was etched in my mind, like waypoints of familiarity that kept me comfortable even as the forest darkened. The climbing tree, the curve to the right, the boardwalk, the ripples.

Even today I can close my eyes, picture them and find my way back home.

* * *

A MONTH INTO MY TIME at Num-Ti-Jah, I was anticipating my adventure quotient would go down after Paul's departure. I had other people to hike with, but he and I had covered a lot of ground together and I had enjoyed his company. He was also the unlikely life of the party, with surprising guitar skills and vocals that would take off in the night around the campfire. You might think the guy had loosened up with a beer or two, but he rarely drank. From James Brown to the Beatles, Radiohead and Bob Dylan, he played it all, often rocking his head, eyes closed in total immersion as he belted out a loud tenor. A stark contrast to his otherwise quiet, deliberate nature.

But one day we crossed paths outside the lodge and he casually mentioned he wasn't leaving.

"My girlfriend and I broke up," he said, without elaborating further. From beneath his long dining room apron I could see his feet shifting in the dirt of the parking lot.

I wasn't sure what to say. I was happy he was staying but surprised at the news.

"I'm sorry to hear that," I replied. "I've got to head in for my shift, but I'll catch up with you later?"

As I walked toward the gift shop I thought about how he hadn't even hinted that his relationship was on the rocks. But I wouldn't pry any further. I got the sense he liked to be left alone to deal with his troubles. Besides, I barely knew him. Why would he want to talk to me about it, anyway? With nowhere else to be, Paul decided he would stay at the lodge for the rest of the season. And whatever his feelings were about his relationship, it was clear he wanted to move on.

Whenever he could, Paul took off into the great outdoors, as though he was hiking off his worries. I was keen to continue exploring the area, so I always joined in when the invitation was extended to me. Though he was quiet on the trail, I enjoyed being with him and he seemed to enjoy being with me. As the summer progressed, I noticed he was going out of his way to come into the gift shop to ask me when my days off were. He was responsible for scheduling staff in the dining room and made every effort to coordinate his days off with mine. During my housekeeping shifts, I dropped by the dining room, often with a question in mind so it would seem like I was there for a purpose. ("How's that trail? If I go up that way, can I drop by that lake?") And from just outside the doorway I watched him serve tables. He moved between them at about the same pace as he hiked: swiftly, briskly, without pause. It was endearing and impressive.

I had never met anyone like him before. Yet it had only been a month since his breakup. I didn't expect either of us to make a move. It hadn't even crossed my mind that I might meet a man when I first set off for Bow Lake. When he told me in mid-July that he wanted to do a circumnavigation of Cirque Peak, I had no idea what that really meant, but I was game. "The trip will take us 15 kilometres, mostly off trail, into the Banff National Park wilderness," he said, running his finger along contour lines on a map. "If we go up this drainage and side valley, we should be able to connect with the basin behind Cirque Peak."

I nodded as he explained our route, but I couldn't envision what we were about to do.

"Let's bring our overnight gear, just in case," he said while folding the map and sliding it into a plastic sleeve.

"Sounds good!" I said, unsure of what I'd just signed up for.

My backpacking experience was minimal, as was my familiarity with sleeping in a tent far away from a road. I had a basic skill set after many summer weeks spent at camp sleeping in an A-frame shelter. Over the years I grew to love paddling and completed a number of flatwater canoe certifications. This took me on a few backcountry canoe trips where I slept in a tent and almost got eaten alive by mosquitoes that swarmed over the Great Lakes. In my last three years of high school, I also took an outdoor education course in which we embarked on hiking trips in Frontenac Provincial Park and whitewater canoe trips down the Madawaska River. We practised our paddling skills on the quarry lake near my high school, portaging our canoes across the overpass that runs over Highway 416 to get there. We also practised orienteering in the same stretch of greenbelt that hugged my childhood home. So my paddling skills were strong and I knew how to use a compass, but relying on my own two feet to get places was a relatively new experience for me. Especially with a big pack on my back.

The cumulative experiences were enough to give me confidence to set foot in more remote reaches of Banff National Park, but my naïveté took me even further.

Fortunately, my fitness was good. My equipment, however, was rudimentary, especially considering the harsh environment and physical output required to travel through the mountains. On my feet I wore low-ankled runners made for hard-packed trails, not scree-laden slopes. I'm not sure who sold me the pack, but I showed up in the mountains with a hostelling backpack that unzipped all the way around like a suitcase. It sat far away from my back, putting strain on my shoulders and threatening to bowl me over backwards. For a jacket I had a lightweight zip-up with no hood – something meant for running (again), not for sleet or cold. My only insulating layer was one I purchased in the lodge gift shop, thankfully a warm alpaca fleece. Otherwise, I had no down layer, no "last resort" barrier to the elements. If I was really cold, I supposed I could pull out my sleeping bag. I didn't consider the impracticalities of hiking wrapped in a body-size blanket that would absorb any moisture that hit it.

Early in the morning, we walked the highway until we reached a drainage that indicated it was time to venture into the backcountry. This would take us through a remote valley west of Cirque Peak to gain access behind it. As always, Paul hiked about 100 metres ahead of me, bushwhacking through the forest before picking his way easily up the bumpy, moss-filled, lower slopes. The distance between us made it hard to have a conversation, so I was often left with my own thoughts. That kind of mental tranquility was new to me and I was learning to appreciate it. But I wondered what Paul was thinking about while he hiked. When I'd manage to catch up, I'd ask him.

"I'm not thinking about much," he'd say. "Just observing what goes by. Soon we'll see the peaks on the other side of the highway."

I was raised in a family that kept up a frantic pace of life, with some occasional downtime to watch a movie with pizza. The idea of muting my thoughts and slowing down so I could observe the present moment was like breaking in a hiking boot. It felt uncomfortable at first. The only version I had known was prayer, and even that was kind of like talking.

When he crested a rocky ridge, Paul snapped some photos on his camera while he waited for me to catch up. From there we saw our only option was to down-climb the other side to reach the snow-filled basin below that would lead us around our objective. The girth of my backpack proved to be a challenge as it pressed me away from the rocks while I was down-climbing a chimney. Paul was beneath me, though. I figured I could lower my pack to him on the next ledge.

A half-metre gap stretched between the bottom of the pack and Paul's hands reaching up.

"Catch!" I yelled as I released my pack, but I'd failed to tell him I was about to let go.

The pack slid for a bit, then ricocheted off a protruding rock in the gulley, flipped well out of Paul's reach and down the mountainside. We watched as my backpack bounced and tumbled, eventually slowing down in the snow of the lower slopes, 200 metres beneath us. I should have been more worried, or angry with myself. Paul didn't seem rattled, but he was hard to read. Losing one's pack might create an unsafe situation, when warmth, food and water disappear out of sight. But I was lucky to catch up with my pack after climbing down the rest of the gulley and following the pack's trail where it skidded through the snow. At least it had proven its durability.

"Everything appears to be intact," I said to Paul, half-embarrassed, half-amused by my mistake.

"That's good news," he said, then he turned in the direction of Cirque Peak and plodded onwards.

A while later, I felt myself slowing down. It had been one of my longest days in the mountains, in unfamiliar territory, and keeping up with Paul, the mountain goat, was tiresome. When we began to post-hole in the snow at the backside of Cirque Peak, I felt frustrated but tried to keep a smile on my face. We hiked in silence. Paul kept trudging, I kept smiling as I sank to my thighs with each step, sugary snow seeping into my runners. *At least I can walk in his footsteps*, I thought. I appreciated his patience.

As the sun tucked behind the mountains to the west, it was obvious we'd be spending the night – we were travelling too slowly to make it back before nightfall. We found a bivy site on an unlikely patch of grass a bit higher up on the peak's shoulder. As we set up our site, I shook off the day's challenges. Whether he knew it or not, Paul had this way of pushing me outside my comfort zone, but so gently that I didn't notice until I was soaked through or watching my backpack bouncing down a mountain. He never made me feel bad about my inexperience. Those trials were behind me now. I was in dry clothes, had a hot meal cooking on the stove and the silence of the backcountry as my soundtrack. It was on my mind, however, that this would be the first time Paul and I shared a tent, just the two of us. I still wasn't certain what was happening between us, but there was *something*. Maybe it was just the rush of adrenaline from a kind of adventure I'd never had before. Or maybe it was a curiosity about this man whom I'd followed into the wilderness, fully trusting him to guide me safely around this mountain.

When it grew colder, we slithered into our sleeping bags and lay side by side. Our bodies didn't touch beyond the bags that were being seamed together in the confines of the small tent. I settled into a restful sleep but woke up in the morning with butterflies in my stomach that never seemed to stop fluttering.

Over breakfast we talked while we ate oatmeal and drank instant coffee, misty clouds swirling in the valley below before the heat of the sun burned them off. Paul grew up in Quebec City as the oldest of two boys, and his parents now lived in a small town near Lac Saint-Jean. His mother's family had been in Quebec for generations and his father's side was from the Czech Republic (hence Paul's last name, Zizka). Paul had taken a year off after CEGEP (Quebec's pre-university program) to live in England and Scotland and tour through Europe. He'd also taken a gap year halfway through his university degree to road-trip through the United States, spend a winter at Num-Ti-Jah Lodge and go backpacking through South America.

I hadn't even considered a gap year. Instead, I went straight into a four-year degree fresh out of high school, as if there was never an option. Paul had seen the options, though. His wanderlust was just as strong after graduation too.

"I finished my degree in Earth and ocean sciences at the University of Victoria and, days later, landed in Iceland for a 1400-kilometre unsupported double crossing of the island," he said. He spoke so nonchalantly about his expedition that he might as well have been talking about a trip to the grocery store. I took this as modesty on his part rather than a lack of excitement. Still, I could tell from the glimmer in his eyes that he lit up when he had the chance to talk about travelling.

After we packed up, we continued our circumnavigation, leaving our backpacks at Dolomite Pass to scramble up Cirque Peak and then picking them up again to zigzag down the endless switchbacks that lead to the highway. We walked the final kilometres to the lodge that day, unable to get a pick up from a passing vehicle. But no matter the discomfort, wet feet, the extra mileage and my inexperience, I returned with a smile. I was officially hooked on backcountry adventures. And, with Paul, a spark had been ignited.

✳ ✳ ✳

WHEN I LEFT OTTAWA that spring, I didn't know I had embarked on a voyage that would help me chart the rest of my life. For two decades I had been paddling the same river. I knew the motions; I knew how to paddle it. I knew how to please. I knew who to be. That is, until I landed in the mountains and my migration west brought me to a fork. A big one.

At first, I didn't even realize the current was pulling my canoe off course. But that backcountry trip around Cirque Peak with Paul pulled me into *his* current. I wanted to spend time with him, as much as possible. I couldn't quite comprehend what was happening when I gazed into his deep brown eyes, but they were magnetic. He was. Like the needle of my compass had landed on *him*.

Yet, in the back of my mind, I could already imagine my family's disapproval. *How would I explain this to them?* Paul, by default, was the forbidden fruit. He wasn't a Christian; he couldn't have even pretended to believe in God. He was raised with good values and to be a kind-hearted, respectful man. But in the world I came from, marrying a non-Christian was off limits. So why bother even starting a relationship with Paul? I felt at odds with myself but didn't even talk to Rachel about it, the one person who perhaps could have understood the two worlds I was bridging.

Yet my attraction to Paul was only a part of the transformation that was occurring.

As the months had gone by since my arrival at Num-Ti-Jah, I began to feel the 3500-kilometre distance between my mountain life and the place where I grew up – not only the physical location but also the landscape of my thoughts that had dominated my existence the previous 21 years. The vastness of the mountains had created a new sense of expansiveness for me to explore my internal musings, my questions about life, about God and religion, my own identity. I had permission to explore the messy, grey middle of things, even if I didn't venture there straight away. When I wanted to, I could question the rules that had previously governed my life. I needed to learn how to navigate this new terrain.

After work I'd often walk down to the rock beach where the creek filters into Bow Lake and spend time watching the sun move across the face of Crowfoot Mountain, relishing in the stillness. I was in unfamiliar territory in all senses of the word, as though my canoe were floating gently downstream with no one controlling it. There was a peacefulness in the floating, but uncertainty about what I might bump into. I still worried what my family would think of my relationship with Paul. But, for the first time, I felt like I was looking at myself from the outside in, and getting to know "Meghan" without a history already attached. Two decades worth of stories, habits, identities, assumptions and beliefs still had a hold on me, but right now the new current was stronger.

The life that met me in the mountains was unlike anything I'd expected. I floated through the rest of the summer as if it were an out-of-body experience. It was filled with adventures, the most unpredictable one being the shift in my internal space. The more I hiked, the more my heart shifted toward new things: mountains, a more open mind, Paul.

I wanted him even if my past told me I couldn't.

From that point forward, I was paddling into more unknowns, charting my way as I went instead of following a route laid out for me.

* * *

I KNEW MY CANOE had officially floated into uncharted territory the night Paul first kissed me, a week before I left to go back to university. It was nearing the end of summer and the nights were cold. The fire in the wood stove of Paul's cabin popped and crackled, with the odd spark flying out onto the metal hearth. Music was playing softly on the iPod Paul had hooked into a battery-operated speaker system. We were tucked in bed, his hand gently sliding across my abdomen. I couldn't see him, except when the warm glow from the fire flickered brightly enough. I closed my eyes and that's when he planted a kiss on my lips. I didn't stop him.

Saying goodbye to Paul felt like I was leaving a piece of my soul behind. It took all my strength to walk away from him, this gorgeous man sitting on a hitching post by the old horse corral. The mountains encircling us required their own goodbyes. They were now familiar to me, like old friends. The wilderness had become my sanctuary. But I had to catch my plane back to Ontario to start my next year at school. Paul couldn't follow me down the road to the car; if he had, I might not have had the courage to leave. When I turned back for one last glance, his eyes were filled with tears.

He'd remain at Num-Ti-Jah while I started my third year at Queen's. A whole country and a world of differences lay between us until we could find the opportunity to reunite.

We departed without a sense of where "we" were going. The map was blank, ready for us to fill it in. The big question was: Would we end up in the same canoe?

2
Adventure Is a Constant

Camping in the Caribbean sounded like fun until I realized how different it was from camping in the mountains. Cool alpine air can be conducive to a great sleep. But now we had swapped that coolness for tropical air; the unabating humidity combined with body heat to turn our tent into a steam room. Sleeping tent-free under the stars would have been an easy solution if it were not for the sandflies and mystery bugs that would visit all night long. So, instead of snuggling inside my sleeping bag, I lay uncovered, on top of my sleeping mat, ensuring no limbs or digits were touching. Add in the exuberant chorus of birds at dusk and dawn and the experience seemed more like passing the dark hours listening to nature's soundtrack.

Sleep or no sleep, it was a cost-effective way to explore some of the more expensive Caribbean islands.

Paul and I left Canada a few days into the new year, and after a brief stay in a hotel in St. John's, Antigua, we moved into our tent on the island of Virgin Gorda – an island famously known for its yacht clubs and luxury villas. Our guidebook mentioned that a guy named Verne was hoping to establish a campground on his property, and we had managed to connect with him prior to our departure. The campground did not yet exist and so he offered us a tent-sized rectangle of patchy grass sprouting from hard-packed mud. There we pitched our two-person tent about 20 metres from the ocean. Fifty metres in the opposite direction sat "The Jumbie Shack," Verne's other business at the time: an open-air club where he'd pump dance tunes into the late-night hours and a gaggle of locals would gather for a drink.

One such character, Brigadier, wore a sailor's cap and talked with an exaggerated accent that left me wondering what he was saying most of the time. But when he laughed, we laughed, not knowing what was so funny except that he thought it was. After a long day of travel, we were knackered but drawn, nonetheless, to that makeshift club at the end of a long dirt road to hang out with Verne and his buddies. They talked small island politics, but they also gave us the inside scoop, like this snorkelling spot a short rowboat ride from where we'd pitched our tent.

The next day, we tracked down Verne's white, somewhat battered boat by the water's edge. Before we carried it to the water, Paul took out his DSLR camera to photograph the boat sitting by the glistening bay. He enjoyed documenting his experiences and, for a few years now, had put more intention and creativity into his compositions. He'd retired his 12-megapixel point-and-shoot camera the year before, so this was his first trip abroad with the real deal.

Paul packed up his gear and we paddled Verne's boat across the crystal-clear water of Little Bay, traversing the lagoon to a stretch of land on the other side. Not wanting to risk being left stranded, we pulled the boat a safe distance onto the sandy shore, then set off for the shallow water. It was there Paul showed me how to use a snorkel.

"You put your face in the water and breathe through the tube," he said, adjusting his goggle strap. "Try to stay relaxed. It's salt water – you'll float!"

I panicked a bit before the act of breathing through the tube felt more natural and rhythmic. Once it did, time stood still as I gazed at the underwater world for the first time in my life. The sea was the sky, and the fish like a deconstructed rainbow – orange, purple, yellow, red and green swimming against an impossibly blue backdrop. I'd come up for a break, take off my mask and stare at the palm trees circling the lagoon, the blue sky showing no hint of rain. I basked in the warmth, in the escape from it all, and thought of my family back in Ontario, experiencing one of the heaviest snowfalls in years. I thought of my oldest sister as she awaited her first-born to make his or her appearance, the first grandchild for my parents. I thought of where I'd normally be in the month of January. Staring at wild sea life through a snorkel while the sun baked my backside felt like a dream compared to the winters I spent watching snow fall past the windows of Queen's University's Stauffer Library.

I wondered if I was even the same girl anymore as I swam, blissfully, through foreign waters. A younger Meghan never would have set off on a trip with a boyfriend. She would have looked down on the idea. To my church community, it might have seemed scandalous, even sinful. I felt self-conscious knowing how my choices might be perceived, but by now I was a bit more used to that. I had broken the dam when I told my family about Paul, by email – I couldn't muster the courage to do it in person. To date, they had been unsure but kind about our relationship. Here in the Caribbean, it felt right to be following my heart, to be swimming amongst these fish with my boyfriend.

We pulled the boat ashore back at Verne's place, carefully placing the oars inside it. Skin wet and salty from our time in the water, we dried off in the sunlight and recounted the splendour of snorkelling, just the two of us, the small bay ours to explore as freely as fish. When night fell, we left our tent when we heard talking from the club, knowing our band of locals had arrived. That night, Brigadier arrived with a fresh catch of the day and he offered some to us. We offered him money, but he wouldn't accept it. Fork flaking through the freshest fish I've ever eaten, I ate as slowly as I could. Until that point, I wasn't into eating fish, perhaps because I grew up far from the ocean. But Brigadier's mahi mahi won me over. He served it grilled without marinade, with a dollop of ketchup and wedge of lime on the side.

We ate our fish and laughed as the men told inside jokes, made even more obscure by their thick Caribbean accents. Time ticked by and I was aware that my chance for a decent night's sleep was dissipating. Paul had plans to leave our site at 5:00 a.m. to walk to the Baths, a famous snorkelling site about 13 kilometres away. But I was enjoying this conversation too much to excuse myself. This was home for these people: the seaside, the fresh catch, the island gossip, the camaraderie. And I was like a fly on the wall or, perhaps more fitting, like fish in the lagoon – swimming, searching, observing.

* * *

I DIDN'T TAKE IT for granted that I had this winter off from school or studies. When the calendar had flipped to September, it was the first time since kindergarten that I wasn't loading my backpack with notebooks, hooking it over my shoulder and heading into a classroom. While many of my friends had returned to campus for teacher's college or a master's program, I was done with formal education, opting to spend the next year exploring my options.

The decision had surprised me. Yet it had been an easy one to make. Applying for a master's program had somehow slipped past my radar, and by the time I got around to downloading program information and figuring out my next steps I discovered I'd already missed the funding deadlines. I took it as a sign. I, the compulsive, careful planner, had missed the boat, yet it didn't bother me. I felt relief. I felt freedom. For the first time ever, I had a truly open slate ahead of me, and no bell ringing me back into the classroom.

The summer after graduating from university had taken me back to the mountains, back to Num-Ti-Jah for the third time and back to Paul. For the previous few years, Paul and I had established a pattern: while I finished up my undergraduate degree, Paul split his time between visiting his family in Quebec and travelling abroad before we'd meet up in the mountains. We'd take our turns visiting each other, braving the 13 hours of buses, bland highways and dingy terminals that spanned between us, then repeating it in reverse when it was time to go home.

At times, our experiences felt polarizing – me scribbling away with class notes, quizzes and essays, while he was off exploring ancient churches and remote mountains in Ethiopia or sipping a Fanta with local school kids in Tonga. But he is older, by five years, and had already paid his university dues. I couldn't hold it against him. While he trotted the globe, my wanderlust outgrew the bubble I was living in on the university campus. I could sense it was about to burst, perhaps one more reason why a postgraduate program was not in the cards. The school-free, open slate was too tantalizing to resist.

I also didn't feel compelled to find a career-oriented job. In fact, I resisted the idea, wanting to keep freedom within my grasp. My degree in drama certainly wasn't a shoo-in for employment straight out of school, nor was my minor in global development studies. Seeing how Paul had been living his life the past few years had opened a door for me – a way out of what I even expected for myself.

While the previous few years had been a pattern, this year, when I left Num-Ti-Jah, I could do anything I wanted. Paul and I decided to return to eastern Canada for the winter months to spend time with our families. But something had shifted for Paul and he was eager to make a more permanent move to the mountains. He had his sights set on the town of Banff. I was unsure of where I wanted to end up.

We were used to being apart, so it wasn't a given that we'd be together for a move back to the mountains either. I had no one, nothing, expecting me to be anywhere. I felt like a bird out of a cage, excitedly flapping its wings and unsure of which direction to start flying. The freedom was disorienting, and while I looked for my bearings there was a part of me that didn't want a compass.

* * *

AFTER THAT LAST SUMMER at Num-Ti-Jah Lodge, before we began to drive east, Paul and I spent a quick stint living with friends in Banff so we could experience the legendary Banff Centre Mountain Film Festival. It was everything we'd dreamed of: days of speakers, films and rubbing shoulders with the world's greatest adventurers. We left the mountains, inspiration oozing out of our pores. Paul dropped me off at my parents' place in Ottawa before continuing on to Quebec. Our plan was to reunite in the new year for a trip abroad – our first together – before deciding whether or not we would move back to the mountains.

As we drove east, the flat plains of the Prairies and endless forests of Ontario guiding us to our roots, we talked about the places our wings could carry us. The Caribbean was calling, and in the previous weeks we'd read the entire *Lonely Planet* book and rated our favourite islands. We'd narrowed it down to seven: Antigua, Sint Maarten, Saba, Dominica, Tortola, Anegada and Virgin Gorda – the last three in the British Virgin Islands. I relished the prospect of abandoning a snowy Canadian winter to snorkel crystal blue seas and bask in the sunshine of perfectly white, sandy beaches. We'd be backpacking and camping, and eating tuna out of resealable packets, but travelling when I would normally be in school was a luxury in itself.

I'd previously only travelled abroad to Trinidad, to work in a camp, and twice to Mexico to work in a home for needy children – all part of various Christian programs. I was entirely new to the idea of backpacking for pleasure.

Three fortunate incidents freed me from any financial responsibilities that winter. The first was my parents' forethought to purchase Canada Savings Bonds back when I was very young, which when cashed in over 20 years later amounted to enough money to carry me into my post-university life. The second was an award I'd won at the convocation I missed on purpose, opting out of the gown and mortarboard in favour of more time spent wearing a waterproof jacket and helmet in the mountains. Through a crackling phone call on the payphone at Num-Ti-Jah, I learned from school administrators that the Rod Robertson Prize for Dramatic Literature and Theatre History came with money – not much, but enough to pay for my island-hopping. Third, I could stay with my parents for a few months, rent-free, while Paul did the same in Quebec.

With surprise money in the bank, and my parents' roof over my head, I spent the next two and a half months exploring the one faint trail that had piqued my interest: writing. In the previous year I'd had a number of people, including two of my professors, ask me if I considered pursuing work in the fields of writing or editing. I had not. But feeling lost as I floated in the black abyss of options, it might have taken just one of those people to convince me to put pen to paper, or fingers to keyboard, more often. *But what kind of writing? And how do you become a "writer"?* I was full of questions. I didn't have my hands full with anything else, so I started to research.

Newspaper writing was of no appeal to me, but my affinity for magazines, particularly in the travel genre, had existed since grade school. As a kid I would sit on an old wooden desk in the dim lights of the basement, wrap myself in a blanket to take the edge off the musty subterranean air, and leaf through my dad's prized collection of *National Geographic*. When I was finished with one issue, I would stand on a chair to reach the magazines neatly arranged on shelves and finger through them, my head tilted sideways so I could scan the spines without going cross-eyed. Yellow and perfect-bound, each was similarly printed with a few phrases that captured what was printed inside: *Fiji. Mount Saint Helens. The Titanic. Wild Tigers. Saturn.* Each one was a portal into a world I had yet to encounter, each concept so galvanizing I lost hours to dreaming and wondering. The stories ignited my fascination with history. I turned the glossy pages, pored over photographs, read until I felt dizzy and absorbed information until I was waterlogged with new learning. I'd have been at school all week long and this was my idea of weekend fun.

Wanderlust burning within me, for now I burrowed my feet into familiarity and cozied up inside the house where I grew up. I needed to plot my next steps. Sitting at the desk in my sister's childhood room, now my self-appointed office, I watched the first snowflakes of winter flutter down and fall past the bedroom window. It felt like a snow globe and I was trapped, not all that unhappily, inside.

Because comfort is, well, comfortable. We can go our whole lives trying to pad our existence with predictability. I needed something strong or sharp to break that glass, and maybe words would get me there. I had the will but didn't have the tools.

Maybe I can travel and write about it for magazines, I thought. It was as cliché as it was naive. I had no idea where to start. So I typed "how to become a freelance writer" in Google and scoured the hits. Articles talked about query letters and editorial calendars, timelines, and nut graphs. I made an elaborate wish list of publications and organized them in a spreadsheet to help me track my pitches. Dozens of queries left my computer by way of emails bound for the overflowing inboxes of editors at magazines like *Outpost* and *Explore.* Surely someone would take interest in my upcoming trip to the Caribbean and I'd see my freelance career take flight.

I never heard back. Disappointed, but not deterred, we departed in early January for the turquoise seas.

* * *

THE SKIES UNLEASHED hurricane-like rains shortly after we disembarked from the ferry to Tortola. After Virgin Gorda, we had three cloudless days on Anegada and departed that island in sunshine. By the time we landed on Tortola, the sun was shrouded by storm clouds. The rain was coming down hard when we left the grocery store, where we were restocking our food stores for camping. Standing sideways under the shelter of the store, our arms loaded with bags, we kept our bodies turned to keep our backpacks from getting soaked. We had no idea how we'd get to our campsite at Brewers Bay. So we leaned on our usual tactic of making no plans, hoping things worked themselves out. They usually did.

"Are you heading to Brewers Bay?" a man's voice called through the rain.

At first I wondered how he'd guessed, but then realized we probably looked like the kind of people who would be camping in the Caribbean. Two unwashed Canadians with 60-litre backpacks, one smaller backpack hooked over our shoulders (our carry-ons) and arms full of groceries were probably not headed to a resort.

"Yeah, we are, actually!" I responded.

His name was Ryan and he had a rental car. Recognizing our conundrum more than we did, he offered us a ride to the campground, where he was also staying. Public transport, he said, wasn't an option and we'd be forking out 30 dollars for a taxi. Hitching a ride was the only way to save us from walking two hours from Road Town to Brewers Bay.

Our no-plan plan had worked.

"It's a bit tight in the car," Ryan said, as we approached his vehicle.

When he opened the trunk, however, it was empty. I was confused but didn't say anything. We filled the trunk with our backpacks and groceries then slammed it shut. I walked around to hop in the front seat.

"This door," Ryan said, pointing to the back seat on the other side of the car. I walked around and noticed the car was indeed full. A woman sat up front.

"This is Anna," Ryan said.

Anna waved with a friendly smile.

"And this is Mila," Ryan said, pointing to his 3-year-old daughter sitting in the back seat. It was dark in the car, but I could see her head of white-blond curls shining in the street lamp.

As we drove the winding roads through the dark night, we went over the basics with the young family. They were from Nantucket Island, Massachusetts, and had rented an apartment for a few weeks on Tortola. Until their place became available, they were camping at Brewers Bay. They asked us where else we'd been in the Caribbean and what our plans were. When they asked me where I was from, I paused for a moment before responding:

"I grew up in Ottawa, our nation's capital," I said. "But I've been living in Kingston for the past four years and spending my summers in Alberta. I'm not really sure where I'll land when I go back to Canada."

"Sometimes it's nice to see an open road ahead," Anna said. That's exactly what I was thinking too.

* * *

WHEN WE ARRIVED, Ryan showed us an available site. We couldn't see much in the darkness, but the rain had subsided, giving us enough time to pitch our tent on the sand. I had never camped on sand before. Ryan warned us about the biting sandflies then disappeared into the darkness to rejoin his family at their tent trailer. We finished pitching then sauntered the 20 metres that stretched between our new little home and the edge of the bay. Everything felt wet and the air was tolerable – still warm and humid, yet the deluge had cooled things down. We found two plastic chairs by the water that didn't seem to have an owner. We sat down and chatted until the stars came out, lights twinkling against an onyx sky. Darkness was our cue to get some sleep.

Morning came and the brightest of blues met my eyes when I peeked through the tent flap. Stepping out, I got my bearings in the daylight. The Brewers Bay campground, it turned out, was a tranquil place, mostly unkempt, right on the edge of the water. Driftwood and low, prickly plants interrupted the sandy beach, but camping on any beach felt like extravagance to me.

I walked to the edge of the water, mindful of the sandflies that were waking up, and took in the quiet, the expanse of blue before me, and the sea air filling my lungs. Quiet, I'd discovered, was necessary to my sanity. The silent hikes with Paul had instilled that in me. When I found it, when I couldn't hear anything but nature and my own rhythmic breaths, I would sink into it like a comfortable armchair and absorb it, as if I was filling up on quiet until the next time I came across it. Lost in the silence, I closed my eyes and breathed. It was bliss until a high-pitched shriek resounded across the bay.

It was Mila playing on the beach. She was bare-bummed, basking in the warmth of the early morning sunlight hitting us from behind. She would run to the water's edge before scurrying back under a large palm tree. I looked on as she picked up coconuts and dumped them back in the water, her legs caked with dirt and dried leaves from running into the ocean and then rolling around on the earth.

She intrigued me, this little girl from Massachusetts traipsing around on foreign soil without a care in the world. Later that day, we sat with Ryan and Anna while Mila played again on the beach. We mentioned we had not encountered people in our lives back home who travelled off the beaten track with their kids.

As we talked, they offered their perspectives on alternative parenting practices. Terms like *free-range parenting, organic* and *Montessori schooling* came up. They seemed to have an opinion about everything mainstream and stood by their own version, usually its opposite. Their perspectives on parenting were a breath of fresh air.

"We like to see the world and figure it's a great education for Mila, even though she's so young," Anna said. "I believe kids still absorb these experiences, even when they can't remember them."

"That's why we've rented a house here for a few weeks," Ryan added. "Mila will grow up having a sense that life is larger than our existence on Nantucket Island."

I had lived a happy, suburban life with everything I could have ever wanted *and* I'd developed an appetite for travel nonetheless. So had Paul. But this was the first time I realized I could create a different kind of upbringing, if I wanted to, should I have my own children.

The blinders were off now. Out of the corner of my eye I saw two little butt cheeks running full tilt for the shallow water as the sun rose higher in the sky.

* * *

"WHY ARE WE PUSHING our bikes up here again?" I asked through laboured breaths and gritted teeth. My arms were outstretched behind the handlebars as if the bike would start rolling back down the hill. Unlike nearby Anegada, a stunted uplift of coral and limestone as flat as a frisbee, Tortola's topography is volcanic in origin. Read: mountainous.

The noonday sun was beginning to beat down on us. *If we're walking anyway, maybe we should just ditch the bikes lower down on the mountain*, I thought. It would mean walking back down to them, but I wasn't sure how much we'd be biking back down these steep, twisted roads as cars skirted around us.

But it was clear Paul was determined to bring the bikes as high up this mountain road as we could and enjoy the ride back down. So we trudged along and pushed our escape vehicles, inching our way up the hot pavement to the boundary of Tortola's Sage Mountain National Park. Near the park gates we leaned our rental bikes against a fence and hoped they'd be there when we returned. We paid our dues then hit the trail for the highest point in the Virgin Islands, all 523 metres of Sage Mountain. By most standards, it's more of a hill. But we'd left from Brewers Bay, where ocean waves lapped the beach near our tent, thus pushing our bikes for seven kilometres from sea level up nearly half a kilometre of vertical relief.

The physical output wasn't *that* great, but mentally I was struggling. I'd already learned that keeping up with Paul means not wasting energy even questioning the purpose behind a mission. Stopping to think means falling behind. After spending a few summers chasing him on hikes and scrambles around the Rockies, I'd learned to just put my head down and eat on the go, lest I spend the day watching him move from 200 metres away. He didn't intend to take off like a rocket; he was just that quick and unrelenting in his natural pace. Something new I learned about him in the Caribbean, however, is that he wanted to walk *everywhere*, even if it meant rising at 4:00 a.m. or walking under the searing hot sun. My subtle suggestions to tone down the adventure quotient often fell on deaf ears. Or maybe he heard me and it was his way of pushing me outside my comfort zone.

It didn't matter because I learned to go along with him. If it wasn't the glint in his eyes, it was the excitement vibrating from his body that told me to *just do it*. Life is short. *Why not push a bike up a mountain just for a ride back down?*

Our sights on the summit, we hiked the muddy trail, soaking our runners through to our socks as we slipped on slick tree roots and tiptoed through deep puddles. Trapped under the canopy of white cedar and mahogany, the cooler air and smells wafting from the trees felt rejuvenating as steam rose from my scalp. We couldn't see out, but we gawked at the twisting trees that welcomed us up the trail, moss carpeting the undergrowth. There wasn't much to see beyond an arm's length, but soon we'd reach the highest point and, as advertised, the 360-degree views would be revealed.

We didn't realize we'd reached the summit until the trail started to dip back down on the other side. We were encircled by armies of trees, as the forest regeneration program had succeeded in growing the forest so fully that it blocked the promised views completely. Beyond the wall of green lay the other Virgin Islands, the Caribbean Sea and the Atlantic. Through gaps in the leaves we could see hints of blue. Maybe it was the sea? Maybe the sky. We would never know.

We looked at each other and laughed. Inside, I let out a deep sigh. Is that not what adventure is all about? Setting off without *any* guarantees?

As it turned out, Paul's insistence that we push our bikes up the mountain was more than an adventure in itself. It was an insurance plan, and I loved him for it. Our summit views had failed us, but our bikes awaited us just outside the national park gates. We hopped on, pointed the bikes downhill, then left our feet idle for the next hour as the scenery zoomed past. My hands went numb as I gripped the brakes, my biggest concerns being that either I'd flip over my handlebars on the steep descent, that my brakes would give out and I'd lose control or that I'd pop a tire and go back to walking my bike. The rental company hadn't given us patch kits, but at least we had helmets.

With no shoulder, we dodged cars and gingerly followed the guardrail around sharp turns, the end of which disappeared into the overgrowth of trees and bushes that lined the road. But the stress was no match for the sea of turquoise in the distance that made my heart skip a beat, or the exhilaration of cruising down a winding road, the wind blowing through my hair, armed with the knowledge that I was reaping the benefits of having pushed the bike up the mountain in the first place.

As we pulled into Brewers Bay I could now confirm that one thing about Paul was certain: if I stayed with him, adventure would be a constant.

* * *

"WHERE ARE YOU HEADING? Can we give you a lift?" A woman's voice pierced through the crowd of taxi drivers haggling with us at the airport. From her accent I figured she was American.

We had just landed on Dominica a few minutes prior and didn't quite have our bearings yet. We knew where we were staying: the 3 Rivers Eco Lodge. But without a sense of where it was on the island and how far away, we couldn't gauge whether the rates the taxi drivers were yelling at us were reasonable.

Turning toward the voice, I saw the woman and approached her so I didn't need to yell.

"Do you know where 3 Rivers is?" I asked.

"Yes, yes, it's on the way to our place. Hop in!" she said, pointing to her Jeep parked not too far from the small terminal. Behind her stood a dark-skinned man wearing a colourful shirt and an equally vibrant smile.

"Yes, it's no problem!" he said.

I looked at their Jeep, clean as a whistle, and looked at Paul as if to ask, *should we?* We were sweaty and stinky; our backpacks were filthy. That seemed obvious to this woman, however, and I figured she wouldn't have offered if she were concerned we'd make a mess. Paul met my gaze and nodded.

"Okay, thanks so much!" I said.

After loading our packs into their trunk, we slid into the back seat and introduced ourselves.

"Nice to meet you," said the woman. "I'm Sheila. And this is Julius."

As we set off, we struck up a conversation with the couple, who turned out to be building an eco resort in Rosalie Bay, not far from where we'd be staying. She was from the United States, he was native to Dominica and the resort they were building together was a labour of love. As the scenery whizzed by, we could see rainforest on both sides, with twisting vines, lush foliage and a canopy that barely let the light in. Everything dripped with moisture from a late-afternoon rain. After some time chit-chatting about where we'd been on our trip so far, and what we were looking forward to seeing in Dominica, the conversation dwindled. It was getting late and I was starting to feel hunger pangs settling in. As the light of the day faded, I closed my eyes and rested.

I didn't sleep and instead reflected on the week we'd just had on Saba. That island was like nothing we'd seen in the Caribbean – or anywhere else for that matter. Out of all the islands we visited, Saba and Dominica fit Paul's criteria for travel to places that were lesser known, even mystical. So after our stint snorkelling the seas off the British Virgin Islands, we left the quintessential Caribbean behind – at least the kind we'd been able to picture before we saw it for ourselves – and ventured into obscure territory. We had split our month of backpacking based on the square mileage of each island, which amounted to a week on Saba and nine days on Dominica.

Saba was spellbinding. The volcanic terrain there reached a height of 887 metres at the summit of Mount Scenery, from which the rest of the island fell away, covered in lush vegetation. An unlikely road wound through the island's folds, like a winding river of concrete. The houses had matching colours with white exteriors, red roofs and either green, white or red shutters on the windows. On Saba, a municipality of the Netherlands, the colours of the homes were once tradition and became the law. The result was charming and slightly creepy. The coastline was devoid of beaches and perilously rugged; it apparently deterred even Christopher Columbus from landing.

We explored what felt like every square inch of that eight-square-kilometre island. Mostly, Saba was easy on us. This was thanks to our accommodations, an eco lodge where we'd rented a little cabin with a bed – one of our only tent-free stays on the trip. Each morning brought us a delicious smoothie, followed by a day of exploring the island's trails and historic sites, a dip in the lodge's pool and an evening spent stargazing or watching open air movies at the local pizzeria. We spent time with the locals, who often picked us up even when we weren't looking to hitch a ride. Over tea or beer they'd tell us about the island's bird life and that most Sabans can trace their roots back to just six families. We explored the lava flows by the airport and watched planes land on the formidably short strip of pavement.

I was having fun, and fell in love with Saba, but I felt a growing frustration with Paul's unrelenting pace. Beyond walking *everywhere*, there seemed to always be something planned. Sometimes what I really wanted was to sit in a hammock, sip a coffee and read a book. I wanted both adventure and downtime, to dig into *A Brief History of the Caribbean*, a book I'd bought on Tortola. Yet I never stayed back. I had a fear of missing out and a fear that Paul would think I was wasting my time. *You came all this way to read?* The truth was, I didn't know what he was thinking or how he'd react if I wanted to slow things down or take a rest day.

The pace was creating tension between us, yet I didn't bring it up.

✳ ✳ ✳

I WAS DEEP IN THOUGHT when the car suddenly stopped at the beginning of a road. In the beam of the headlights I could see it had eroded down the middle.

"3 Rivers is down that way," Julius said, pointing into the darkness.

I didn't blame them for wanting to avoid busting the undercarriage of their Jeep. Water ran down the road as a permanent creek, leaving tire-deep ruts amidst rocks and gravel. It was getting late, and at this point we were wearing our headlamps as we waved goodbye.

"Come by sometime!" Sheila said. "We'd love to treat you to breakfast."

"Thanks again," we both said as we hoisted our packs onto our backs and fronts to walk the rest of the way.

The darkness obscured my sense of distance and time. When we reached a wide stream that washed over the road, we stopped to make sure we were heading in the right direction. With no other roads in sight we kept walking. Eventually, we came upon a cabin with a light on and knocked gently on the door. The proprietor greeted us with a British accent.

"I was wondering when you'd arrive!" he said. "I'm Jem. I just need you to sign some papers and then I'll give you a proper introduction tomorrow. We've got a bit of a walk to do from here."

We still aren't there? I was confused but followed along. Packs loaded back onto my body, I followed behind Jem and Paul as we began trudging down a path that soon climbed along the Rosalie River. I could feel my energy fading by the minute.

"In the daytime, you'll see this is the Mermaid's Pool," he pointed out, speaking a bit more loudly over the splash of the falls. "A great swimming hole!"

We could hear the enthusiasm in his voice, even if we couldn't see his face. We'd learn later that he fell in love with Dominica as a backpacker in his 20s and eventually bought land there and started work on an eco lodge.

We kept walking. The trail was reinforced with rocks and boardwalks; it was obvious the area flooded regularly. Soon we were hiking straight into the rainforest. Against the canopy I could see the tree houses Jem had built for accommodations. But we weren't staying there. Eventually, he parted some bushes and pointed to a small clearing.

"The forest grows so quickly that I cleared this for you this morning!" he said.

We stared at a gap in the undergrowth where we were meant to pitch our tent. Water dripped from overhead, even though it wasn't raining.

As Paul slid the tent out of his pack, I looked around us at the forest. *What is this place?* I felt disoriented and excited, all at the same time.

* * *

JEM MET US the next morning to give us an official orientation now that we could actually see. Nearby, there was a communal table for all the guests, a small cabin where the cook worked, a shower that ran on rainwater warmed in a barrel, and an outhouse. All guests, except us, were staying in one of the tree house cabins. We were mostly cooking for ourselves but met the other guests at breakfast: an older couple and a young one on their honeymoon. The bride didn't look too impressed. She may have been envisioning a beachfront Caribbean vacation. I couldn't blame her; I was eager to explore but already missing our beach camping.

Our first order of business was to bus to Roseau to pick up our rental car. The bus was crowded and passengers bobbed their heads to reggae music as they shifted back and forth with the turns in the road. We didn't notice the harrowing, pot-hole-filled roads with makeshift "guardrails" lining the steeper sections until Paul was driving our vehicle: a small Toyota with barely any clearance. He'd lay on the horn as he went around corners since the narrow roads often didn't accommodate two-way traffic. He navigated around potholes so big they could swallow the whole car. I had never seen him so nervous and uptight before. But with wheels we had freedom. Walking the roads around Dominica was both impractical and dangerous.

Dominica prided itself in being *the* island for adventure and independent travel, yet everywhere we went we were told we needed to hire a guide. We didn't have the budget for that, so we ventured out on our own. Had I not been with Paul, I likely wouldn't have been so adventurous, but he had this way of pulling that out of me. I was motivated by this new desire to explore but also felt compelled to keep up, as if I needed to prove to him I could push as hard as he could. We were still new in our relationship. If I didn't keep up, would he want to stay with me?

So, with Paul leading the way, we hiked "trails" that merged abruptly with shallow, rock-filled rivers, which we then followed to waterfalls cascading out of the jungle. One such waterfall, at Ravine Cyrique, required climbing down (and up) a series of rope ladders affixed to roots jutting out of the cliffside. It was an accident waiting to happen, but we went for it anyways. Or should I say, Paul went for it and I reluctantly followed.

"This feels sketchy!" I exclaimed with a touch of panic in my voice as I negotiated the wet, slippery ladder rungs.

But my comments fell on deaf ears. Paul was already at the bottom. "Oh, wow!" he yelled up to me. "This is just amazing!"

By now I was halfway and could either go down or up. My heart thumping, I finished the rest of the obstacle course and landed in the sand at the bottom. *Everything will be all right.*

To my left, Paul was standing as far out as he could to see the waterfall. It was high tide, so we couldn't get close. As I approached I saw that it was, indeed, amazing. The waterfall came right out of the sea cliffs with an arc of water that sprayed into the sea, as if someone had turned on a garden hose from 30 metres above. I was trembling from having clung onto the ropes and ladders so tightly, but took a moment to appreciate this wonder of nature.

"It's cool, eh?" Paul said.

"Yeah!" I said, forcing my enthusiasm somewhat. I was happy to be there. I was also not sure how I felt about the precarious climb down.

After some photos, we ascended back up without incident. I felt relieved when we reached the road above. It wouldn't be the first time I did something involving tangible dangers. Perhaps the key was *not* to think about it.

* * *

FOR OUR NEXT BIG EXCURSION, we both agreed that Boiling Lake was on the bucket list. The world's second-largest hot lake, this bubbling pool of water in a steam-filled basin in Morne Trois Pitons National Park is the most popular trek on Dominica. The hardest part was finding the trailhead. Our guidebook got us close enough and friendly locals pointed the way to the actual trail, as though we were playing a game of hot and cold. *Warmer, warmer, hot, hot, hot!* We stepped onto the muddy trail, which led us for over six kilometres past steaming volcanic features to the lake. Little route finding was needed.

The smell of sulphur filled the air as we gazed upon the grey-blue water, vapour rising to obscure it. And then the rain began. The clouds emptied like a firehose, soaking us to the bone with rain so fierce we couldn't keep our eyes open. Water sloshed and oozed out of our hiking shoes as we retraced our path back to the car. We smiled and laughed, but beneath it we were tired of being wet all the time.

Each day we returned to our campsite, nervously fording the creek with our rental car so we didn't need to park it in plain sight. At the Mermaid's Pool we would wash off the day's sweat with a dip in cool, crystal-clear water. Then we'd arrive, sopping wet, at our campsite, which had never dried out. The canopy had grown back somewhat since Hurricane Dean had ravaged the area the previous summer, and little sunlight came in.

The water hadn't totally soaked our spirits until the fifth day, when I lifted my camping mattress to discover it was covered in white mould.

"*Tabarnak!*" came flying out of Paul's mouth. I looked at him, startled. I had rarely heard him swear, but when he did he swore in French. His mattress had mould too, but I could sense his outburst was about more than that.

I promptly smeared hand sanitizer all over them and wiped them down with a cloth, hoping it would keep the fungus at bay.

"What if we left early?" I blurted out.

I was done with the dampness, the white-knuckle driving, the bags of tuna. I wanted a real meal and a dry bed. A few days prior I'd felt so weak from lack of proper nutrition that I demanded, rather uncharacteristically, to spend some of our travel budget on a meal made by the eco lodge's resident cook. Paul seemed to think I was being melodramatic, but the hypoglycemia won over. I ordered some vegetable fritters and instantly felt better.

Now we both had short fuses.

I had rarely seen Paul cry, but I think the stress of driving on the island had done him in. Between the hairpin turns, potholes and one-lane roads through towns with two-way traffic, he had grown tenser by the day. His usual razor-sharp sense of humour had dulled. That week, his camera lens also fogged up while he was taking photographs at Mas Domnik, the annual Dominican carnival. I had never seen him so frustrated, and not only with the camera but also my attempts to help.

I wasn't surprised when he said, through tears, that he'd had enough too.

"It's more complicated to try to leave, though," he responded as he hung a shirt up to air out on the line we'd installed in our tent. "How will we book new flights? Where would we even go?"

Without the internet, we had no way of changing our plans. We could perhaps get Jem to help us, but it would seem ungrateful when he'd been such a kind host to us.

We lay on our camping mattresses, reeking of hand sanitizer, and discussed our prospects. We could go to Antigua early, but it was out of the budget. Paul was right: it was too complicated to try to leave.

Reluctantly, we stayed put. We had just four more days left so we tried to be positive. I spent time with Jem, learning about eco-tourism. I had an article in mind that I wanted to write and I interviewed him for details. We visited Sheila and Julius, who had driven us from the airport on that first day, and they treated us to brunch. We drove up the east coast of Dominica to purchase handicrafts from the Kalinago, also known as Caribs – a once-dominant Indigenous group who resided in the area before colonizers decimated their population, and for whom the island region is named.

We swam in the Mermaid Pool a few more times and enjoyed the cool, soothing water.

✳ ✳ ✳

BY THE TIME WE GOT TO ANTIGUA, our final stopping point before flying back to Canada, it felt like Paul and I were riding on different wavelengths. The driving on Dominica had shredded his nerves. The pace of the trip had run me ragged. On the surface, we were still having fun, but in truth we'd lost sight of each other and fallen into cyclical habits.

The conflicts were perhaps typical of any relationship, but they were new to us. He was being impatient, I was being oversensitive – a vicious combination. I was still feeling somewhat resentful about keeping up with his pace and ambitions and had yet to communicate that to him in a productive way. On our last dinner in Antigua we splurged on some fish at a restaurant by the harbour, where lights shining from the boats reflected on the water and a periwinkle sky signalled dusk. It seemed like a momentous, even romantic, occasion, our last meal before taking off, but I felt like there was an ocean between us. Our conversation felt stilted. I was feeling hurt and didn't want to go home without at least touching on the topic.

"I don't want to dwell on this because I've loved our time together and want to end on a good note. But at times I feel like you've been insensitive with me," I said, before taking a sip of water. "I'm glad you've pushed me. It's just that at times I've felt like I was pushed too far."

Paul looked out at the boats nearby that bobbed gently with the waves. After a pause, he spoke up. "I know...I know I'm like that," he said.

It turned out he knew his tendencies but didn't have a way of tempering them. I had suspected this about him and already had enough evidence from our other adventures together. But after our month of backpacking, I saw in him something special – an almost superhuman quality that could be both good and bad. His determination could take him to places no one else could imagine; it would also be the thorn in his side.

"I'm sorry," he said.

"I'm sorry I didn't speak up earlier," I said.

And we left our conversation to float over the harbour with the breeze.

* * *

WE SPENT THE NEXT MORNING at a beach before we called a taxi for a drive to the airport. While I soaked in the sun, aware I was about to return to a Canadian winter, my thoughts drifted to the central question I now needed to answer: whether or not I'd move to the mountains and join Paul there come springtime. I didn't have a valid reason not to. Paul or not, *I* wanted to go back. I had nowhere else to be, and the prospect of living in Banff was exciting. I hadn't spent much time there, but I liked the idea of living in a larger community that was still within the national park.

Paul and I would also have time apart before meeting up in the mountains, and perhaps that could ease some of the tension between us. We parted ways in Toronto, and I flew to Ottawa while he flew back to Quebec. When I landed, my oldest sister was in the hospital for a C-section. A baby boy, Carter, was born that night. I spent the next six weeks helping her and working on pitching more articles about our backpacking trip.

A few weeks later, I had one article on ecotourism at 3 Rivers published by an online travel magazine. It didn't pay me, but I had been published and had my first byline. This gave me a small boost of confidence. Shortly after, I packed my life into two suitcases and got on a plane bound for Calgary. I was grateful for my time with my family and ready to reunite with the mountains, to explore new terrain.

Paul and I had decided: We would give Banff a year and see what happened. That would be enough time, we thought. We didn't say how much time we'd give our relationship. That would be an adventure without a timeline.

3

Going Solo

COSTA RICA, SPRING 2009-WINTER 2010

Calling it the "Green Season" is Costa Rica's way of advertising the less expensive rainy season that spans from May until November each year. True, everything is greener and more lush, though it would be hard to imagine that country without its canopies of green, twisting vines, and forests where birds sing their happy tunes. It's a fitting advertising spin for a country where everything is *pura vida*, the pure life, which I have always taken to mean life is good, make the most of it.

Make the most of the rainy season.

It was the Green Season when I flew down to Costa Rica alone, when I slept on Mexican airport benches waiting for my flight, when I went in search of *pesos* so I could buy a coffee. When I waited after dark for the shuttle to my hostel in San José that never showed up. When, after midnight, I climbed into a vehicle that the driver said was sent by the guy back at the hostel and I forced him to call the guy so I could hear him confirm my details (still not very reassuring). It was Green Season when I left my hostel and walked into Banco Nacional to use my broken Spanish to send a wire transfer of funds to secure permits to hike Cerro Chirripó; when I bought an *empanada* with unknown fillings at the local *mercado*; when a guy told me I shouldn't wear a backpack because pickpockets would target me;

when I sat in my room and stared at the wall, unsure of what to do with myself. It was Green Season when I hid away from other travellers at the hostel by sticking my nose in a book or writing in my journal, warding off all conversation because I didn't feel like talking.

Let's face it: it was called Green Season because I, the greenest of solo travellers, had arrived in Costa Rica.

I hadn't intended to be alone, but my travel companion had to bail because of a job and Paul couldn't take time off either. I had managed to negotiate time off from my jobs in June and I wanted to stick with it. It would be my first time travelling abroad since Paul and I had backpacked the Caribbean, and my first time travelling alone. And this time it would be in a country whose official language I only slightly understood. Eight weeks of Spanish classes back in Banff had given me a basic knowledge. I could say *"sí"* and *"no."* I could buy a bus ticket or check into a hostel. And I could ask the most important question: *"¿Puedo tomar un café?"* (May I please have a coffee?)

Fortunately, Ticos (Costa Ricans) are some of the friendliest people I've met on the planet. The country is not without its problems, but it has largely escaped the violence that has plagued other Central American countries in the past 50 years. In fact, Costa Rica dismantled its military in the late 1940s and simultaneously granted universal suffrage. To this day, it is one of only a few democracies to operate without an army. Tourism is monumentally important to the nation's GDP. For a first-time solo backpacker, and a woman, the low levels of violence and crime in the nation were reassuring.

Costa Rica is also the producer of some of the world's highest quality coffee beans. This is where I would learn to drink my coffee black. And if I could learn to drink my coffee without milk and sugar, I could learn how to live my life in *pura vida*, not trying to sweeten the bitterness of the things that were hurting me, not softening the sharpness of the unanswered questions that were confusing me.

I could be with myself for three whole weeks and come out with more clarity than when I went in.

I could find myself again. Or maybe even discover someone new.

* * *

MY JOURNEY TO THE TRAILHEAD for Cerro Chirripó was about as straightforward as my bus rides in Costa Rica thus far. What should take a few hours as the crow flies would take an entire day as the winding roads slowed the pace and added extra kilometres between villages and towns. It was common for a 20-kilometre stretch of road to take an hour or more to cover. If it weren't for my iPod and some scenic parts of the countryside, I would have been bored out of my mind. But I used those long rides to contemplate and dream, think through my next steps and get lost in the meditation of Not Doing Anything.

Back in San José I had waited at a bus terminal, which also served as a hole-in-the-wall arcade, local television room and marketplace where vendors strolled by attempting to sell me everything from nail clippers to underwear. From there I journeyed a full day, all the way toward the southern tip of Costa Rica, to Puerto Jiménez. Nearby you'll find the famous Corcovado National Park, one of the most biodiverse places on the planet. I didn't explore the park and instead took in the sights and sounds of the forest reserve and explored where I could without a guide...and crocodiles. After a few days I hopped on a bus and rode north again toward San Isidro, where I would hopefully find someone who could drive me to San Gerardo de Rivas, the gateway village for the trail to the summit of Cerro Chirripó.

My destination for the night was a guest house called Albergue Uran. I was sure we'd missed it when my taxi driver, Alain, continued driving higher and higher up the mountainside, the undercarriage of his vehicle barely clearing the uneven cobblestones that made up the road. He didn't seem fazed and was enjoying my company. He called me his *amiga* and also told me I was "sexy" – the extent of his English. When I saw how populated the area was, and how slowly we were actually driving, I decided he wasn't a threat and let him keep driving me to the guest house. Because the truth was I had no idea how much further it was. If I got out now, I might be walking for a while.

We turned a corner and there was the sign for Albergue Uran. I handed Alain some money and said farewell. Then my hostess came running out of the guest house, dressed to the nines as most Costa Rican women are, and the first thing I noticed was that she was navigating the rocky terrain in platform heels like she was on a dance floor. She showed me my room and in fast Spanish explained something to me about asking for my dinner because I was the only guest for the night.

I ate tacos as I read a massive 578-page hardcover novel I'd brought along (which unfortunately turned out to be one of the worst books I've ever endured). A chihuahua looked on with sad eyes. Maybe he pitied me at the thought I'd be lugging that book up the country's highest peak.

Tomorrow I'd be sleeping at Crestones Base Lodge, which sits in the alpine air at 3400 metres. But first I had to get there.

* * *

EVEN IN MY LIMITED AMOUNT of time spent abroad, I discovered I was a thorough planner when it came to travelling. My theory was the more I planned for the *important* things, the more I could make the most of my experiences. Over time, I learned to distinguish what was important to research or arrange in advance. The rest could flow so long as those important pieces were in place, like a foundation to build upon. Items like passports and permits simply couldn't be left to chance.

Our trip to the Caribbean taught me that some pieces of the puzzle would remain a mystery until the answers fell into place on their own. Serendipity could play a role in travel as much as careful planning. But one aspect of travelling to Costa Rica that I wanted to arrange in advance, especially being a woman travelling alone, was the accommodation. That way no matter what happened during the day, I would know where I was laying my head at night. It took some spontaneity out of the equation, but for the Green Traveller it was perfect.

Amidst all of my objectives, the one that had captured my imagination was my intention to climb Cerro Chirripó, Costa Rica's highest point, nestled in Chirripó National Park. It felt like curiosity had guided me there. Paul's adventurous spirit was rubbing off on me. This time, however, I was on my own to determine just how adventurous things would get. And perhaps the curiosity and drive was to see if *I* could do it.

My guidebook had recommended the hike, and back then I leaned on those guidebooks as much as I wanted to write them. I took thorough notes when we went on trips and sent my updates to the publishers. For many years, they'd send me free guidebooks or discount cards as a thank you for my meticulous reporting.

Cerro Chirripó rises to 3820 metres, higher than I had ever stood in the Canadian Rockies. The 20-kilometre trail to the highest point climbs over 2200 metres, starting in San Gerardo de Rivas, yet it comes with a reward. On a clear day, the view from the summit reaches to both the Pacific Ocean and the Caribbean Sea. The hike sounded hard but doable. And with a backpacking pack? I could do that. After all, I could leave my belongings at the Crestones Base Lodge and go light for the final summit push.

I could do this.

My high spirits woke me up at 4:00 a.m. and I set off 45 minutes later, confident the day would be challenging but enjoyable. I started off at a quick and ambitious clip until the weight of my backpack tired my legs and gravity slowed down my pace. Each kilometre was marked by a wooden signpost. At first they were a welcome sight, but the weight of my pack slowed my pace and the signposts came at a progressively slower rate. *I can do this, I can do this*, I encouraged myself, knowing there was no one else on the trail to distract me with conversation or to help keep me motivated.

I reached the fourth kilometre and realized I was averaging about 30 minutes per kilometre, or slower. My backpack dug into my shoulders and the early morning dew of the lower montane forest made me feel both sweaty and cold. I felt annoyed with myself; I had experience in the outdoors but had knowingly packed quite poorly.

All three pounds of the world's worst book were sitting on my back, as was a large glass jar of Nutella. There was too much weight sitting on top. A heavy pack might have been okay on a trail that flattened from time to time, but the trail up Chirripó went relentlessly uphill as it contoured the lower portions of the volcano. As the day progressed, humidity settled into the air and I began to sweat so much no amount of water consumed could offset the water I was losing.

I had my iPod for music, but knowing there were pumas and other wild creatures in the forest – not to mention the fact I was hiking totally alone – I didn't dare put my earbuds in. Instead, I listened to the sounds of the canopy overhead as unfamiliar birds sang back and forth, their songs creating a soundtrack for my footsteps. Four hundred bird species call Chirripó National Park home, as well as jaguars, monkeys and 260 species of amphibians and reptiles. The park is considered a biologist's paradise, and the melodies floating out of the forest combined with stories of animals I'd yet to see.

Just after kilometre seven, I reached Llano Bonito Refuge, a place where I couldn't stay but could get more water if I needed to. It was there I discovered I had seven more kilometres to go to Crestones Base Lodge, not three, as my guidebook indicated. *WHAT?* I felt despondent and reeled with a sense of defeat, even anger. I'd be sure to add this error to the list of corrections I'd later send to the publishers. But then I couldn't only blame the guidebook.

Why had I come up here? Was I trying to prove something?

I didn't really feel like I had anything to prove to anyone, not even myself. I just liked a challenge and Chirripó was the one I chose for myself, in addition to all the other challenges I was facing in Costa Rica: navigating bus systems, finding my accommodations, overcoming fears of travelling alone, staying healthy, learning to be alone with my thoughts for long periods of time.

I knew I'd eventually get to Crestones, but so far the trek hadn't been enjoyable. As I sat at Llano Bonito Refuge eating snacks and resting my back and shoulders from my monstrous pack, I heard a chatter approaching me through the trees. It was a group of adolescent boys, about ten of them, with a few men accompanying them – the first people I'd seen all day. They were from the United States, a leader explained, and this was a group of delinquent boys who were destined for the detention system if they didn't get their act together. A journey up Chirripó was part of a trip that would remove them from their "usual" lives and challenge them by taking them outside their comfort zones. For the moment, I could relate. I hated to admit I felt like I was in over my head.

When the group departed the refuge, I decided it was time for me to move on too. Maybe the trail would ease off as I got higher.

I was wrong. The hardest portions of the trail were yet to come. The first few rugged kilometres were only a taste of the strenuous hiking that awaited me between the two refuges. Amongst these sections, Cuesta de los Arrepentidos (The slope of regret) left me sitting on my pack by the side of the trail hoping no one would come by. When a guy bounced past me down the trail en route back to San Gerardo de Rivas, I promptly sat up smiling, pretending to be taking a quick snack break. In actuality, I was looking for the strength to keep going.

Eventually, I stood again, hoisted my pack onto my back and slid my hand under the right-hand strap to ease the sharp pain that had developed in my shoulder. The last quarter of the trail to Crestones took me through the remains of a forest fire that had left the land a cemetery of trees, their leaves charred away and remaining stumps and branches sticking skeleton-like out of the shrubby vegetation. The landscape looked just like how I felt inside. I had no one watching, yet I felt humiliated by my lack of preparation for the ascent.

Seven hours after I had set off I arrived at the lodge and relief swept over me. Crestones Base Camp looked like a green-roofed, multi-tiered bunker cleverly tucked into a hillside and surrounded by low, bristly brush. The lodge keepers showed me my room. It housed four bunks, but I had no one to share it with. I chose a top bunk for sleeping, thinking it might be warmer than sleeping on the bottom. The temperature would drop that night and I didn't have my warm sleeping bag. Later, I sat in the dining room writing by the dim light of my headlamp and I finally felt at home, here in the alpine. It reminded me of many of the alpine huts back in the Rockies. And the others sharing the dining room with me came from all over: United States, Canada, Israel and Spain. They took pity on me as I ate my stale bread and Nutella, and fed me their leftover pasta.

I shivered through the night. Tomorrow I would rent a sleeping bag. No matter, I was getting up at 2:30 a.m. to hike to the summit in time for sunrise. It would be the grand crescendo to my challenging hike thus far. I would see the Caribbean and Pacific and it would all be worth it.

* * *

MY ALARM SOUNDED and within 20 minutes of waking up I was already hiking into the cool alpine air. I had a few snacks in my bag but no desire to eat so early in the morning. Five and a half kilometres spanned between the lodge and the summit and nothing was rushing me apart from my wanting to be there for sunrise. In the not-too-far distance I could see a lightning storm, and I stopped to see which direction it was coming. The skies above me were made up of moody, swirling clouds that threatened rain. My chances of seeing much of anything from the summit were quickly diminishing. I'd come this far, though. I'd go to the summit so long as I wouldn't get hit by lightning.

Tony, a guy from the United Kingdom I'd met the night before, came up behind me as I stopped to gaze at the flashing lights.

"What do you make of the lightning?" I asked.

"I think we're fine if we're not too high when it moves in," he said. "We have good visibility from here, so we can head back down if things are getting dodgy." I nodded in agreement. "Mind if I tag along?"

"Not at all," I said.

I welcomed his company after my solo hike the day before. With a light pack on, this time I was flying up the trail, which concluded with some rocky terrain that reminded me of scrambling back in the Rockies. The sky was an opaque grey by the time we reached the summit and the ground was dark and wet, with no sign of the pink and orange hues of sunrise – certainly no sign of the Pacific or Caribbean. I'd made it, though, and I felt proud.

I arrived back at the lodge by breakfast. I didn't plan on hiking down to the base until the following day, so I had the rest of the day at Crestones. Having no travel companions with me, I discovered I was craving human interaction. I felt restless and lonely but pushed the feelings aside by keeping myself busy. I went to the reception area to rent a sleeping bag for the night so I wouldn't freeze again. I finished the beast of a book and left it in the dining room "give or take" library, now sure that over ten years later that book is still sitting there. I wrote for a while to recap my ascent of Chirripó. I wrote about Paul.

We'd been together for nearly four years. Like all couples, we'd had our ups and downs, ebbs and flows. Adventure had been a common denominator. Paul had also discovered he not only enjoyed photography but was quite good at it. A year prior, he'd quit his bartending job to pursue photography as a full-time career. I was thrilled for his new venture and proudly took up pompoms as his most enthusiastic cheerleader. He was supportive of my personal and professional goals, but the stress of his new business at times came between us. After many years together, we were the best of friends, yet I wasn't sure where "we" were going, as though we were climbing a mountain with no sense of where the summit was.

Then there was the question of my falling off the wagon of my faith by choosing to be with a non-Christian, not that I could define myself as a capital *C* Christian anymore. My spiritual explorations had led me to read texts like the *Tao Te Ching* and the writings of Eckhart Tolle – concepts that in my mind complemented the teachings of Christianity and simultaneously opened my eyes to other ways of looking at the human experience. I didn't go to church in Banff. We were often climbing on weekends and, the truth was, I didn't want to go. I needed space to explore the grey. And while I could explore these philosophies and practices in private, I couldn't hide my relationship with Paul. Even four years into our relationship, I was being told I couldn't marry him. My dear grandmother, whom I saw once or twice a year, was sure to remind me of this as lovingly as possible. An uncle joked about it. I knew from the way my church community talked about other "unequally yoked" couples that I was in for a life of hardship. Worse, it was seen as downright disobedient.

Ever the pleaser, I felt unsure about my choice as much as I fought hard for the relationship. I discussed some of these feelings with my dad over breakfasts at a local greasy spoon diner and he listened without judgment. He became my sounding board. He never forbade the relationship, nor explicitly said anything to the effect of "go for it." He always left it to be my decision.

I wished someone I loved would just tell me to go running to the man I loved and marry him. I could tell that my family loved Paul, they loved "us," but at times it felt like I was asking them to bend their beliefs to accept us wholeheartedly.

If there was one thing I held onto from my roots, though, it was that commitment looked like marriage. Whether or not I thought we should get married was irrelevant. I couldn't handle the shame I'd feel if I didn't, when I knew it was so important to my family. For Paul, commitment meant something different, as though he needed to figure out other parts of his life before he could figure out how I fit into the big picture. In his family, marriage wasn't a given. It wasn't expected. His parents were married, and had adhered to some Catholic traditions. But Quebec had become an increasingly secular province by Paul's generation. Most of his cousins, for instance, would not marry their long-term partners.

I'd ended up in Costa Rica alone and took it as a chance to take some space from trying to decipher what my future with Paul might hold. *Could I be content on my own, not just in a foreign country but also in life? Would I be happier on my own rather than waiting for him to commit?*

I didn't like to ask these questions, but deep down I knew they were necessary.

Part of it was that I felt I'd never truly been out in the world on my own, so I had nothing to compare it to. I had gone from my childhood home to university, where I lived with a childhood friend. I moved to Bow Lake with another close friend and met Paul. We'd been together ever since. I felt like my independent "adult" life hadn't truly started until I was out of school, and now here I was, four years later, attached to another human being without any sense of who I was in the middle of it all. My time in Costa Rica was an opportunity to get to know myself again. Make decisions for myself.

What did *I* want?

I felt uncomfortable at times amidst the endless hours with only *me*. For three weeks, I had no responsibility to anyone. When people asked me the predictable question, "What do you do?" I struggled to answer. "I'm a travel writer," I'd sometimes say, knowing it wasn't entirely accurate. Back in Banff, I was working as a sales coordinator, serving in a restaurant in the evenings, and freelance writing on the side, mainly paid gigs for tourism bureaus and some magazines. I felt like a fake calling myself a writer, though simultaneously believed I had to play the part or I'd never make it.

It was refreshing to be amongst a group of vagabonds, backpackers and serial travellers with no care for what the world told them they could or couldn't do. Tony, with whom I'd hiked to the summit of Cerro Chirripó, looked to be about 30 years old and had his own approach.

Back at the lodge, after our hike, he inquired as to what my blog weblink was. I had been writing blogs throughout my trip, mainly for family and friends to read.

"Can I have your email address?" I asked. We had no internet service at Crestones, so I planned to email him my information later.

"Sure," he said. "It's tony@i-dont-work-anymore.com."

"Are you serious?" He shrugged in response.

I later tried the email address and wasn't surprised to discover it didn't work either.

He was perhaps travelling to get away from something, not only see something new. All I could get from him was that he had left his job and hopped on a plane bound for Central America. His story was one more reminder to me that there are many ways of going about life. The life I grew up with, as wonderful as it was, did not determine the one I could adopt for myself later. Tony reminded me of a guy who once picked me up hitchhiking on the Icefields Parkway back in the Rockies. I was supposed to climb Mount Athabasca with friends and woke up with a migraine. My partners set off for their climb and I agreed to hitch a ride back to Bow Lake. I was picked up by a guy from Toronto who had just quit the nine-to-five work life he'd been living for 20 years. He sold his house and most of his belongings and put rubber to pavement, travelling across Canada and living off his savings until he figured out his next steps. As with Tony, I have no idea where he ended up, but they both inspired me in a small way, cracking open the window of possibility as I considered my future, not just with Paul but as a professional.

I hadn't yet fully engaged in the nine-to-five life, but I didn't need to in order to know it wasn't going to be the life for me. I needed to find a way to work for myself, to have a flexible schedule and the freedom to see the world. The idea of "two weeks vacation per year," as so many jobs allowed, felt horribly restricting to me. I knew Paul would be on board with the idea of less financial certainty if it meant we'd have more control over how we spent our hours. Still, the question lingered: Would Paul and I ever come around to agree on the same concept of commitment to each other?

That night at Crestones, I gathered in the dining room with people from all over the globe. We had a potluck dinner of hot foods that everyone, except me, contributed to (I offered up some of my Nutella for dessert). We played a rendition of rummy that we called "Chirripó Rummy," and laughed and laughed.

The best part was, for a few hours I forgot about who I was supposed to be around these people. I simply was.

* * *

THE NEXT DAY I woke up around 5:30 a.m., packed my things and began to descend the trail to San Gerardo de Rivas. With the world's worst novel conveniently left behind at the lodge, and my jar of

Nutella almost empty, my pack was lighter and I felt a thousand times better than I had on the ascent. I breathed deeply, no longer encumbered by the weight of my pack. But I breathed more deeply because life felt lighter too, like I'd taken small steps in my journey to understand myself more intimately. I wasn't with anyone, but didn't feel so alone on the trail anymore. My own presence was a comfort and a joy. And I certainly didn't feel alone when I heard the snapping of a twig and saw the shadow of a creature swing through the forest, about 30 metres from where I stopped in my tracks.

I knew exactly what it was as its gangly limbs flopped and floated tree to tree: a spider monkey. Three more soon joined the troop and their shadows danced and swung against the mist occupying the gap between branches. I pulled out my camera and set it to video mode to capture the magic of the moment, then watched in awe and bewilderment as a child-like sense of glee came over me. Within a few minutes they were gone and the letdown of their departure was quickly replaced by a sense of gratitude. It had been a tough trip to the summit of Chirripó, but the hard part was behind me. Thirty-nine kilometres down, only one to go.

* * *

AFTER CHIRRIPÓ, I moved through the country, spending two to four days in each place: back to San José, onward to La Fortuna and its views of Arenal Volcano, into the cloud forest of Monteverde, and out to the small seaside town of Santa Teresa. As I hopped around, I gradually let go of expectations for myself. I became familiar with the sound of silence and less uncomfortable when I had nothing to think about. As I travelled, I felt less of a need, or desire, to socialize. I had come to prefer my own sweet company to the company of strangers who were friendly but eager to ask the predictable questions: Where are you from? What do you do? How long are you in Costa Rica for?

I discovered that, when I travel, as it is in life in general, people I encounter might fulfill a very short but purposeful role. Some friendships last decades, while others are out of my life as quickly as they came in.

And the only person with me the *whole* time is…me.

As I sat in the swaying shadows of a palm tree on the beach in Santa Teresa, staring out at the grey waves of the ocean and the surfers in the distance riding toward the shore, I contemplated the aloneness of the past three weeks once more. It turned out time and distance really did make the heart grow fonder. In Costa Rica I had learned to appreciate myself, and had come to know myself as an *individual*, but while I would be okay being alone, I preferred not to be single. I preferred to keep climbing this mountain with Paul. Back in Canada, a wonderful man loved me and wanted to share life experiences with me each and every day. While I didn't know what the future held, travel had reminded me to live in the moment and take each experience as it comes.

Yet I also learned that happiness can neither depend on a future moment nor be compromised for the sake of something that is wonderful day to day but wouldn't be if it never evolved. All in all, the questions I had before I went to Costa Rica still remained unanswered. What was clearer, however, was who I was and who I was not. Who remained after three weeks on my own was a woman who could take care of herself and be content in her own company. As I rode countless buses, navigated through new towns and embarked on small daily adventures, I learned to love myself.

Going beyond my usual comforts had exposed parts of me that had been hidden or lying dormant beneath years of accumulated assumptions. I realized that familiarity had forced me into a form that I assumed around the people I loved, at my jobs, in my community and group of friends. Still the "good girl," afraid of making mistakes or upsetting anyone. I was still upholding the appearance, even if I no longer looked the same.

"What part of you have you let go of for the sake of fitting in?" I wrote in my journal on the beach that day. "The characteristics that we shed are often what set us apart, so go pick up the pieces of you that you left behind!"

I found a gentle and quiet spirit that thirsts for solitude and peace. And I came to know for myself that in order to be happy with Paul, with anyone, I first needed to be happy with myself.

As I departed for San José it felt like I was closing a chapter of my life that I could never have written even if I tried. In closing that chapter I also closed my practice of writing in a journal. It would be about 12 years before I picked one up again, except for when I'd take research notes for magazine articles or other projects. Looking back, my journals had been filled with angst, anger, confusion. What I needed was positivity, accountability, clarity. I had not yet been able to cultivate these with pen and paper.

This was the end of the trip, but the beginning of something else – the beginning of what, I didn't know. I just knew I was ready for a change.

* * *

OUR COURSE TO COMMITMENT looked like an episode of *American Gladiators*, with each of us navigating the best route there in our own unique way. Paul fought against the societal views of marriage, while I fought the feeling that his apprehension was a sign he didn't love me or prioritize our relationship. Underneath, I knew he did. It was the bridge between us. We just had to find a way to cross to the other side.

The following winter, we were still in limbo. Paul took an eight-week solo trip to the South Pacific. He'd previously been alone in many countries and it was something he looked forward to. But, before he left, we sat on the bed of his one-room cabin and had a simple conversation.

"I'm not giving you an ultimatum," I said, "but I don't know how much longer I can wait."

"What are you saying, Meg?" Paul asked.

"I'm just saying that I'm ready for our commitment to each other to be official. I want us to be number one in each other's lives. Just think about it while you're away."

I didn't want to pressure him, but I needed to make my needs known.

While the eight weeks went by, I tried to park my thoughts about the topic, knowing I wouldn't have any answers before he returned. He occasionally checked in by email but made no mention of it. To distract myself, I put my energy into my jobs, one in retail and one as a waitress, as I continued to write articles on the side. I went out into the mountains ski touring with friends, including Rachel. She'd come out for a visit and kept me company just before Paul returned.

Shortly after he came home, Paul and I went out for a meal together. The topic never came up on its own, so I finally asked if he'd taken some time to think about "us."

Casually, almost as though I'd asked him to pass the dinner rolls, he said, "Yes, I think I just needed to take some time to look at my priorities. I'm ready."

I knew with Paul that a simple response didn't mean insincerity. In his own way, he was committed to the idea of securing our future together with a more intentional move, like marriage.

* * *

A FEW DAYS LATER, I received a strange text from Paul.

"Can you come over?" he asked.

"I'll be there in a bit," I wrote back. I was living in an apartment about a 20-minute walk away. I took a shower and gradually made my way to his place, without a sense of hurry.

Then he called.

"Where are you?" he asked. He sounded annoyed that I hadn't gotten there yet. Confused, I told him I was just around the corner.

When I arrived, I discovered he was in a total panic. A wound in his foot that he'd received trekking in the jungle of Vanuatu had become infected. After a visit to the doctor, he'd gone down the Dr. Google rabbit hole and convinced himself he was going to lose his foot.

"I saw the family doctor write down that it might be osteomy-elitis," he said. Google told him this was an infection of the bone, a rare and serious condition that in extreme cases required the foot to be amputated.

"She said they'd have the results of the blood work and X-rays on Monday. I can't wait that long!"

It was Thursday. His foot certainly didn't look very good. It was very swollen and the skin had toughened in a way I'd never seen before.

"Why don't we go to emergency?" I said. "If it's quiet, I bet they'll expedite your results."

He hobbled into the emergency room and, fortunately, it was quiet – one of the many benefits of a small town. It only took a few minutes to see a doctor, who was able to view his charts and lab results.

"You've got cellulitis, likely from a staph infection," the doctor said. "That's a deep tissue bacterial infection, but not in the bone."

Treatment required an intravenous antibiotic drip at the hospital every day, and his foot became even more swollen, the skin rock hard. Paul knew he'd dodged a bit of a bullet, but at least he'd make a full recovery.

In its own strange way, the scare brought us closer. I rented him a Nintendo and we bonded as we passed the hours together, worry-ing less about missing out on some winter adventures and more on ensuring he came out of the ordeal with two functional feet.

Our day-to-day interactions became smoother now that we'd come to a mutual agreement that we wanted to commit to each other for real. I'd always thought we'd get married on the shores of Bow Lake, if we ever did get married, but by June I was crunching numbers and realizing how expensive it would be to get our families out west to celebrate with us. Then I had an idea. We planned to go east for Christmas. Quebec City, one of our favourite cities in the world, was located partway between his family in Alma and my family in Ottawa. I had already left my sales coordinator job, so didn't need to request time off. I'd have to quit my retail job, as my employers wouldn't let me take a break over the holidays. And on the writing side I was ready to dive in full-time. I had enough contract work to convince me to take the leap, with corporate gigs, magazine articles and blogging filling up my time.

Perhaps we could marry in Quebec City instead?

We would.

4

Into the Arctic

BAFFIN ISLAND, SPRING 2011

Flick. Flick. Flick. Even the simplest tasks were being compromised by the cold. Our situation was becoming dire. Yet the pain of flicking a lighter with frozen fingers was only half the problem. That the flame, when I managed to produce one, wouldn't light the stove after repeated efforts meant we had no food or water. Without a functioning stove, our trip was over. All we had were dehydrated meals. And with all sources of water still frozen in the sub-zero temperatures of April in the Arctic, snow would be our only source of hydration.

Our outfitter, Peter Kilabuk, had shown us how to light his stove, an old Coleman that ran on white gas, the only gas available in Pangnirtung. It was to replace the two lightweight stoves we brought with us to Baffin Island after being assured we'd find propane for purchase. When we failed to find it in town, Peter graciously borrowed this stove for us, which, of course, lit when he showed us how to prime and light it. But after trying for hours in the dark of night, freezing cold on the tundra at the gateway to Auyuittuq National Park, the stove wouldn't ignite. Though it was nearing midnight, we had no choice but to call Peter on the satellite phone.

"Hello!" his voice called back. It felt surreal to be speaking to him from the wilderness of Baffin Island while he was back in Pangnirtung, likely curled up in a warm bed.

"Peter, the stove won't work!" I yelled into the phone, not out of anger but in an effort to overcome the wind and ensure my message got through. "We've tried everything. We did everything you showed us."

"I'll be there in three hours," he said, without any additional questions or suggestions. *Click* and the phone went silent.

At this point we weren't sure if he was coming to retrieve us or to bring us a replacement stove.

* * *

HOW WE ENDED UP in the Arctic was quite fortuitous. We never could have afforded to travel to Baffin Island. The flights alone would have cost us more than $4,000 each. But Paul had entered a photography contest with the Canadian Tourism Commission and the prizes, 13 of them, were all-expenses-paid trips to each of the provinces and territories. Paul happened to win second, third and eighth place. The grand prize winner chose the trip to Manitoba and Paul quickly scooped up the two places that met his personal criteria for being more off the beaten track and expensive to travel to: Northwest Territories and Nunavut. For his final prize he chose a food and wine tour of Nova Scotia and we ate like pigs for a week. He took his dad up to the Northwest Territories and saved Nunavut for me.

When he saw that the pre-set itinerary included a side trip to Pangnirtung and a snowmobile ride into the Arctic Circle, his wheels started to turn.

"What if we got dropped off in the Arctic Circle and went ski touring for a week?" he casually recommended. He made it sound like he'd just thought of it, but it was apparent he'd already tracked down some maps, done a fly-through on Google Earth and earmarked potential photo locations.

I wasn't feeling very confident about the idea, but I decided that vocalizing all my fears would make them too real. Instead, I fed off Paul's enthusiasm as if it were my own. *Fake it 'til you make it.* I had learned to appreciate the fact that, without Paul, I didn't conjure up such adventurous plans on my own.

"Sure, babe," I said. "Sounds like an amazing place!"

The funny part was this was our pseudo-honeymoon. Paul had proposed to me on a rainy August day at Noseeum Lake in the back-country of Banff National Park. His attempts to propose on Mount Barbette using an entry in the summit register were kiboshed by a thunderstorm that left us running down the backside of a mountain and hiding under boulders as lightning flashed around us. Noseeum was still true to our style and he managed to find enough elongated rocks to spell out the words, "Will You Marry Me?" by the lake-shore. We built a cairn out of them before we left and set our sights on a December wedding in Quebec City.

I prided myself in my resourcefulness in keeping our wedding plans simple and capitalizing on the allure of an already romantic city filled with holiday glitter and twinkle lights. And though I still felt subtle pangs of guilt and unease that I was marrying someone outside my family's faith, I asked my dad to marry us. I'd realized the guilt was a habit, a relic of my upbringing. But it was never enough to hold me back from pursuing the man I knew was right for me. If my family had concerns, they were no longer shared with me. And though my dad needed to obtain an out-of-province permit to officiate the wedding, he generously agreed to handle the paperwork and perform the ceremony.

On December 28, 2010, we gathered with our immediate families and a handful of friends for a small wedding at La Crémaillère, a French restaurant in Old Quebec. It was everything I hoped it would be. Paul and I had wanted to give the night a personal touch and customized our vows to each other: "I will endeavour to meet your needs before my own, comfort and encourage you, listen to you with patience and understanding, and be your most loyal companion through all of life's adventures as long as we both shall live."

After a memorable night with our loved ones, we scurried off to a bed and breakfast down by the water. We had two days together as a married couple, which included eating breakfast with a group of strangers, before we travelled up to Alma to spend time with his folks. So a *real* honeymoon never quite took place. Instead, "all of life's adventures" would include a journey into frozen land on Baffin Island, the closest we came to a honeymoon in the months following our marriage.

* * *

WE ZIPPED OURSELVES into thick expedition suits with fur-lined hoods for the 35-kilometre, bone-chilling ride across the fjord and past the Arctic Circle to our starting point for our ski trip. The thickness of the army-green suit (a "one size fits all") reduced my mobility to an awkward, noisy shuffle as the material rubbed between my knees. We hoisted ourselves over the side of the *qamutiik*, or sled, and settled in behind the snowmobile with our equipment in the sled in front of us. We tried not to breathe in too much of the gas and fumes wafting our way. As Peter revved the engine, swerving around rocks jutting out of the ice and up slick, frozen ramps, our bodies jolted and hit the wooden sides of the sled with every manoeuvre. Still, nothing could prevent us from appreciating the scenery.

On either side of us, under a blue, sunlit sky, Auyuittuq's notable mountains grew from bumps in the distance to jaw-dropping peaks. In Akshayuk Pass, we were in a kind of broad half-pipe hemmed in by mountains whose shapes defied anything I could have ever imagined. To our right, the 1250-metre west face of Mount Thor – the highest vertical drop in the world – leaned toward us. To our left stood the highest peak on Baffin Island, Mount Odin, a broad peak named after the main god in Norse mythology. Just beyond, Breadablik Peak rose out of the land like a glacier-capped molar. The pass between them had been carved by now-absent glaciers as they receded in this place the Inuit called the *land that never melts*.

I was star-struck by the land and tried not to think of how far the snowmobile was dragging us, so far from any civilization, any help, anyone.

When we dismounted at Windy Lake shelter, Peter was quick with his goodbye, an abrupt end to our journey with him to this point. But perhaps he knew the longer we lingered there, the less we'd be willing to step out of the expedition suits we wore for the drive in. We peeled off our suits and felt the immediate chill of arctic air. Peter waved his goodbye and was off in a cloud of exhaust, quickly disappearing into the distance. The vulnerability of that moment, being left on the ice with nothing but wilderness surrounding us, forced me into autopilot. For the first time, I noticed crystals lingering in the air, like a constant haze of sparkles. Diamond dust.

Keeping my fears and doubts at bay, I hoisted my 80-litre pack on my back, clicked into my skis and started moving to ward off the cold.

We'd opted not to use pulks, mainly because we didn't own any, had never used them and weren't sure if the tundra would be snow-covered enough to make pulling them easier than carrying our gear on our backs. The added warmth was welcome, though the calorie-burning effect of carrying extra weight crossed my mind several times. Not wanting to expose my hands in the sub-zero temperatures, let alone try to eat some frozen granola bar, I set my mind to skiing and watching the mountains and glaciers of Auyuittuq float past, much more slowly than from the back of the snowmobile.

I was hungry and thirsty but figured I could refuel once we had stopped for the night at Thor shelter.

It was there that the troubles began. We hadn't planned to sleep in the emergency shelters, each built roughly eight to ten kilometres apart through Akshayuk Pass, which carves the way through Auyuittuq. So we pitched our tent just outside the shelter but moved into the wooden structure to melt snow and cook our dinner by the open door. With no source of heat other than our own bodies, even the shelter felt like a refrigerator. When it came to lighting the stove, we had matches, which might have been easier on our fingers. But when the stove failed to light, the matches would be quickly wasted, so we chose the lighter as our source of fire. It also became a small source of torture on my worn, frozen fingertips.

After our call to Peter, we tucked into our sleeping bags in the tent, feeling tired, hungry and frustrated. I managed to sleep until the sound of an engine approaching us in the night reverberated through the flimsy walls of the tent and roused me to full consciousness.

The conversation was short. Peter was apologetic. It turned out the fuel lines were dirty, and the stove had been compromised. We were disappointed, but his midnight trip into Auyuittuq to meet us remedied any hard feelings. At least we weren't further into the pass when it failed.

But when he pulled out our replacement stove – a two-burner Coleman barbeque the size of a briefcase – I laughed out loud.

"We'll make it work!" Paul said, before I could even vocalize my concerns about us carrying it.

This time, the stove was thoroughly tested and seemed rock-solid. The idea of carrying a barbecue for the rest of our trip seemed ridiculous. But on the upside, we had two pots with us, one for collecting snow, the other for cooking, so now we would be able to double our melting.

Before he left, Peter encouraged us to sleep in the shelter usually reserved for emergencies.

"The only other people in the park are skiing the opposite direction as you," he said. "You might see them in a few days, but you're unlikely to be sleeping in the same place."

Armed with that information, we moved into the shelter and from then on never pulled out the tent again. We said goodbye to Peter for a second time and he drove off into the frigid night, the light on his snowmobile his only guide through the darkness.

With the shelter cutting the wind, we got a system going melting snow over the stove, which sat by the open door, taking turns crawling out of our sleeping bags to check on it and fill our water bottles and resealable dehydrated dinner packs. Once they were filled, we placed the bottles and bags inside our sleeping bags, warming us from the outside before we could eat and warm our bodies from within. It was 3:00 a.m. before we finally filled our bellies. The temperature had dropped to 40 degrees below Celsius. With only ten kilometres to ski to Summit Lakes shelter the next day, we let ourselves sleep in, cocooned in our sleeping bags, denying the moment would ever come that we'd need to slide out into the arctic cold and start moving again.

* * *

AKSHAYUK PASS IS KNOWN, rather notoriously, for its biting northerly winds that scour the landscape and any skin left open to exposure. Prior to our mission to ski to Summit Lake, we stayed the night in the small village of Pangnirtung at the Auyuittuq Lodge, where the hotel proprietor barely spoke with us and never cracked a smile. Still, it was a decent place to stay with most meals included, an essential amenity in a town with few dining options. The day before embarking on the trip we attended an obligatory orientation at the Parks Canada office in Pangnirtung, where a young staff member named Matthew told us about the perils of Auyuittuq. For three hours he hammered the words "hypothermia" and "frostbite" into our skulls, in as nice a way as possible, while recounting endless tales of rescue and disaster. Having come from Banff National Park, which gets over four million visitors a year, my head spun at the idea of doing an orientation for every person who crossed through the park gates. But here it was essential, and I knew it: I'd nearly gotten frostbite on a dog-sledding excursion back in Iqaluit before we'd come to this part of Baffin Island. While a group of Inuit Elders gathered in another room in the building to drink tea and tell stories, we watched videos, filled out paperwork and purchased our national park permits.

"This winter season, 12 parties have entered the park and half have been rescued," Matthew told us, explaining that the reasons for evacuation ranged from severe frostbite to crevasse falls.

The odds weren't in our favour, and suddenly the idea of skiing on Baffin Island felt like a really bad one. When he handed us more mandatory reading – a brochure crammed to the margins with as much text as they could jam into two pages about *Safety in Polar Bear Country* – my mouth went dry. The possibility of seeing a polar bear wasn't news to me, but I wasn't as familiar with the tactics of dealing with North America's largest land carnivore as I was with grizzlies and black bears back in Banff. Matthew said it was unlikely we'd see one since it was mid-April and polar bears were now on the sea ice hunting seals by the floe edge, not inland where we'd be skiing. But it's illegal to carry a firearm in a national park and bear spray in those temperatures likely wouldn't deploy. We also didn't carry an electric fence. "Any potential weapon must be considered, such as skis, poles, rocks, blocks of ice or even knives," read the brochure. Using any of these as weapons would mean I was in a *very* close encounter.

Now I was thoroughly scared. But I did what I always do in the face of doubt and total fear: pretended I was cool with the plan, convincing myself more than anyone else. It wasn't that I was totally unprepared: I'd skied on the Wapta Icefield, a large glacial system back in the Canadian Rockies, and done many overnight ski touring trips. I had climbed peaks in winter conditions and dealt with cold since I was a little girl kicking through snow in the yard for hours on end. I had encountered bears in the wild and managed each situation well. I was savvy and cautious. But the breadth of wilderness in the Arctic was new.

Compared to the Inuit, I was *far* out of my league. The Inuit People have lived in northern Canada and its arctic reaches since around 1000 CE, when their predecessors, the Thule People, first emerged from western Alaska. While Europeans had a "bird's-eye" sense of the landscape, as we do today with our maps and GPS technologies, the Inuit see their surroundings from their perspective as the traveller. The framework through which they view the landscape – one that can seem flat and featureless at times – is more like a "memoryscape." They remember their experiences with various elements, such as the sun, stars, wind, moving ice and snow, and what it was like to move through the landscape. Traditionally, they have shared this knowledge with members of their community, which then gets passed down through generations. All of this was done orally, without the use of maps or writing, and their descriptions would be filled with vivid details about the land rather than the cross-section of latitude and longitude that we're familiar with.

I could see how, in a whiteout, with all visual references stripped away, Paul and I might have been helpless if it were not for our GPS.

In Auyuittuq I had the physical skills and some knowledge to feel confident skiing in such remote, unforgiving wilderness. But if I were going to get home safely, I would need to take a cue from the people who had travelled this land for millennia. The Inuit have a term for a good wayfinder, which is *aangaittuq* (attentive). We can miss the small, seemingly indistinguishable details on the horizon because we don't pause to look. Essentially, we can travel through the land (and life, for that matter) and miss what's transpiring around us because we're focused on *getting somewhere*.

I would need to take things slowly and deliberately. Watch for cues. Stay mentally strong and believe in my abilities. And if the expedition was going to mean anything to me later in life, I wanted to absorb the experience of travelling through a landscape I might never see again.

* * *

THE REALITY OF JUST HOW COLD it could be in the Arctic in the month of April hit when it came time to get out of my sleeping bag the morning after our stove failure. My sleeping bag was crusted with frost. As my breath hit the air, it puffed a cloud of crystallized vapour with each uttered syllable.

"I guess we should start boiling water," I said, half-hoping Paul would interpret it as a request.

But then, once I was awake, I was more prone to feel the cold. Movement would get the blood flowing, so we both set our minds to tasks: Paul collecting snow to boil and me quickly packing our sleeping bags into their stuff sacks so we wouldn't be tempted to crawl back in. While the barbecue worked its magic melting enough water for our breakfast, hot drinks and one water bottle each, we packed up the rest of our gear, mostly in silence to conserve energy. It wasn't much to pack, considering we hadn't yet taken off any layers, but we needed to reorganize to make space for the double-burner Coleman that would be joining us on the track.

The best approach, we decided, was for me to take all of the bulk from Paul's pack to clear out at least a third of the contents. The results were miraculous, with the barbecue sliding in as if the backpack had been designed to harbour the exact dimensions of the oversize stove. My load wasn't so exact, with extra layers, sleeping pads and sleeping bags bulging out wherever the pack allowed. By the time we skied away from the Thor cabin, Paul's pack looked like a filing cabinet and mine as though I'd stuffed the Michelin baby inside. As awkward as it was, it worked, and we set off for the next cabin.

A few hours later, we still hadn't shed any layers, despite the heat-building effects of skiing. The air temperature had perhaps risen to –30° Celsius. On my upper half, I wore a merino layer, followed by two fleece layers, my shell and my thickest down jacket. On my bottom half, I wore long underwear, two fleece pairs of pants and snow pants. A hat, fleece neck warmer and goggles saved my face from the freezing temperatures. But my hands and feet were what I worried about most. I kept my boots somewhat loose around my thickest ski socks to keep my circulation from cutting off. And inside my mittens I used chemical heat packs to combat what had been a chronic issue for me in the mountains: cold fingers that turn to pins and needles when I didn't stop to take care of them.

With nothing to do but ski, the movements became rhythmic and my mind fell into a meditative state. The absolute quiet of the landscape made even the swish of a ski sound deafening, and even then I had various layers on my head muffling it. I followed not too far behind Paul, being sure to keep up so he didn't need to turn around too often to see if I was close by. With no changes in the terrain – just a thin layer of snow on the tundra – I could gaze up and around, learning the features of the peaks as they slowly passed me by.

We had been skiing for only a few hours when we arrived at the Summit Lakes shelter. Again, we were prepared to move outside into our tent if anyone came along. But knowing the park was empty, we settled in without concern, thankful for the firm walls that cut the wind. Inside, however, it was chilly until our bodies began to warm the small structure. We set up our two-burner barbecue just outside and out of the wind, and melted snow for tea. We didn't talk much or discuss anything beyond the basics. Even talking felt like an expense of warmth and energy. Yet it was also because we didn't need to talk in order to accomplish our tasks. As a couple we'd found a rhythm on our adventures and had a sense of who did what, and when. We could also enjoy our experience in the moment without talking about it, simply knowing the other person was experiencing it too. After the trip, we could reminisce and look at photographs, recount stories to our friends and family.

When Paul ventured off to take photos, I happily slid into my sleeping bag and pulled out a paperback to read. I was content settling into a book for a while as it took my mind off of some of my fears about my circumstances. Our gear had made it safely from Banff to Pangnirtung on numerous flights. But a broken binding out here could be deadly. At least we had Peter on the other end of a satellite phone. And when we'd skied our distances for the day, I could shimmy into my sleeping bag wearing all my layers and snow gear, sip tea and warm myself from the inside out. Later, I could worry, if there was even a point to that.

* * *

OUR DAILY RHYTHM changed somewhat on the third day, when we decided to do a round-trip ski to Summit Lake and Mount Asgard before returning back to the same cabin for the night – a 30-kilometre excursion with lightweight packs.

Asgard seemed like the perfect end point to our ski into Akshayuk Pass, seeing as we only had a few days to accomplish our mission. Famous for its sheer rock faces and cylindrically shaped twin towers, Asgard was most famously featured in the opening sequence of the 1976 James Bond film *The Spy Who Loved Me*, standing in for the Austrian Alps when stuntman Rick Sylvester skied off the mountain into a BASE jump and opened a Union Jack parachute on his way down. Climbers might also remember the 2009 film produced by Alastair Lee, *The Asgard Project*, which follows Leo Houlding's attempt to make the first free ascent of the peak's North Tower before making a wingsuit descent from the summit. I'd seen the film at the Banff Centre Mountain Film Festival that year. It's tough to forget a mountain as impressive and beautiful as Asgard, and it had stayed with me ever since.

It was another bone-chilling morning, about −25° Celsius, with a whitewashed sky and low fog as we skied in the direction of Summit Lake and Mount Asgard. As he did on other such days, Paul kept his camera batteries in the inside pocket of his fleece, inside his down-filled jacket. I knew he'd seen a photo opportunity when I heard a zipper open, followed by another zipper, and then the outer layer being zipped back up. Then a *click, click* of the camera body opening so he could insert the batteries before creating his images and then doing the steps in reverse. The only time I took off my mittens was to open the lid on a thermos of soup I'd brought. The cold air outside had somehow permeated my thermos and the soup was tepid by the time we stopped for lunch. I hid behind the only boulder I could find to shelter myself from the wind, sipping the lukewarm soup, while Paul walked along the terminal moraine, taking photos and looking more closely at a route that would get us to the base of Mount Asgard. I don't think he ate anything on that excursion and I ate very little, opting not to try our teeth on a frozen granola bar or rock-hard jerky. Eating a hot meal back at the shelter was more appealing than risking a broken tooth.

As I packed up my things and rejoined Paul, we saw two figures coming at us from the opposite end of Akshayuk Pass, across Summit Lake. My heart skipped a beat at the surprise of actually seeing the two other people we knew were in the park. They dragged pulks behind them and were in front of us sooner than we thought they would be. We detoured from our route a bit so we could talk to them, but kept our conversation short, knowing we needed to keep moving to stave off the chill. Through balaclavas they told us, in French, that they were visiting from France. They'd skied down from Qikiqtarjuaq, the northern entry point for Auyuittuq National Park, and were on their way to Pangnirtung.

"*Mais, mon Dieu, il fait froid!*" (It's cold!) the woman said.

While I couldn't see much of their faces, they seemed to be in great spirits despite the frigid temperatures. They'd arrive back before us, so this short, two-minute interaction was the extent of our human contact during our five days in the pass.

We parted ways and Paul and I turned back toward Asgard. We couldn't see the twin summits, and to get a better look we'd need to climb a moraine and up a glacier that descends from the 6000-square-kilometre Penny Ice Cap. We'd never make it to the mountain's base that day, but Paul at least wanted a closer look. After strapping our skis onto our packs (fearing they might disappear if we left them behind), we started up the steep moraine. About 100 metres up, I could feel my energy starting to dwindle. I thought about the 15 kilometres we still needed to cover to get back to the Summit Lakes cabin.

"You go ahead," I told Paul. "I'll wait here for you."

I wasn't thrilled about waiting alone, but I also didn't like to feel guilty about holding Paul up when he had an objective in mind. Over the years, I'd learned to communicate with him when I'd hit the wall. I also learned that, unless there was an emergency or I was adamant about not splitting up, Paul would continue without me for a little while. There were many times I still willingly pushed myself (now with less resentment than I'd had pushing that bike up Sage Mountain), but there were also times when I put the brakes on when I knew I'd had enough.

"I'll be quick," he said, before trudging up the moraine.

As he departed from sight, I pulled out my down jacket and also kept moving. When I felt warm enough, I sat down for a little while then started the process again, moving and shaking to keep my blood circulating, then resting again.

I couldn't check my watch under my layers of jackets and time was passing slowly. I realized Paul might be waiting for better conditions for photography, seeing as we had lots of cloud cover and the light was flat. I put my pack down and started to do laps in my ski boots up the moraine for 20 metres and then down for 20, up and down again until I had adequate warmth. I windmilled my arms and wiggled my toes, though I also had chemical heat packs in each mitten and boot. Finally, I sat down again with my back resting against my pack and closed my eyes, breathing in the crisp air through my fleece neck warmer.

Still waiting. It had been about an hour, and I wasn't surprised that Paul was still gone; after six years of adventures with him, I knew he was happy and productive with his photography when he had time to roam and explore his options. I knew the rhythms and what it required to take great photos. But, sitting alone on the moraine, the arctic wilderness was starting to feel much bigger, more remote and desolate by the minute. I sat staring out at the scenery and down toward the flat surface of the pass below, visible through a wide gap in the moraine beneath me. My thoughts began to wander. *What if he doesn't come back? What if there was an accident?* I reminded myself that I had the satellite phone on me and I was only a few hours away from a shelter with a radio. Our sleeping bags, dehydrated food and stove were in the shelter, not with Paul. I was perfectly capable of handling myself in the wilderness, and had Peter on the other end of a satellite call if I needed it.

But I'd need to carry the barbeque. Now my thoughts wandered to a vision of me skiing through the Arctic with an 80-litre pack on my back, stuffed to the brim, with one ski pole in one hand and a Coleman camping barbecue in the other.

I didn't let my thoughts wander to what it would actually mean to go home *alone*.

Down below, a dark figure galloped across the gap beneath me and I snapped back to reality. I had just enough time to acknowledge its presence to see it run the final few metres before the slope of the moraine blocked my view. I quickly replayed the image of it running past, its gait, its four limbs striding by. It looked to be on the small side. *A wolverine?* I wondered. *Do they have wolverines in the Arctic? Yes...but I don't think wolverines gallop like that.* Then I clued into my sense of scale as I sat there, about 80 metres above the pass, and it dawned on me that the animal that looked so small was actually my worst fear of travelling through the arctic wilderness in the first place: a polar bear.

My heart stopped and my mouth, already pasty from dehydration, went paper dry. I wasn't sure whether to yell for Paul or stay quiet. *Would a polar bear be attracted to noise? Did it know I was there?* Of course, it did; a polar bear can smell a seal from 32 kilometres away. Surely it could smell me.

At the very least, I needed to get Paul's attention *and* a view of the bear, so I began to clamber up the moraine as quickly as I could, backsliding in my ski boots with each desperate step. I'd decided to stay as quiet as possible until I suddenly let out an involuntary, "PAUL!!"

With no response, I continued upward until I could feel myself sweating inside my jackets. This was also not a great situation to be in while travelling through the Arctic, as sweat can lead to hypothermia when the moisture cools off. But, for now, the bear was a more pressing matter. I turned back and still couldn't see it, so I waited, holding one ski pole in my hands like a spear, knees bent, ready for battle. After a few minutes, I was confident the bear wasn't climbing the moraine, but I still couldn't see it down below or further up the pass. Eventually, I sat down, still gripping my pole in my hand – my only weapon if it came down to it.

Twenty minutes later, Paul arrived; of course, unaware of everything that had transpired. He hadn't heard my desperate cry, nor seen me scaling the moraine.

"I think I just saw a bear," I said, my voice breathless, without expression. Exhaustion and depletion had settled in alongside a sense of relief that the immediate threat was over.

"You what!?" he said, in disbelief.

We'd been told the bears would be by the floe edge at this time of year. I explained to Paul that the bear, whatever I saw, was dark in colour.

"Maybe it was in a shadow and only appeared to be so dark," I reasoned.

Still bewildered and apprehensive about descending back into the pass, we slowly made our way down the moraine. There was no sight of the bear. Still, I stopped every ten metres to look around. A cold wind blew through Akshayuk Pass and, apart from the sounds of our boots grinding into the shale as we adjusted our packs, the world around us was completely quiet. The fog we woke up to had yet to lift, and jagged peaks stood out above it on the other side of Summit Lake. I started to wonder if I'd been hallucinating – not completely far-fetched seeing as I was tired and hungry. But, no, I'd been lucid when I saw it run by – cold and uncomfortable but very much aware. I was certain of it.

We got to the bottom of the moraine and there they were: polar bear tracks. Deep depressions had marked the snow. They were unquestionably the paws of a polar bear, giving away its presence as it disappeared out of sight, fortunately in the opposite direction of our route back to the Summit Lakes shelter.

A few hours later, we arrived back at the shelter. I picked up the radio at the scheduled call time and reported my polar bear sighting. The conversation coming from the other end was minimal. I answered a few details about the bear and the dialogue ended when I reported there'd been no close encounter. We melted snow to boil water and filled our dehydrated dinner packages, stuffed our sleeping bags with the zip-locked bags from our previous meals and chowed down on a backcountry version of Hawaiian chicken with rice. I could rest easy in the safety of the shelter, but took a quick glance at the door to make sure it was bolted before I drifted off to sleep.

* * *

WE NEVER SAW the polar bear again. In fact, I never saw another animal, not even the Arctic fox that Paul said followed me most of our way from Summit Lakes shelter back toward Mount Thor. Skiing back toward Pangnirtung put us on a slight downhill. The pass was wind-scoured and icy. For many kilometres we simply slid, even on what looked like completely flat terrain. Our return was quick and effortless, but the bitter cold was unrelenting. Occasionally, when I'd stop to take a photo, I'd also remove my goggles to take a picture of my face. It was the only place on my body where I feared I'd have skin exposed in the gap between my goggles and neck warmer. Zooming in on the picture display, I'd search for traces of frostbite because I couldn't feel my skin numbing.

The sky waffled between a brilliant blue and clouds that would roll through the pass, minimize our visibility and shroud the peaks in mist before dissipating again. We skied in silence as we retraced our route and familiar peaks slid by us. I was grateful to be moving slowly enough to absorb my surroundings.

We were still far from Pangnirtung, but I had a smile on my face knowing we'd so far survived three nights of −30° temperatures. We still had all of our digits. We'd reached our objective and we were still enjoying each other's company. In all that silent gliding there had been a conversation, a connection. We didn't need to verbalize how much we trusted each other, nor how much awe we felt about the arctic landscape.

Perhaps our ability to function with few words exchanged – even under the most challenging of circumstances – was indicative of a unique strength in our relationship.

On our final morning in the Arctic Circle, we began skiing toward Pangnirtung but stopped to wait for Peter at Windy Lake Cabin in case anything delayed him from picking us up. We felt safer waiting by one of the emergency shelters. Even if the conditions didn't seem extreme, we were prudent, especially knowing that half the parties that ventured into Auyuittuq that season had been rescued. We'd been managing the cold by this point, but just so. Now we had four day's worth of dehydrated dinner packs to use as makeshift heaters. In the shelter we would be safe.

It was around noon when we heard the *put put* of an engine sputtering as Peter's snowmobile zoomed toward the shelter. When he was finally in front of us, the gleeful look on his face said it all: genuine happiness to see us, and also relief that we had emerged from our adventure unscathed.

We were closer to Pangnirtung than when he'd dropped us off, but we'd still need the expedition suits for the ride back. After fighting the chill for days on end – I hadn't realized how much energy I expended keeping warm until I ventured out onto the arctic tundra – zipping into the suits felt like stepping into a sauna. The cold couldn't get to me anymore, and with the fur-lined hood pulled around my face, even the space between my goggles and neck warmer was impenetrable. With our gear loaded into one *qamutiik* and us loaded into the other, we set off for the village. The landscape flashed by much faster than it did when we were powering ourselves through the pass. Still, with the wideness of the pass and distance to the peaks, we could gaze at them for long enough before they slipped out of sight, etching the details of their summits, smooth rock faces, cracks and couloirs into our minds as we slid along.

* * *

BACK IN PANGNIRTUNG we had a few matters to attend to before we could shower and eat a proper meal. We first swung by the Auyuittuq Lodge to dump our ski gear before dropping by the Parks Canada office. We met the hotel proprietor in the hallway, who also smiled at us when he saw us, his cold disposition melting slightly at the sign of our safe return.

"*Je suis soulagé de vous voir*," he said. (I'm relieved to see you.) He'd picked up on the fact that Paul was from Quebec and I understood too, so he spoke to us in his native tongue. I felt that our "adventure" into the Arctic had been a tame one, so was starting to wonder about all the fuss of us actually returning.

When he continued, we started to understand his concern. The French couple had been in good shape when we saw them at Summit Lake, but by the time they arrived in Pangnirtung, the man's cheeks had turned purple and grey, the skin critically damaged with severe frostbite. They'd been evacuated to Iqaluit and on to Ottawa to seek treatment and try to save his skin. Though they hadn't been evacuated from the park itself, Auyuittuq's statistics of "victims" that winter had remained intact with our two parties. It could have easily been us had we let down our guard. The most frostbite I had suffered was a crescent-shaped sliver of purple on my right cheekbone where my neck warmer hadn't always been tucked under my goggles.

Matthew was also happy to see us when we went to deregister at the Parks Canada office. By the time we left his office, and heard more of his stories of accidents in the park, I was feeling even more relieved that our mission to ski into Akshayuk Pass was complete. He was an expert at cautionary tales and I was thankful we'd taken him seriously.

Our final mission was a simple one: tea with Peter and his family at his home in Pangnirtung. Then a long, hot shower, but not before taking a picture of our wild hat hair and wind-scoured faces. In the photo we are grinning from ear to ear – equal parts joy and relief.

After a hot meal, we climbed into bed early, grateful to be snuggled tightly under blankets in our hotel, no longer thwarting the constant chill from sleeping outside in the Arctic Circle. I sat up briefly to take some notes while the trip was fresh in my mind. They would come in handy when I returned to Banff and prepared some story pitches for magazines. (Paul and I would later land our first co-created feature in *IMPACT*, a fitness magazine, which combined my storytelling with his images to bring our short expedition to a larger audience.) When I began to nod off, I put my notebook aside, turned the light off and pulled the blankets up once more.

As my body warmed under the covers, I reflected on how I'd felt coming home from our backpacking trip in the Caribbean, when the challenges we'd faced caused us to drift apart or lose sight of each other. But here in the Arctic, on our "honeymoon" adventure, the story ended differently. Our time in the Arctic had showed me, fresh into my marriage, that we could be wonderful companions in life and on adventures, especially if I could surrender to Paul's preposterous ideas. We had survived the landscape and I had managed my fears. Our teamwork had preserved us.

In all our silent skiing, amongst legendary peaks and diamond dust, Paul and I had grown closer.

5

Freedom amongst Giants

NEPAL, FALL 2011

Something woke me up early – probably one of the sounds of
Kathmandu stretching its arms at sunrise. I lay there for a while
trying to eke out a few more minutes of sleep. But the air in the
room was sticky and stale, and my thoughts had woken up too. I
gazed at the ceiling while I pondered: *I feel like I've been hit by a
truck...I need to pack for our trek into Mustang...I wonder if we can
leave some gear at the hotel?*

Suddenly aware that I'd been sweating in my sheets, I quietly
crawled out of bed, slipped into different clothes and headed out onto
the rooftop porch overlooking the cross-section of streets below.

It was still quiet compared to the bustle that would explode from
the city in just a few hours. Looking out, I gazed upon a sea of the
same: power lines and multi-storey apartment buildings hugging
shoulder to shoulder along the maze of roads; vibrantly coloured
signs for trekking agencies poking out at right angles amidst trinket
shops, restaurants and airline offices. It was October, but the city,
sitting under its layer of incubating smog, felt warm. The air was
thick with the yellow tinge of pollution, yet its odour was strangely
pleasant. Sandalwood and nag champa had somehow won the battle
over cigarette smoke and dung.

This was Thamel, the commercial heartbeat of Kathmandu. It was, and continues to be, the tourist district. Expats tend to avoid venturing into it, but as a visitor in this city of a million, I was grateful to find my footing here.

A lone shopkeeper made his way up the narrow street below, soon to be overrun with motorcycles and scooters and women wearing saris in every colour of the rainbow. There, under the prayer flags that zigzagged above the cobblestones, across the garage-style shop doors hiding mala beads, pashminas and knock-off outerwear, the shopkeeper started his morning routine. Stopping mid-stride, he forcefully cleared his throat, making sure to reach the hidden depths of his sinuses, and spit phlegm into the street. He took a few more steps then stopped again. Expertly placing his index finger over the opposing side of his nose, he cleared one nostril then the other, the mucus landing where I'd soon be walking in flip-flops. The sounds reverberated through the empty alley, and I realized I was contorting my face with disgust. After a moment of quiet, just enough for me to think the performance was over, he cleared the first nostril again, just for good measure.

The same scene unfolded three more times in as many minutes and it quickly became apparent that the habit of spitting in the street and shooting snot rockets, as we called them, was a common practice in Nepal.

The action below began to unfold like a time lapse, an alarm clock for all five senses. Elements joined in increments, until the sum of them exploded into a kind of coordinated chaos. Passing cars blew their horns every few seconds as a courtesy to pedestrians walking ahead (that they'd surely hit otherwise). Habituated locals, unfazed by the hazards, barely looked up from their flip phones as they stepped inches aside to avoid a collision. Scooters honked with a quick *beep-beep*, but mostly turned slalom-style between people. I held my breath as one passed by a child who was kneeling on the road, creating ripples in a puddle with his fingertips. Women wove effortlessly between *tuk-tuks* (rickshaws) and fruit stands – a delicate, daily dance they'd mastered – and their colourful clothing highlighted their presence as they walked their usual path to work, to errands, to...*I wonder where?*

I was so engrossed in the scene I hardly noticed my travel companions – my husband Paul and friends Rachel, Adam and Dave – had joined me on the rooftop. I knew all of them through Num-Ti-Jah Lodge, though we had not all worked together at the same time. We'd travelled from various parts of Canada to meet up in Nepal.

There was talk of breakfast and my attention was quickly diverted. Hunger pangs hit me like the heat wave that overwhelmed us the day before as we descended from plane to tarmac at Kathmandu's Tribhuvan International Airport. Now jet-lagged and hungry, we were ready to start our own day exploring the labyrinth of shops and shrines before meeting with a trekking agency back at the hotel.

Soon I was on the street that I had been so keenly observing from above. I listened for car horns warning me to leap out of the way. I breathed in the incense, a constant cloud of cinnamon, lemongrass, cedar and mint. I tasted milk tea at a shop selling woodcarvings, where the merchant asked if I was married and I hoped the water was properly boiled. I observed the *sadhus*, or Hindu holy men, with their corn-coloured garb and intricately painted faces. I felt the warp and weft of fabrics as I strolled by, ran my fingers along the bellies of tiny Buddha carvings and stroked the rims of singing bowls. I tried not to think about where I was stepping.

I didn't say it aloud to my friends or my husband, but this was the farthest I'd ever been from home and by far the most culture shock I'd ever experienced. I was 27 years old but felt like a kid starting school for the first time – uneasy and excited. My world, as I knew it, was on the other side of the planet.

* * *

PRIOR TO PLANNING our trip to Nepal, I knew very little of this small country wedged between two giants: China to the north, and India on the remaining three sides. What I did know intrigued me.

Mount Everest had grabbed my imagination as a middle-schooler and never let go. Like millions who read Jon Krakauer's *Into Thin Air*, I became enthralled by the idea of high-altitude climbing and the extremes of the Himalayas. Then just 12 years old, I chose that book for an in-depth analysis for a school project, using a map of Nepal photocopied from my atlas and hand-drawn diagrams to introduce my classmates to the world's highest peak and the process of acclimatizing before the summit could be attempted. That world felt so foreign, so exotic in contrast to my suburban life in Kanata. But, like the hours I spent with my nose in *National Geographic* magazines, *Into Thin Air* had planted a seed that grew into a fascination as an adult.

My collection of mountain literature had expanded by the time I relocated permanently to Banff, and soon my shelves were filled with stories of dramatic rescues, the psychology of climbing and other tales of adventure. Krakauer's book sat on my shelf with many on the topic of Everest, including other accounts of the 1996 tragedy. I joined the throngs of mountain enthusiasts at the Banff Centre Mountain Film and Book Festival each year, where every story and slideshow was like water and sunlight to my growing passion. I attended workshops and seminars on how to get published and how to get funding for an expedition. I was surrounded by people who understood my interest in the complexities and often polarizing aspects of mountain culture. I listened to authors who had embarked on self-propelled journeys across oceans and deserts, or tracked the history of notable ascents. I wanted to *be* them. I wanted to *do* what they were doing. I wanted it so badly my heart was bursting with possibility by the time the festival was over each year. Paul felt the same way and our shared passion kept the flames ignited, the loftiest of goals just within reach.

We had no idea what we were doing at times, but we were good at dreaming. We wanted to pursue careers as creative freelancers with a flexible schedule that would enable us to take time for adventure and exploration. Our exploits could then become the fodder for our creativity. We could pay the bills with work produced for corporate clients and tourism organizations. Client by client, over the course of two years, we built up enough work to kiss our stable sources of income goodbye, clocking out from our retail and restaurant jobs for the last time by the end of 2010. While Paul hauled the camera along on climbing trips and backcountry hikes, I fine-tuned my writing to specialize in outdoor, travel and adventure. I started to call myself "a writer" when people asked me what I did for work. The corporate work continued to come, as did an internship with *Alpinist Magazine*, where I devoted six months to writing news articles and online features.

It helped that Paul and I were in it together, that we shared the sense of drive and determination required for not just one of us but both of us to pursue freelance careers. By the time we left for Nepal, we still had no certainty as to where the money would come from each month, only that it would. We could also safely exit our working lives and check into emails every two weeks when we'd emerge from the trail and into a larger town or city with an internet connection. As freelancers, we had the luxury of disconnecting from the world back home for two full months and not suffering any professional repercussions. At this point in our lives, we only had ourselves to worry about.

It was a good thing we didn't need to check in more often, because our trekking itinerary left little time for working anyway. We had nine weeks in Nepal with a jam-packed itinerary: the Kingdom of Mustang, the Dhaulagiri Circuit, Annapurna Sanctuary and Everest Base Camp. We also needed to build in a buffer in case our flights out of Lukla (the gateway to Everest) were postponed just prior to our flight back home. With any luck, we'd get out of there in time to explore Chitwan National Park in south-central Nepal, home to more than 700 species of wildlife, including the Bengal tiger, rhinoceroses and sloth bears.

* * *

PAUL LIKED REMOTENESS, so it wasn't surprising that he suggested we visit the Upper Mustang region of Nepal. Formerly the Kingdom of Lo, Mustang was recognized as a separate kingdom within Nepal's borders until 1950, and until 1992 it was inaccessible to foreigners. Its kingdom status and isolated location served to protect and preserve its Tibetan culture. It had been open to foreign trekkers for only two decades when we purchased special permits for about $500 each to hike through the area. The journey into this sacred land would take us on foot from the gateway town of Jomsom to Mustang's capital, Lo Manthang – a round trip of 125 kilometres.

In order to do so, we also needed to trek with a government-appointed official and we welcomed the opportunity to learn about the local area from someone who lived there. When we descended from the small plane in Jomsom, we expected to see someone in uniform. Standing there on the pavement was a guy so slight in stature it made him look even younger than his mid-20s. He wore running shoes, blue jeans and a white T-shirt with "New York City" written across it. Shaggy black hair crept up from under a grey ball cap. He wore black-rimmed glasses and a timid smile. We knew from the way he greeted us that this was our official.

For the duration of our ten days with Tsewang (TSEH-wahng) it's likely we butchered the pronunciation of his name, but he never corrected us. He was kind, gentle and an ideal guide, though full of surprises – like the time he unzipped his backpack on Day 4 to reveal he'd only been carrying a sweater and a bag full of apples! There wasn't much navigating to do. We mainly walked on well-worn trails from centuries of use, or a dusty road that was being built, which would forever change the pace of the Upper Mustang region. But the Mustang where Tsewang grew up had been largely closed off from the world. He went to Kathmandu for school for part of the year, but returned to Mustang to introduce trekkers like us to the Tibetan culture and his hometown of Lo Manthang.

To get to our turnaround point, we would walk along the Kali Gandaki River at the bottom of a large valley before crossing it at the village of Chele, then up and over Chogo La (pass). We set off with barely a cloud in the sky over a region that seemed larger than life. Perhaps it was being in the rain shadow of the Himalayas, with terrain right in front of us that looked more like the Tibetan Plateau. By the river, the land was irrigated and laid out in a patchwork of terraced farmland where villagers grew buckwheat, barley, potato and mustard. The foreground terrain was arid, each mountain in the distance a varying shade of yellow and brown. Shadows and light danced as hoodoos clung precariously to steep slopes, the vestiges of taller mountains crumbling toward the river below. And, in the distance, the Himalayas rose higher and higher still. A mirage of a monstrous scale, peaks like the tops of temples, snow-capped and shimmering against a baby blue sky.

* * *

NEPAL SLIPPED ON like a well-worn boot. Especially when we left the noise, fast pace and crowding of the cities behind and settled into a slow rhythm on the trail to Lo Manthang. This trip was the first time I'd be trekking for almost two solid months; prior to that, the longest trip I'd done on foot was four days. But my body was strong and nimble after a summer of mountain activities. For now I also didn't need to worry about high altitude sickness. The trek to Lo Manthang would take us to a maximum elevation of 4280 metres as we crested Chogo La – a height that didn't concern us considering we were being mindful not to gain too much elevation in a single day. One of our group members, Adam, was using Diamox to help him better acclimatize. The rest of us planned to take things slowly and see how our bodies adapted, though we all carried medication for emergencies. Dave was the tallest of our group, at six foot five inches, with Adam's tall, lanky frame taking second place. Paul wasn't a big guy, but he had unwavering energy. I was habituated to hiking in the mountains with these three. They had pushed my fitness to the brink many times. Rachel needed to build up her mountain legs in Mustang, having come to Nepal from the lower lands of Ontario. Once she found her stride, she was as strong as any of us.

The altitude challenges would likely come later when we'd ascend to elevations that far exceeded anything we had encountered
before. For now, we could relax. Walking, I discovered, was like a
meditation. The trail was wide, the valley broad. I sensed the spa-
ciousness in my mind as much as my environment: the chance to
explore my thoughts, engage with my inner dialogue more expan-
sively, more freely. There were many parts of Mustang where we
walked that dusty road, and the views, albeit magnificent, changed
slowly. I didn't need to concentrate on my footing or the scenery. I
let my thoughts wander.

For the first time in my adult life I had total confidence in the
career I had created, even if it felt unconventional to me. My first
year of writing full-time, without any supplemental income, had
proven to me it was possible to make a career out of creative work.
Both Paul and I had found bread-and-butter contracts with regional
tourism and government agencies, which left some time for freelance work with magazines and other projects on the side. While
we were in Nepal, a friend back in Banff was depositing cheques for
contracts we had completed just prior to leaving. We didn't need to
work for the two months we were away – a sure sign the freelance
gigs were moving in the right direction. And our relationship was
strong. We had both been working from home – a two-bedroom,
ground-level apartment in downtown Banff – and that worked for
us. We lived together, worked in the same space and played in the
mountains together on weekends. It was a lot of time *together*, but
perhaps our five years of dating prior to marriage helped us to avoid
some of the first-year obstacles that many newlyweds face. Also
ideal was the fact we were working two-thirds time to make our
income. Our schedule was our own to make, so every weekend was
a long weekend. We hiked, we camped, we climbed.

I was happy to be trekking in Nepal, though, and not scaling a
scary peak. That previous summer, my nerves took a beating. I'd
scrambled up many peaks, using hands and feet to get up low-
angled terrain without the use of a rope. That kind of climbing
rarely bothered me. For a few years I'd also been roping up for more

involved climbing: Assiniboine, Mount Fay, Athabasca, Hector, the Lyells and a dozen more. I even made an attempt on Mount Rainier that took me within 300 metres of the summit on a climb through sub-zero temperatures and 70 km/h winds. But, somewhat out of the blue, my last two alpine climbs in the summer, prior to Nepal, had started a downward spiral in my confidence as a mountaineer.

It started on Mount Louis, a limestone spire that rises to just 2682 metres but presents some of the most exposed and challenging climbing in Banff National Park. Adam, Paul and I opted to climb the Kain Route, the easiest line. But being a group of three, with two climbers following the lead, made for some slow climbing. We bivouacked closer to the base of the route to shave time off the approach in the morning. It wasn't enough to prevent us coming home in the dark, though.

Nothing particularly life-threatening happened on the climb. I could just tell that my nerves were frayed. The scramble to the base of the route was dicey. I couldn't muster the courage to lead. The rappels felt like they took ages.

On the third to last rappel, I reached the end of the rope and landed on my feet where Paul and Adam had set up the next rappel station.

"You okay?" Paul asked.

"I'm at the end of my rope!" I shouted. My voice wavered and my nose burned the way it does when I'm fighting back tears.

Paul laughed out loud at the irony of my outcry. On any other day, I might have too, but in this moment his response only made me feel more on edge.

There were still more challenges to come. We had rockfall on our final rappel, which also took me through a small waterfall due to snowmelt coming off the mountain. Once we had retrieved our camping gear, we marched down the Mount Edith trail that circles roughly seven kilometres back to the parking lot. It was pitch black and the guys were hiking way ahead of me. I screamed through the dark for them to let me catch up. I didn't mind the dark; it was bears or other wildlife I was worried about.

Twenty-three hours after leaving our campsite that morning, we finally got back to the car.

Mount Sir Douglas was the last straw. I set off with Paul, Adam and Dave, knowing I had reservations about my ability to tolerate alpine climbing, but I wanted to test those nerves. Maybe to prove I was still in the game and could keep up with Paul, my climbing comrades and the other alpinists in the mountain community. *Was it all in my head?* I knew I was physically capable. But it felt like I didn't want to be there anymore.

As with our climb on Louis, there was no near-death experience, just a crumbling mountain, softening snow and a dodgy summit ridge traverse to cap it off. As we descended, I remember sitting in the snow waiting as we down-climbed one section, one climber at a time.

"I just want to get off this mountain," I muttered under my breath. I was too far away from any of my partners for them to actually hear me.

I'd felt that way on climbs before, but not scared out of my mind. This time, I was nearly paralyzed by fear and I had no choice but to keep going. Meanwhile, Paul and the others seemed to plod along without issue. Perhaps they were panicking inside about the melting snow and how much farther we needed to descend, but they weren't letting on. Frankly, neither was I, on the outside. But when we stepped off the glacier and reunited with our bivy gear, I felt like I'd just escaped death. Nothing bad had actually happened. But it demonstrated a mental shift I couldn't ignore.

I had chosen to be on that mountain that day, but moving forward I would make decisions differently. I didn't want to be stressed or scared. Of course, adventure wouldn't be adventure without the occasional injection of those ingredients. But I wanted to focus on the mountain activities that offered me more enjoyment than fear-fuelled adrenaline, such as hiking, backpacking and scrambling. This would mean I wouldn't be as hardcore anymore, that perhaps Paul and I would sometimes need to pursue different types of climbing. I would also need to let go of what I thought a mountain

enthusiast was supposed to be. It had taken me being scared out of
my wits to come to that point, but this choice was authentic to my
true sense of adventure.

Later, Paul posted his pictures from the climb. There was one of
me taken shortly after coiling the rope, just as the sun was coming
up on the shoulder of Sir Douglas. The sky is a watercolour painting
with rose-pink clouds hovering above brown, glaciated peaks. I've
got one hand leaning into the mountain as I stand on a rubbly, hard-
packed slope. I'm looking straight into the camera and the expression
on my face says it all. You can feel my discomfort, my uncertainty.
Looking at the photograph later, I saw how perhaps I shouldn't have
been on Sir Douglas at all. I had gone up, tagged the summit like I
was stealing something, then gingerly climbed back down.

I have never climbed like that again.

* * *

EACH DAY OF OUR TREK in Mustang ended in a similar way. We
unpacked our belongings and, when dinnertime came, we gathered
to drink milk tea so sugary it left me shaking. It felt good after a
big day on the trail, though. We couldn't speak the language, but
Tsewang explained things to us. He often translated our food orders
to our wonderful hosts, usually short-statured women with dark
hair and weathered faces. They would smile and nod, then scurry
away with their feet shuffling out from a woollen *bangdian* – a
colourful Tibetan apron that draped like a rainbow cascading
down from the waist. They'd return a short while later with chow
mein and more milk tea, and I wished I had the language to speak
with them.

We purified our own water using an ultraviolet light system,
which meant a nightly routine of swirling water in a Nalgene around
a light contraption that screwed in in place of the cap. Trusting science would save our stomachs.

Unfortunately, nothing could protect us from the food we didn't
cook for ourselves, or the drinks that were offered to us. About four

days into the trek, some uncooked meat got into my system and wrecked my intestines. Maybe it was the Tibetan butter tea.

In the village of Charang, we had dropped off our packs in the trekking lodge and set off with Tsewang to visit the local monastery. After a short tour and view from the rooftop, it turned out that Rachel and I needed to wait outside; only the men could visit a particularly sacred room. Outside, a group of monks had gathered by some trees.

"*Po cha*? Tea?" one called out to us from amidst the cluster of shaved heads and raspberry-red gowns.

I had heard plenty about this traditional drink but had yet to try it. It might have also been rude to decline the offer, so Rachel and I both nodded, "yes." Made with black tea leaves, water and salt, *po cha* tastes exactly as you might think it should: bitter and salty. That is, until they add a glob of yak butter, so now you're drinking liquid popcorn. I could see why the tea was a staple at these elevations, with its warmth, saltiness and natural fats. But it was obviously an acquired taste. I gagged a bit then tried to sip slowly, not wanting to be impolite to the smiling monks watching us. When our friends returned, I enthusiastically pointed to my cup then gave the monks a thumbs-up. They happily poured three more cups for the guys.

I was the only victim of tummy troubles in Mustang (the rest of the group would have their own problems later in the trip). I was grateful to have my husband with me, rubbing my back and comforting me through my sickness. The next day, we were supposed to walk the rest of the way to Lo Manthang, but I didn't feel up for it. The rest of the route was accessible by Jeep on this new road being built, and Paul agreed to join me for the bumpy ride.

Upper Mustang had long been an important transit zone for trading, but it was on the verge of tremendous change as the road being constructed also paved the way to greater connectivity to the outside world. Electricity, modernity, opportunity, but also the ills that come with *more*. We were there in the infancy of that process and were able to witness life as though frozen in time. I walked and observed the quiet busyness of the women in their daily routines, washing clothes in the river or sweeping a porch. Men tilling the fields or clip-clopping by on horseback, monks filing out from the village monastery. Children playing, giggling the way all children do. Their lives held hardships I could not understand. Did they ever grow tired of the hard physical work? What happened in the case of a medical emergency? Yet I could also sense the appeal and need for the simplicity they'd found in subsistence living: the repetition, the cycles, the season.

"My people worry about our culture," Tsewang explained as our group sat around the table of our guest house in Lo Manthang. "Too many tourists could change things."

I had read in an article prior to leaving Canada that Mustang residents had worked closely with the Nepali government to restrict tourism to 1,000 people per year, which provided revenue for the region without swamping it.

I asked Tsewang about it: "Do you think that's effective?"

"My ancestors have lived here for hundreds of years. Changes are always happening, but now they come faster. Some changes are good; they make life easier. But some...I don't know. The kids here want American music. There is more connection to *out there*." Tsewang pushed his hands outwards. "Some want to leave Mustang forever. I'm not sure who will keep working, who will go to the monasteries."

"We say in English this kind of change is a double-edged sword. Have you heard that expression?" I asked Tsewang.

He paused and looked to the side to ponder for a moment. "No, but I understand," he said.

I was afraid this sword would cut too deep. It made me question my own presence in Mustang. Was it compromising the cultural heritage of such a precious place? Or did my personal cash injection actually help to preserve it?

All the same, Tsewang was clearly proud to be showing us his home and I was grateful for his generosity. We met his sweet mother, with whom we could not converse, but I could tell she was proud of her son. We had tea with the unofficial king of Mustang, now since passed away, who gave each of us a *khata*, a white ceremonial scarf.

Tsewang provided us with horses for a day and guided us from Lo Manthang along ancient trade routes to the cave dwellings of Garphu.

En route home, we stopped at a monastery where monks were engaged in a *puja*, a ceremony that featured chanting and horns called *dung chen* that made elephant-like sounds. It was the first of many *puja* we'd experience in Nepal and I remarked how distant I felt from the kind of "church" ceremonies I was accustomed to. In all my self-exploration, and floating away from the faith of my childhood, I had learned to accept there were many possibilities in life and countless ways of expressing one's spirituality (or lack thereof). My belief system, once confined to a singular truth, no longer impeded me from seeing validity in other faiths. I could close my eyes and meditate. I could listen and observe. I saw a kind of devotion I'd previously witnessed within my Christian circles.

When we departed Lo Manthang, we would, for the most part, retrace our steps back to Jomsom. For the final stretch we rode in a Jeep to avoid hiking the dusty, shadeless road. A lineup of Canadians blared from the car speakers: Justin Bieber, Celine Dion, Avril Lavigne. This connection to "out there," as Tsewang had put it, was my connection to home. It was strangely comforting to me, but I didn't actually need any comfort. I was enjoying being far from it all, far from life as I knew it. Our first two weeks in Nepal had given me confidence. I felt strong and capable, even after the sickness.

The harder trekking lay ahead as we set our sights on Dhaulagiri, Annapurna and Everest Base Camp. I just needed to keep the rhythm going.

* * *

WEEKS LATER, we arrived at Gorak Shep, the last trekking lodge en route to Everest Base Camp. The next morning we set off for the final stretch of trail. The trekking lodge had been full the night before and we noticed that most hikers stopped at a mountain of prayer flags. There was a sign inscribed with "Everest Base Camp," but we knew the actual camp was a bit farther. We descended to the glacier and walked for another kilometre to find total tranquility. There, we found ourselves staring up in astonishment at the Khumbu Icefall, an endless wall of shimmering, crumbling blocks of ice the size of houses. There was not another soul in sight. The bluest of skies had been our backdrop to the Himalayan peaks for nearly two weeks in a row and the sun beat down on us, reflecting off snow in every direction. Had I not peeked down a crack in the hardened snow to see garbage and batteries wedged within it I might never have believed this place would be filled with hundreds of tents when climbers took advantage of the few weather windows available to attempt the summit. But it was early December and climbing season was over. Dave had gone back to Canada already, so it was just Adam, Paul, Rachel and I standing at our highest elevation to date – 5500 metres – in a place that had captured my imagination a long time ago.

After Mustang, we trekked the Dhaulagiri Circuit and into the Annapurna Sanctuary. Both took my breath away with their ruggedness and beauty. But I felt a personal connection with Mount Everest, which also goes by the names Chomolungma (Tibetan) and Sagarmatha (Nepali). I now finally had the chance to see it for myself. I had no desire to climb the 8848-metre-high mountain. For me, standing in its presence was enough. Paul, on the other hand, had mentioned he'd sacrifice a few toes for the opportunity to climb it.

Everest Base Camp also marked the farthest location we'd be reaching in the Khumbu region prior to trekking back toward Lukla, where we'd board a plane for Kathmandu. We were close to ending our time in Nepal and I wasn't ready to leave.

The evening after our trek to Everest Base Camp we set our sights on Kala Patthar, a hill on the other side of the narrow, rock-filled valley. We'd been at the base of Everest but still couldn't see the summit. The 5644-metre highpoint of Kala Patthar would give us the vantage point we needed.

"We should bring our headlamps," Paul said. "We'll be descending after sundown."

We took our time hiking up higher and higher. Everest appeared in the distance, a heavyset triangular summit flanked by a good-looking Nuptse. Paul led the group at the front, with Adam hiking steadily behind him. Rachel was a methodical hiker, choosing each step in a calculated fashion. At the back, I kept up my pace but stopped to breathe deeply and slowly to keep the oxygen flowing. We all hiked unhurriedly, knowing we were pushing our bodies to new altitudes. I'd been experiencing some lightheadedness and headaches, which subsided quickly enough with water and rest. But shy of the summit of Kala Patthar, about 150 metres below the prayer flags that flapped in the wind, I grew suddenly nauseous and knew I'd reached my stopping point.

"You guys go ahead," I said. "I'm not feeling well and I think I'll stop here."

"You sure, Meg?" Adam asked.

"Absolutely. I don't feel awful, just unwell. I'll go down a bit and join up with you when you come down from the summit. If for some reason I'm not on the trail, you can assume I've gone back to the trekking lodge."

"Okay, Megs. Enjoy the sunset," Rachel said.

As they continued upwards, I hiked down a bit, ensuring I could still see the summit of Everest while the sun was setting. Then I sat off the trail, freed the tube of my water bladder so I could sip on it, and set my back against my pack.

A few minutes later, the show began. As the sun set, it lit up the South Face of Everest like a spotlight. It burned bright and yellow, then orange, as shadows from neighbouring peaks crept upwards. Soon the only thing glowing was the summit of Everest, a golden pyramid against a grey-blue sky. I sat and waited for the sun to disappear, the stars to come up. I sat in total solitude as the sky darkened to a midnight blue, a single bright star broadcasting its presence as the mountains shone as though lit from within.

I felt total contentment even as the air grew colder. I sat and waited for the rest of the group. Soon I saw headlamps dancing down the trail toward me and reunited with my friends on their descent.

Later that night, I couldn't sleep. Various trekkers had succumbed to the altitude, perhaps because they hiked too quickly. Through the thin walls I could hear them retching. High altitude had already made me an insomniac. I gave up on trying to rest and stepped out of the trekking lodge to take in some fresh air.

I'll never forget the stars that night. I stared up at Nuptse, lit up by the moon, and the millions of stars surrounding it. Each one was crystal clear and sparkling like a diamond. I breathed the fresh air in deeply and lingered as long as I could withstand the cold.

I'm going to think of this moment when life gets hectic back home, I thought. The quiet, the remoteness, the guiding lights in the sky. Nepal had become my baseline for what my life at its simplest could look like. Those stars would be forever imprinted on my memory.

I reflected on home, on the meaning of home. How it's a frame of mind as much as a physical structure. It's where I feel at ease, where familiarity rules. It's my tiny corner of the planet where I store my belongings. It is safety and comfort after a big adventure. It's the "real life" juxtaposition to the "escape" that travel warrants us.

And home isn't a single place. There are many places where I can feel at home. It's where my outer environment meshes seamlessly with the inner, where I can release the anchor and stay put for a while knowing I can always venture back out again.

* * *

MORNING CAME and we began the multi-day trek back to Lukla, but we could hike faster now that we were descending into thicker air. We had plenty of time, even with the built-in buffer in case flights didn't depart from the tiny, cliffside airport. We'd be able to tack on a quick trip to Chitwan before flying back to Canada. We also had time for a side trip on our way back to Namche Bazaar from Everest Base Camp. We set our sights on the Gokyo region, which required a high-altitude trek over Cho-La Pass. But Adam got food poisoning at Dzongla, the town we'd be departing from to climb over the pass. We needed to weigh our options.

"You three should go to Gokyo," Adam said. He still looked green, sitting there on his bunk. "I'll meet up with you in Namche Bazaar in a few days."

"I don't know, Adam," Rachel responded. "We have no way of communicating with one another."

"We could wait an extra day for you?" I said. "We're not in a rush. We have plenty of time to get back to Lukla."

We were reluctant to separate. Back on the Dhaulagiri Circuit, our group had split into two groups after leaving Dhaulagiri Base Camp. A snowstorm descended on us later that day and the first group ended up off-trail, pitching their tent where we couldn't see it. The next morning, our group hiked past them without knowing it, and a game of cat and mouse ensued for nearly two days before we serendipitously reunited in a village. Without a satellite phone we had no way of reaching each other. If Adam went off on his own, the same thing might happen.

"Yeah, no problem, man," said Paul. "This is such a beautiful area. I definitely don't mind hanging around a bit longer."

"No, really, it's okay," said Adam. "I'm looking forward to a shower. I'm good to rest here and then get to Namche on my own."

The forecast looked stable and the trails back to Namche were quite straightforward. We deliberated some more, but Adam insisted it was okay. He would wait for us to arrive before continuing to Lukla.

The next day, Paul, Rachel and I got an early start to hike over Cho La, down to the village of Dragnag, across the complicated structures of the Ngozumpa Glacier before reaching the stunning village of Gokyo. It was the only lakeside village we'd seen in Nepal, made up of two dozen buildings that faced the shimmering turquoise water of Gokyo Lake and a backdrop of jagged peaks. Together, Rachel, Paul and I explored the other lakes of the region and hiked up Gokyo Ri for another view of Everest. I made it to the top of the 5357-metre summit without any altitude issues, and we popped a can of Pringles as a celebration.

Back at the trekking lodge we met a father and his teenaged son – he must have been about 14 years old. They were on a "road schooling" trip as a family and the duo was hiking in Gokyo and Khumbu while Mom was off at a yoga retreat. During the mornings they'd trek and the afternoons would be time for homework. The boy had a proper textbook, which he was lugging around the Himalayas, but his father admitted it was really the world around him that was his education. They just wanted to keep up with some arithmetic and linguistic exercises. Meeting them was like fast-forwarding from meeting Ryan, Anna and Mila three years prior. I put the "road schooling" idea in my back pocket for future reference.

When we set our sights on returning to Namche Bazaar, Paul wanted to check out a side valley, so Rachel and I set off just the two of us for the two-day trek back to the largest village in the Khumbu. Now our group had split into three. To ease my concerns, I leaned into the idea that this time we knew the trajectory of each group and had a plan to reunite in Namche. On the Dhaulagiri Circuit it was one big guessing game.

As we hiked, Rachel and I bickered a bit, the way we had since childhood. The way sisters do. Naturally, we had grown a bit tired of being around each other for weeks on end. On the flip side, it had been nearly two months and we'd barely spent time just the two of us – perhaps this was part of the issue. For that matter, Paul and I hadn't had much time alone either. I didn't think to ask for it, assuming that travelling with friends meant sticking together. This late in the trip a break from the larger group was good for me. My spirit craved a feminine connection and the kind of vulnerable conversation I could have with a close girlfriend. When Rachel and I reached our stop for the night, a trekking lodge near Phortse Tenga within earshot of the rushing Dudh Koshi River, we settled in like we were having a sleepover.

We had the afternoon to relax, so we found a spot by the river's edge where we could decompress to the pounding flow of the Dudh Koshi and let the water wash away the tension that had grown between us. When the valley fell into shade and our down jackets no longer thwarted the chill of early December, we found warmth and refuge at a table in the trekking lodge, and ordered a steaming

Thermos of milk tea. We sipped tea, read our books, wrote in our journals and chatted about our favourite parts of our trip. Home was on the horizon and our conversation drifted toward life back in Canada, what kind of careers appealed to us, and the paths we'd taken so far. And though it came somewhat out of the blue, I wasn't surprised when she asked me a question I'd been toying with in my subconscious:

"Do you think you want to have kids?" she asked.

Kids. It was tough to even think about when I'd just come through a few weeks living out of a backpack with barely a care in the world. But I had anticipated the question would arise. It wasn't out of place considering Paul and I had already been together for six years. Nor was it out of place for a friend like Rachel to ask me.

"We've talked about it a bit," I replied. "But neither of us feels ready."

I often figured I would have kids but didn't aspire to be a mother. Plus, how would I keep exploring and travelling with kids to take care of? How would we balance kids and the lifestyle we were in the process of creating?

I warmed my hands on my mug and shared these thoughts with Rachel.

"That's understandable," she said. She didn't seem to have an opinion, more a sense of curiosity about the topic.

"I noticed some kids as young as 8 or 10 hiking the Annapurna Sanctuary trail," I added. "And I know of a few people who have continued to pursue adventures, even with kids in the picture. Only a few though. Maybe I just don't know the right people."

The truth was I had a hard time picturing it all – a hard time picturing either Paul or me as parents.

We finished our tea and ate an early dinner before tucking into our sleeping bags. Tomorrow we would hike to Namche to meet up with Paul and Adam.

This time, our group reunited as anticipated. No cat and mouse.

* * *

WE RETURNED HOME TO CANADA just prior to Christmas. My backpack was brimming compared to when I'd departed, with singing bowls wrapped in yak wool blankets stuffed inside it. I had tucked pashminas, jewelry, scarves and other gifts into the interior pockets, and hoped the dollars I spent helped those who needed it.

In Banff I unpacked my bag and remarked how little I had needed for over two months on the trail. I hadn't even used all the gear I'd brought with me, opting to stash it in hotels along the way when I knew it would go unused on the next stretch of trekking. I had given other gear to porters and hosts I met throughout Nepal: a trekking pole when I didn't need it anymore, a helmet I could re-place back home, a pair of socks as a show of gratitude when my pathetic handle on the language failed to communicate it otherwise. Nepalese people seemed happy, but most were very poor. Some of the porters I had seen on the Dhaulagiri Circuit were wearing only socks on their feet for the 14-day journey. Others wore flip-flops. While they carried generators or tables across icy boulder fields, I carried a backpack that contained contingency items. The disparity felt concerning to me, yet impossible to narrow. Still, it stayed with me, like the stars above Nuptse. Forever a baseline, an awareness of my privilege.

I also left about ten pounds behind in Nepal. I didn't have much to lose off my frame after a summer of climbing, so I came home as pure, lean muscle. My pants had started to fall off me about halfway through the trip, and I kept them up by tucking them under the weight of my 80-litre pack. But I had also developed a pinched nerve in my hip, which was only relieved by undoing the hip strap of my pack. By the end of the trip, either I was losing my pants or couldn't feel my right leg.

Re-entry was tough. I missed the trail, pinched nerve and all. And my whole body seemed to be rejecting the idea of being home. About ten days after our return, when we were visiting Paul's family in Quebec, I remarked I'd skipped my period. By Christmas Eve, I was about five days late. My lower tummy had a fluttering feeling and my hormones raged. When I googled my symptoms, it seemed either I had a parasite (possible) or I was pregnant (also possible). The thought of both frightened me, especially the second option.

"I'm not ready to go through that," I said to Paul as we lay in bed that night. "I'm not ready for that kind of transformation."

I was talking about my body but also the lifestyle shift.

Paul also seemed a bit shell-shocked, but was being supportive.

"It will be okay, babe," he said. "We'll figure it out."

"Well, it's too early to take a pregnancy test," I said. "I can't stand waiting."

I tried to hide my anxiety from his family for the rest of the week as the symptoms grew stronger. Thoughts plagued me through all the holiday cheer. *If we weren't planning this, it means we aren't ready for it!*

When we relocated to Ottawa to visit my family, I was just about to take a pregnancy test when I finally got my period, ten days late. All that hiking in Nepal, about 500 kilometres in total, must have thrown off my body's rhythms. We breathed a sigh of relief, like we'd dodged a bullet, but it got me thinking.

Later that week, Paul and I went to a burger joint for lunch, just the two of us.

"Life is kind of funny," I said. "That little scare made me realize maybe I'm more ready to have a family than I thought I was. I'm not ready now, but maybe sometime this year."

"Me too," Paul replied, the corner of his lips curling into a smile.

It was a simple conversation about one of the biggest decisions we'd ever make. And the first time either of us had acknowledged that maybe, just maybe, we'd like to have children.

The trip to Nepal, it turned out, was the end of an era. All the independence, the luxury of getting lost in one's thoughts for days, even weeks on end. The freedom from responsibility, whether work or otherwise. The simplicity in our existence and daily task of hiking a trail from A to B.

It was the last trip we took abroad before everything changed.

part two

TWO BECOMES THREE

May your choices reflect your hopes,
not your fears.

—NELSON MANDELA

6

The Next Great Adventure

CANADA, FALL 2012-SUMMER 2013

My skin felt clammy as the sweat droplets on my brow hit the crisp
air of an October morning in Banff National Park. We were hiking
to Healy Pass – Paul, his dad, Jacques, who had come out for a visit
from Quebec, and me. The trail to the pass was a typical one in
the mountain park, starting down below treeline, climbing steadily
to thinning forest, flattening out through subalpine meadows and
emerging above anything that grows more than half a foot high. I
felt impatient on trails like this. They spend so much time in the
trees before the views finally unfold in the alpine, where my spirit
was ignited. But good things come to those who wait, and that day
my pace was slow anyway.

My body was hurting. Gravity was starting to work its forces on
the next generation in our team of hikers, our first baby, cocooned
inside me. Every feeling, every grinding joint, was a new sensation.
What normally felt like an easy cruise up a well-trodden trail now
felt like a bad idea. The baby was only 16 weeks in gestation but felt
like a bowling ball, cradled by my pelvis. I was determined to make
it to the pass, another eight kilometres away. I was determined not
to let this new family member derail me from pursuing the things
I loved.

Paul and I talked about dreams and ideas as his father hiked ahead. Our conversations tended toward lofty goals and creative projects – something that perhaps grated on people around us. But for us it was exhilarating; it was no different on the trail. Sometimes a dirt path through the wilderness offered us a time to be silent with each other. At other times it was our opportunity to discuss things at length, our ideas running wild in the boundless outdoors. As we stepped over rocks and roots, I held the underside of my slightly rounded belly – less of an affectionate acknowledgement and more an attempt to relieve some pressure – and we conjured up our plans for the upcoming year.

"Sometime in the first year, I'd like to take this baby abroad," I said, knowing it was unlikely Paul would disagree. "I've been reading about couples who take their babies to more exotic or off-the-beaten-track places. It can be done, it just requires some adjustments from the usual way we travel."

Paul's animated response told me he was game, and he immediately started tossing ideas around for where we should go. His tendency to throw a new one on the table before I processed the previous one had been an ongoing theme in our adventurous lives as a couple. His voice intensified and his accent grew thicker when he was in planning mode.

"Kamchatka would be so cool," he said, and I attempted to visualize our family amidst volcanoes and grizzly bears. "Or Kyrgyzstan or Uzbekistan – any of the "Stans," he added.

Now I didn't know what to imagine. Mountains?

"Somewhere in Africa could be cool too."

Our family travel plans were propelled by naysayers and, mostly, our own ambitions. We had only recently announced we were expecting, yet had already heard the gamut of assumptions: "So I guess you won't be travelling for a while?" or "Just you wait..." a phrase completed by various horrors or changes we could expect. For two people so strongly driven as us, these kinds of comments only fuelled the fire. So we hiked, we talked, we dreamed.

I put some of my criteria on the table.

"We can take the baby somewhere far away, but perhaps without so much culture shock," I said, stepping carefully over a tree root. "And somewhere warm."

We want to do this trip in winter, and I didn't want to be freezing with a baby.

"How about New Zealand?" I said. "It's far away but similar enough to Canada. Plus, I've always wanted to go. Seems like a friendly place to take a baby."

Paul had been there before. Five years prior, while I finished my last semester of university, he was solo trekking through fjordland, mountains, forests and twisting Kiwi highways. He didn't like to repeat destinations. He was willing to explore it, though, if we could tag on some other islands in the South Pacific. He'd already been to Tonga, Vanuatu, Fiji and New Caledonia, so maybe French Polynesia? We let that plan simmer.

After a few hours, we reached Healy Meadows. Castilleja (paintbrushes) and purple fleabane had transformed from their pinks and purples to a lifeless grey-brown. The wildflowers were long gone, but the larch trees illuminated the landscape, their bright golden needles reaching improbable shades of yellow before falling to the ground. Larches are coniferous trees that shed their needles – long, soft needles that splay out from branches that billow, unlike the usual downward inclination of evergreen boughs. Contrasted against a blue sky dabbed with clouds, the scene looked like a living Group of Seven painting where paint swirled and swayed in the wind.

This season of yellow-hued change was my favourite next to the height of summer glory in the Rockies. It is the grand finale before the snow descends and puts an abrupt end to autumn. It signals a change. And that day I was feeling the incumbent changes more than ever.

At last the trail climbed toward the sky, hiding what lay beyond. This is a wonderful thing about mountain passes; they trigger our curiosity in that final stretch, tease us in those last moments before the vista on the other side is revealed. Another surprise lay right beside me, followed me, in fact. The midday sun had started to cast longer shadows and mine stopped me on the trail. I knew what it felt like to be *in* my body, and I've looked in the mirror as the changes in pregnancy unfolded. But a glance at the curved outline of my midsection made me chuckle. I rotated left and right to fine-tune the angle. It was a shadow play telling a story on the earth beside my feet. The circle of life cast in a dark patch atop drying grasses and maroon-tinged shrubs. I snapped a photo of my bulging profile to remember it by.

* * *

EARLY ON IN OUR RELATIONSHIP, Paul told me he wasn't sure if he wanted kids. For a time the possibility seemed off the table altogether. I wasn't heart set on becoming a parent, but in some part of my mind I figured I'd eventually have children, the way I cut pictures out of magazines when I was a kid and collaged them into my future life. My Christian upbringing had reinforced this assumption, even if it was only an illusion that everyone was following a more traditional path.

My conversations with Paul about kids had started a year or two into our dating relationship, when we corresponded with handwritten letters during our long-distance stints. The topic was important to me – essential, even, as I explored our prospects into the future. Talking about it in person felt too vulnerable. But I could hide behind the words scribbled on the page, free myself from any immediate reactions, his or mine. The writing was therapeutic and honest, and through the printed word we discussed some of life's most polarizing topics for couples: children, marriage, religion. When we met, by outward appearances, we found ourselves on opposite sides of each issue, but my own previously held convictions were no longer impenetrable and Paul was too open-minded to write off the idea of marriage and children altogether.

Years later, the conversations had still not come full circle. Four years after we decided to "give it a year" in Banff, we were still there, enamoured by the mountains. Yet many loose ends still dangled from our relationship, unfinished thoughts floating out in the ether. Our relationship had survived a number of scenarios that threatened to pull us apart, our dissimilarities sometimes as deep and wide as the oceans we'd crossed to explore the world together. Our families of origin were drastically different from each other in ways I often didn't grasp until Paul and I had a disagreement and I couldn't pinpoint where it was coming from. We'd grown up speaking different languages (fortunately, we both spoke French and English). I learned over time that Quebec has a distinct culture from the rest of Canada. Going there to visit his family sometimes felt like visiting a foreign country. I learned to appreciate it, though I never quite felt like I fit in – perhaps the way Paul felt with the Christian traditions that permeated my home life. We also grew up dancing to a different rhythm of life. My household was a revolving door of activity and emotion; his had seemed to err on the side of simplicity. And when it wasn't our upbringings that were different, it was the way we handled stress or conflict as adults. Paul went into his cave; I wanted to talk.

In the midst of those challenges we'd crack a bit at the seams and doubt and misunderstanding would seep in. But the glue was adventure, always adventure. By lacing up our hiking boots, we could mend our brokenness, bridge the gaps on journeys through the wilderness, trudging through muddy trails and up the backsliding scree of the Canadian Rockies. We'd strap on our skis and tour into unknown terrain together, the sound of our swishing skis joined only by the sounds of our deep exhales. There was often no conversation about it, this wilderness therapy, but it was the language Paul and I learned to speak together.

As I'd learned through our dating years, and in marriage, part of being in a relationship with Paul was accepting that he's like a cloud I can't pin down. It was hard – borderline impossible – to imagine how he'd fare adding the heavy responsibility of children into his daily existence. I was not so different. I'd taken a liking to the mountain lifestyle that so pervasively existed in Banff. Before setting down roots in the Bow Valley, I had never before encountered such a dense concentration of people who thrived on a freedom-filled lifestyle, a deviance from tradition and a nonstop quest for adventure. The upside? Constant inspiration and a community of misfits – other people who had found a new life in the mountains. The downside? No one ever wanted to commit to anything. Bow Valley dwellers are notorious for saying "maybe" to everything.

As I neared my 30s, the same conversations about kids kept recurring, like a commercial on repeat at every break. Friends, peers, acquaintances talked about their lack of desire to see any offspring on the planet. The idea of kids was like the crux of a climb, threatening to put an end to the adventure. I wondered: *People say parenting is an adventure in and of itself, but is that really true? How do you make it work without giving up everything you love?*

The questions nagged at us from that pivotal conversation over burgers until a cold winter's day in February 2012 while we were skating loops around a rink on the Bow River. As our blades scraped the ice, etching lines with each glide, we started to voice our questions aloud.

This time, we talked openly, triggered for the first time by a shared desire to explore the idea of having our own kids. But we also shared the same concerns. Ever the inquisitive mind, I came up with an idea.

"What if I interviewed other couples who have made the transition to parenthood, and blogged about it?" I said.

Paul, also curious about what people would have to say, thought it was a great plan.

"I bet there would be a lot of interest in that," he said.

I let my thoughts swirl as we skated laps on the river.

It turned out that people loved to talk about it. I fired off a few emails and wound up interviewing two dozen people, including IFMGA-certified mountain guide Caroline George; ski mountaineer Hilaree Nelson; and documentary filmmaker Leanne Allison and her partner Karsten Heuer, a biologist and conservationist. A few years prior I had interviewed Leanne after her film *Finding Farley* (which featured her voyage across Canada with Heuer and their

2-year-old son) won the Grand Prize and People's Choice Award at the 2009 Banff Centre Mountain Film Festival. Our interview formed the basis for an article for a local magazine titled "The Land of Why: Quest for Adventure, Family-Style." The idea of bringing children along for the adventure intrigued me, the way watching Mila run into the shallow waters of Brewers Bay on Tortola had caught my imagination years prior.

My blog interviews spanned from high-profile athletes to families living off the grid, embarking on permanent road trips or travelling abroad with their kids. They featured mothers who kept climbing or ski touring through pregnancy to fathers who quit their high-paying corporate jobs to focus on adventures with their kids. Though a few answers trended across all interviews (mainly that the transition was tough but worth it), too many factors caused divergences to offer me any "guarantees." Each couple had a different way of coping with the changes, integrating adventures and freeing up the time to even get outdoors to begin with. The ability to keep adventure alive through parenthood, I discovered, was as much a matter of willpower as it was about managing finances, health, the work-life balance and personal crises. Only one thing was clear: like all the people I had interviewed, Paul and I would need to find our own way through it.

Eventually, we made a firm decision.

"I don't want to wait too long and make it harder to give up our independence and freedom later on," I said one night as we sat together on the couch. "Especially once we've become accustomed to having that kind of a lifestyle."

Paul agreed. "If we don't have kids soon, we probably won't ever. I feel like the sooner we integrate a family into our lives as adventurous people, the better."

There would never be a perfect time to have kids.

We didn't intend for it to happen so quickly, but by midsummer we were expecting. It was time to make some space in our canoe for a little human.

* * *

JACQUES WAS THE FIRST to reach the pass and sat on top of a large rock that has been adopted by many as a lunch spot. Paul was next. As I approached the highest point, I intentionally slowed down, allowing the scene on the other side to unfold one element at a time – a gradient of peaks and pinnacles, lakes and forested valleys. I saw Egypt Lakes, the three-summited Pharaohs, Mount Ball in the distance and far into parts of Kootenay National Park I'd never been to. The view, and the fetus, left me feeling breathless.

I joined Jacques on the rock and pulled my lunch out. I couldn't believe how ravenous I was all the time, especially after nearly nine kilometres of hiking. Aware I needed energy to hike back down, I put a few snacks aside, though it was tempting to eat it all.

"There's Assiniboine," Paul said.

His comment distracted me from my hunger.

It looked much different from this vantage point, its signature triangle of a summit rounded and heavy-set. But, there it was, the peak of my dreams, the one people call the "Matterhorn of the Rockies." Assiniboine was remarkable in every way: a beautiful peak, striking in stature, aesthetic for climbers and also the highest point in the area. It stands 3618 metres tall, head and shoulders above the rest. I bit into my wrap and sank into a moment of contemplation.

Just over two years before, I stood on the summit of Mount Assiniboine after the strongest climb of my life. Our team of four – Paul and me, and our main climbing partners, Dave and Adam – had opted to climb the less-visited southwest face. After a summer of hiking and climbing, I was at the peak of my fitness and my mindset was rock solid. Like many mountaineers, I had struggled with moments of doubt, a milder version of what I'd later experience on Mounts Louis and Sir Douglas. But on Assiniboine I was cruising. Panic never set in. It was as meditative a climb as I've ever experienced – one step, one powerful swing of the ice axe at a time. We woke at midnight, reached the summit by 9:00 a.m., and were back at our campsite at noon and hiking the seven kilometres back to the car a few hours later. If I needed to go into that extra gear, it was on the drive home as my eyelids threatened to close and deer lined Highway 93 South, ready to bounce across the road without warning.

Climbing Assiniboine had been a lofty goal and still stands as a proud moment amidst many such times I've stood on summits throughout the Rockies.

Being the highest in the region, it is a beacon, a waypoint in the wilderness, and a guardian keeping watch over all that lies below. That day, from Healy Pass, it was a crystal ball in the shape of a mountain.

I wonder if I'll ever climb like that again, I asked myself, uncertain of what life would look like once the child arrived. I had already decided I didn't like being scared in the mountains anymore, but now I wasn't only considering myself in the equation.

I lost seven pounds in the span of three days when I climbed Assiniboine; today my growing belly was swinging me the opposite direction and not just with my weight. Part of my feeling of lightness in climbing Assiniboine was the weightlessness of being uninhibited by any "real" responsibility. I was living the good life, free as a bird, manoeuvring between retail and restaurant jobs while I grew my freelance writing career. But there were no children to leave behind – whether for a weekend climb or forever – had something gone horribly wrong.

Even without children, I had loved ones who would have been shattered if anything happened as a result of my risk taking. Earlier that year, a friend of mine, Carlyle, was killed in a climbing accident in Patagonia. Her death shook me; she was the closest friend I'd lost to the mountains. Climbing or skiing accidents were common enough in the Rockies community, but we never really got used to it. Each time, they left someone – a spouse, children, parents, friends – behind. This was the dark underbelly of mountain life. The epitome of "they died doing what they loved."

But was it all worth it? Mountaineers know the answer isn't simple. I didn't have an answer for myself, even as I stood at the start line of parenthood.

As we hiked back down from Healy Pass, my body ached even more. I vowed I wouldn't hike that far again until the pregnancy was done. I was disappointed, and feeling defeated, that other women could keep exercising at high levels right up until they delivered. My body felt cumbersome, like a foreign entity.

Ever the researcher, I had read articles and books about *everything*, from pregnancy to labour and delivery to breastfeeding to adventuring with kids. I hiked, holding my belly again to take the weight off my pelvis, and thought about the couple that raised their three kids on a sailboat, stepping ashore to birth each one before venturing back out to sea. Another couple had embarked on an expedition across an Alaskan glacier with two young children, including a baby who slept most of the way, strapped to her mama's back. Another couple had still embarked on a year-long country hop around the world with a baby they had somehow potty trained a few months after birth.

Each story left me feeling beyond impressed, somewhat hopeful and totally overwhelmed.

If they could do it, surely we could too?

* * *

THE CONTRACTIONS STARTED with mild cramping, all night long. I didn't sleep, yet I felt a rush of energy. A midwife, or anyone experienced with the common patterns of labour and delivery, would have recognized this as a telltale sign the body was ripe, labour approaching. But I didn't know what was happening.

On the morning of March 20, after that sleepless night, I got up and made a breakfast of fried eggs. A few minutes later as I was flipping an egg, pain shot through my lower back and I bent over in half.

"Whoa, that was intense!" I said to Paul, my right hand still gripping the frying pan, my left rubbing my back, then around to feel my swollen belly.

He was sitting, back turned to me, at his living room work station — the one we'd cobbled together after we turned his office, our only other bedroom, into a nursery. I downplayed the episode, figuring it was a fluke contraction. I was already three days overdue and wasn't about to trick myself into thinking it was finally "go time." Paul turned around to check on me, but the pain had already abated.

Then *wham*. Another wave of pain in my lower back. Now I knew something was up, but I wasn't sure exactly what it was. *Was this pre-labour? Early labour? Why didn't I feel anything in my abdomen?*

Paul was in the process of selecting photographs for a coffee table book, his first. He'd whittled thousands of images down to 300 or so, but still needed to select the ones that would make the final cut. With book deadlines looming, he had no option but to work "business as usual" until that baby was officially on its way out.

Every ten minutes or so, my back would seize and I'd be left gasping for air as the pain moved through my body like a tidal wave. The pain itself had no particular sharpness to it. It felt more like a full-body muscle spasm that squeezed, unrelenting, for ten seconds and then fully released as if it had never happened. We started to google my symptoms, swapping Paul's photo catalogue software with various webpages describing early labour. I thought contractions would be felt on my front, not exhibit themselves like symptoms of a kidney infection. None of our Google hits gave us definitive answers.

"We'll know when it's getting real, right?" I kept saying.

The mind games were worse than the pain itself.

As the day progressed, so did the back spasms. Still, I didn't think to call my doula (birthing support) for fear it was a false alarm. I watched movies while bouncing on an exercise ball. I helped Paul with photo selections, blurting out "yes!" and "no!" between breaths growing shallower and more desperate by the minute.

By 8:30 p.m., symptoms hadn't intensified out of control, but they weren't subsiding. Our doula, Julia, suggested we go to the hospital to get checked. Around 9:30 p.m. we arrived at the acute care nursing station in Canmore, hospital bag in hand, while Paul's computer uploaded files to the online folder containing all of his book selections.

The next 29 hours put any mountain climb, any long-distance hike, to shame. I was halfway dilated when we arrived at the hospital, but the baby's position prevented things from progressing. After intolerable pain and several interventions, including an epidural that allowed me to sleep and rest, I was finally ready to deliver.

Just after 2:00 a.m., on March 22, 2013, a little girl joined us earthside, just as the sun moved north across the celestial equator.

* * *

WE CALLED HER MISTAYA (nickname Maya) Joy Zizka – named after the Mistaya[1] River that courses through a dramatic, thundering canyon not too far from where Paul and I met at Bow Lake. Joy is my middle name, and my mother's. And Zizka was chosen over Ward to honour both our families' traditions of passing on a father's last name. Ward-Zizka just didn't roll off the tongue.

If there was ever a perfect metaphor for what was transpiring in our lives, as individuals and a couple, it was a baby born as the world transformed from winter into spring. We were no longer two untethered, adventure-seeking souls, at least not in the way we'd previously defined it. As for that book we were working on while I bounced my way through contractions, the result of our image selection was Paul's first book of photography, *Summits & Starlight: The Canadian Rockies*. We didn't know it at the time, but that book was the beginning of something incredible. It had put his name amongst others on a bookshelf, but from there his photography would also take off online. In the next few years his work would be seen by a global audience, which would catapult his photo career beyond anything we could have ever imagined.

The birth of a child also births the parents. While I had carried Maya for the better part of a year, it wasn't until I held her in my arms after a long, tedious delivery that I understood the immense responsibility and privilege of being a mother. And if her birth was any indication – that she'd been too stubborn for hours on end to simply tuck her chin and make her way into the world – we were

---

1   Mistaya comes from the Cree word for grizzly bear, *mistahaya*.

in for many years of paddling upstream against her current. From day one, she was fixated on doing things her way, no matter the struggle that inevitably ensued. From day one, we experienced the yin and yang of parenthood, that in a matter of nanoseconds you can go from feeling your deepest frustrations to feeling the overflow of joy and love, so deep it cuts through you like a canyon, oozing your heart out the other end and forever carving you into something new. From day one, we learned you can look at yourself in the mirror and wonder where "you" went.

It would take years to recognize myself again amidst all the sculpting, the stretch marks, the sacrifices, the surprises. Motherhood became the new adventure I didn't know I was on until I saw a resemblance between life with a child and my previous expeditions: that it's better to plan for things not to go according to plan; that just when I think I've figured something out, another challenge comes knocking; that the moments that fill my heart can come in the most unexpected ways, gently tapping me on the shoulder to remind me to stop, absorb the moment and revel in the miracle of the here and now.

* * *

OUR FIRST SIX MONTHS as parents were a blur. No one, nothing, could have prepared me for that kind of sleep deprivation, especially when I had a baby who resisted sleep. We spent countless hours bouncing on an exercise ball because she loved the motion.

When Maya was 3 months old, we flew to meet my family at my uncle's cottage in Ontario's beautiful lake country, Muskoka. Returning to Muskoka was significant for me. This place held many childhood memories: weeks of carefree living, swimming in the lake, learning to water ski and playing cottage games with our lively group of siblings, parents, aunts, uncles and cousins.

More than that, it was where, a year prior, I had discovered I would become a mother. I had travelled there on my own to reunite with my parents, my oldest sister and her family. Rachel was there too. As I left to catch my airplane, I knew something was feeling different. I had a fluttering feeling in my belly and my emotions were all over the place. So I grabbed two pregnancy tests and shoved them in my bag. A day into the cottage visit my symptoms had intensified. My period never came. I peed on a stick when I was certain my body was past the point of a false negative and two blue lines showed up: pregnant. Knowing I'd have a hard time keeping the news to myself, I ran from the boathouse, where we were staying, up the 122 steps to the cottage so I could use the landline and make a call to Paul.

"If all goes well, you're going to be a dad!" I said. It felt strange not to be sharing the moment together in person. Especially after it had been such a huge decision for us.

"Really?" he said. I could sense the mix of tenderness, joy, surprise and excitement all at once. After a pause: "I can't believe it."

"I know...it's very surreal to me too," I said. "Especially because you're not even here for me to tell you the news in person." I switched the receiver to the other ear.

"Wow. It's going to take some time for this to sink in," Paul said.

"Well, you've got the week before 'we' arrive," I quipped.

Paul let out a short laugh. Another pause. "So are you going to tell your family?"

"I think I'd like to," I said. "I mean, I'm here with them. It would be special to tell them in person."

"Yeah, that makes sense."

"Okay, well, I'm going to head back down. I love you babe. This is very exciting."

"I love you too."

There was more to discuss, but it was best to save the lengthier conversation for when I returned to Banff. I bounced back down the steps to the boathouse.

That evening, unable to keep the news a secret from my family, I wrapped not one but two positive pregnancy tests (the cap firmly back on the "pee on this" end) in Christmas paper and gave them to my parents, saying they were souvenirs from Nepal I had forgotten to give them.

Smiles and laughter ensued, and a bit of disbelief. On both their parts and mine.

Fast-forward a year and I was back with the baby, back to some of my old stomping grounds in Ontario. For the rest of our child's life we'd likely be living far from family. Any chance we could get to see our kin would become very precious. But this cottage visit, with a 3-month-old bundle of gurgles and cries, wasn't very relaxed. I felt frumpy and tired. I got out in the kayak once while my mom stood on the dock, bouncing the wailing baby, and the noise reverberated across the water. Life was different now, and I was adjusting – kind of.

One night a tremendously loud rainstorm broke out and water gushed from the skies. Thunder and lightning crashed around the boathouse where we were staying and I lay awake, listening. We didn't get storms like that very often in the Rockies. It was a treat, as long as the baby kept sleeping. It took me back to my childhood, listening to thunderstorms as I lay on top of my covers on those hot and humid Ontario nights. This baby wouldn't be an Ontario kid. But these were her roots as long as she was a part of me.

* * *

A COOL WIND WHIPPED through the air, sending the familiar chill of autumn down my body as we prepared our gear at the trailhead. It was now mid-September, and while the fall season had not yet officially arrived, the cooler temperatures had, and with them the beginnings of a change in colour. The larches had turned and there was almost nowhere as prime to see them as in the Skoki Valley of Banff National Park.

Of course, changing colours also meant winter was coming. In the mountains, a September day can feel like summer, fall or winter. On this particular trip, we were heading off wearing warm hats and puffy coats. And inside my coat I wore a 6-month-old Maya.

The soft carrier allowed me to carry her on my front, almost as if I was still pregnant but with the baby outside of me instead of inside, and further up my chest than in my belly. This way she could curl her body into a fetal position around my front, rest her head on my chest and doze off while I patted her rump. Before we set off, I twisted the legs of my hiking pole until they locked into place. One pole would give me enough stability and free up a hand for me to support the baby.

As we hiked, Maya looked up and around, her big brown eyes absorbing a world of rock, browning grasses and incoming snow. From the look in her eyes – one of curiosity, not fear – she was obviously aware that this was outside the ordinary. We'd been hiking with her throughout the summer, but this was different. Eleven kilometres from where we stood was a mountain lodge that would be our home for two nights in the backcountry, our first backcountry trip with Maya since she was born.

The amenities at the lodge allowed us to leave our big pack behind and bring only a few snacks, a change of clothes and toiletries. We also needed to bring diapers. It was hardly roughing it, with cozy cabins, warm duvets, gourmet meals and a structure that oozed history alongside the oils in the logs. But the idea of hiking back there with a baby was adventurous to us. It also felt like a rite of passage, that, as mountain-loving parents, we could now expose our child to our same love for areas farther from the road.

This was our fourth trip into Skoki Lodge. We'd previously visited on media trips and this one was also a media gig. I was working on a piece about "roughing it without really roughing it" in Banff National Park, and Skoki Lodge perfectly fit the bill. Plus, it gave us an excuse to go spend time with our friend who ran the place.

The journey in was largely uneventful, unless I considered all the things I wouldn't have been doing unless I brought a baby along. Like changing diapers on the side of the trail and nursing beside a huge rock at Boulder Pass to avoid the wind. We arrived in one piece, and for me just the physical output felt like an accomplishment since I hadn't quite caught up to my pre-baby self. In fact, I was far from it. Still, something about Skoki felt like "home," as though when Paul and I arrived we reunited with a part of ourselves we'd lost along the trail to parenthood. By the light of the kerosene lamps, we were treated to delicious meals. We chatted with other guests who took a genuine interest in us and didn't put down our desire to travel the globe with the little girl squirming on my lap.

"So many people have told us to say goodbye to travelling for a while," I mentioned, sensing I might get some validation from the people sitting at the table. Most were wealthy and retired, and seemed like they'd seen the world for themselves.

Paul chimed in. "It's funny how much unsolicited advice you get. It's annoying."

"Travel is not the same, but that doesn't mean you can't do it," one woman explained. I didn't catch what her own background was, but I knew her husband ran a private investment firm. "We took our kids to many places. It definitely got easier as they grew older, but we still had a lot of fun."

I wondered what kind of travelling they had done but didn't want to pry into their financials. A five-star resort with all the comforts of home was a wildly different experience from the kind we were more likely to embark on at this point in our lives. Perhaps these people had once travelled on a shoestring, as we would be. At the moment, Paul and I were down to one income while I was on a self-employed maternity leave that allowed me to take freelance writing jobs when I wanted. We'd decided Paul's photography business would shoulder the load and I'd be Maya's primary caregiver, at least for her first year. Still, in our seven years together, we had prioritized experiences over things and therefore always had a budget for travel. We could still afford it, but we'd be foregoing a lot of comforts that might make things easier while travelling with a baby.

"Sometimes I wonder if it'll be worth it in the end," I said. "Of course, I knew when we became parents that we would need to give up some things. But we've enjoyed our trips so much in the past because of the freedom we had while we were there."

"We really like to make the most of places," Paul said. "With a baby, it might feel like spending the same kind of money for 50 per cent of the experience. I don't know. Maybe we should wait until she's older."

In the first five months of Maya's life, we'd taken her to parts of Canada to visit family: Vancouver, Winnipeg, parts of Quebec and Ontario. Each time, we experienced an amplification of the challenges we had at home. Nap schedules. Nursing. Our own tiredness. Opting out of activities because it felt too complicated. We were dealing with the same here at Skoki. Wouldn't a trip overseas amplify it that much more?

"Perhaps the travel experience could actually be enriched by bringing a child along," the woman responded. Looking at Maya, I noticed how the candlelight flickered in her eyes.

"That's the hope," I said. Then I smiled. *That's the hope.*

Maybe I needed to redefine what travel meant to me or what was important about the experience.

Our friend who managed the lodge had raised her own kids in the wilderness, a concept that had always intrigued me. I knew of many people who ran backcountry lodges and also had kids. What sounded so exotic to me was mostly a necessity for them if they wanted to have children *and* keep doing what they were passionate about. And the children seemed to adapt to their upbringing. Perhaps the more we exposed Maya to the idea of travel and all the joys, excitement, discomfort and uncertainty that might bring, the more she could adapt to the idea that this was our way of doing things as a family.

Time would tell. We had yet to firm up our travel plans, but we had New Zealand and the South Pacific on our minds. A stay at Skoki Lodge, as short as it was, could be like a mini-bootcamp for travel abroad.

As dinner wrapped up, it was well past Maya's bedtime. We were exhausted after a full day of hiking, with little time to relax. But a restful sleep was not in the cards. Maya wouldn't settle in her crib, one the lodge had provided in our cabin. Hours later, she was still awake, the light of the lamp illuminating her drool-drenched, chubby-cheeked face as she crawled across the bed. In my tiredness, I stayed lying down while I reached out to stop her by the ankles before she went over the side of the bed and onto the hardwood floor. She'd then scurry to the other side where Paul would catch her.

This was the child I was determined to travel with.

Back and forth she went, her eyes bright with wonder, curiosity and mischief.

7

Where I Begin

Paul Zizka. I'd see his name in my inbox and nearly jump out of my chair with excitement. With my heart pounding – *Was this what it felt to be lovestruck?* – I'd read his latest report from his solo expedition and miss him more than I thought I was capable of. Days later, I would take a break from labouring over research essays for my final semester at Queen's University to reopen the few photographs he had attached. He sometimes turned the camera on himself, to his face dripping with sweat, beard growing in over a big smile while the scenery reflected in his sunglasses: a glacier, a scenic viewpoint, the ocean beyond.

He had 1488 kilometres to walk. I had eight weeks to endure, getting intermittent contact while I plugged away at courses like theatre history and biomedical ethics. I loved school, but I wanted to be with him. Part of me felt like I was missing out on a grand adventure.

Sometimes he checked in with a phone call and I talked to him through the night, not caring that my morning classes would require a large coffee to keep me alert. Each time that I knew where he was, I traced his route with a black marker on a map of New Zealand, which I had pinned to the wall above my desk in the century-old home I was renting with friends. Sometimes I waited to colour parts of the route, even though I knew he'd covered those stretches. It gave me the satisfaction of bringing him closer to his end point in one fell swoop, as though I could make him move faster. He completed his trek as planned and even had a week to spare, so he flew over to the island of Tonga. He later landed in Montreal and I drove his car to pick him up. The anticipation gave me a heavy foot. When I glanced down at my speed, I realized I was going nearly 30 kilometres over the speed limit. I arrived early and waited impatiently for his face to appear in the crowd. He arrived looking tan, lean and tired. His feet and gear smelled so bad they stunk up the car, but I didn't mind. This was love.

Fast-forward seven years and now we were *together* for a New Zealand adventure. But this trip would barely resemble Paul's solo trek – especially not with a baby in tow. While Paul had walked along the South Island's mountainous spine, we would be bound to the highways, perhaps tackling short hikes. Our itinerary wasn't all that adventurous, but Paul had been willing to compromise as long as we could venture off the beaten track after our time in New Zealand. So, after a month of exploring the South and North Islands by car, we'd continue on for another five weeks of island-hopping in Niue, French Polynesia and Hawaii.

Our original itinerary was a lot more ambitious until I bumped into a friend one day in Banff who had spent the previous year in Wānaka. When I told her our rough plans, she offered a cautionary tale about how driving distances in New Zealand were deceptively foreshortened by Google Maps. A 100-kilometre distance could take an hour and a half on open roads, or upwards of three hours when the roads begin to wind around mountainous features. With switchbacks and turns built in to lessen the gradient, you get the impression that you're driving sideways more than straight. I promptly adjusted our plans.

We got our first glimpse of the hairpin turns on our very first day of driving in New Zealand. We started the trip on the South Island, which required a domestic flight from Auckland to Christchurch shortly after we had landed from an epic day of travel: Banff to Calgary by car, Calgary to Vancouver by air, and then a 15-hour overnight flight from there to Auckland with a baby who barely slept. But the journey didn't end there. Our first booking was on the Akaroa Peninsula, an hour and a half drive from Christchurch International Airport. After a quick breakfast at a cafe near the airport, Paul navigated the busy roads that skirted around Christ-church and into the countryside, his eyes still drooping and blurry despite the coffee we guzzled. Driving on the unfamiliar side of the road and around endless traffic circles that operated in the opposite direction than we were accustomed to were enough to give him a quick, and understandable, temper.

We finally made it to the peninsula, baby screaming in her car seat in the back. The road, and my stomach, began to switchback. I've long been cursed with carsickness, but not wanting to take the wheel I tried to stick it out until I nearly tossed my cookies.

"Pull over!" I yelled.

He did, and I quickly left the vehicle to get some air. Stopping the motion also let me take in the panorama of rounded hillsides falling into deep blue seas around the peninsula, the low sun high-lighting the yellows and faded greens of an approaching autumn. I took some deep breaths until I felt better.

From there, I braved driving on the "wrong" side of the road, inching close to the shoulder for fear I was too close to the centre line and wincing every time a car passed. When we couldn't find the holiday park we'd booked, we stopped at a nearby cafe and quickly booked a spot at the Akaroa Top 10 Holiday Park, then backtracked to find it. We finally arrived at a stopping point a full 24 hours after we'd left Canada. I had yet to sleep, and Maya had barely closed her eyes. I was all too aware of what happened when our baby was over-tired: the less she slept, the more she would struggle to fall asleep.

At this holiday park, we had booked a simple cabin, with benefits that greatly outweighed the small price difference from a campsite: a solid roof, mini fridge and kettle, bunk bed and double bed, and access to a communal camp kitchen. When the park managers of-fered us a travel bed for the baby, I took it, not knowing how much it would save us while we adjusted to the time change.

For the next few days we tried, unsuccessfully, to get into a travel rhythm. Our baby, who resisted sleep at home, was no different on the road. And now we were dealing with jet lag – something I'd overlooked despite our self-imposed plan to fly to the other side of the world. It turned out you can't tell a baby to go to sleep when their body is telling them it's time to be awake. So Maya had fitful naps during the day and then she was up at all hours of the night, ready to party. When we didn't join her, she screamed at us from her travel bed, ensuring no one got any sleep at all. At least she couldn't go anywhere, trapped in the tiny padded prison of her cot. Four walls meant decreased supervision when we were trying to close our eyes. Around 3:00 a.m. on our first night, I watched with incredulity as Paul sat on the lower bunk bed in his underwear with his eyes half-closed, cutting grapes into quarters on a plate. Maya shovelled them into her mouth like it was an afternoon snack before she began to scurry around the cabin.

The next day, torrential rains poured down, leaving us with no option but to keep ourselves, and an 11-month-old, entertained in a tiny cabin with nothing but six stacking cups to play with. We hadn't packed much by way of toys, opting to find things in nature to play with or purchase something along the way. Still, we were happy to have a solid roof over our heads instead of a tent fly, and at lunchtime I whisked over to the camp kitchen to make us some macaroni and cheese.

When the skies cleared, we went for a drive, hoping Maya would sleep in the car. She cried as we wound our way back up switchbacks to Summit Road, which then traced the rugged topography of the peninsula's highest points. She fell into hysterics as we inched higher, gaining views of the gulf to one side, the Pacific to the other. Still more crying as we crested the highest point, her wails and undecipherable babble comprising the soundtrack to our sightseeing. I could feel my anxiety heightening as we reached our highest point on the road.

As we began to retrace our route back toward Akaroa, she finally fell asleep but managed to do so with her eyes open. So I did what any parent would do, staring at their lifeless child in the back seat, eyes open but unmoving.

"Wake up!" I blurted out as I prodded at her belly until she started to cry again.

* * *

DESPITE THE CALM, quiet and sweeping views of the peninsula, and our excitement to be travelling, I felt a sense of hopelessness. Paul did too. Back at the holiday park, we sat outside at a picnic table while Maya played in the grass.

"I think we need to pause sightseeing plans and take turns sleeping," he suggested.

"Yeah," I said. I was at a loss, but any plan to catch up on sleep sounded appealing.

When it was Paul's turn to catch up on shut-eye, I took the 15-minute walk into Akaroa with Maya. We didn't travel with a stroller, but thankfully she liked the soft carrier, where I could wear her on my back like a backpack now that she was nearly a year old. I stumbled upon a health food store, and bee lined it to the sleep supplements, hoping there was something baby-friendly I could give Maya to help her get on track. I found some homeopathic sleep tablets, safe for infants, and figured it was our best bet. Perhaps the adults should have been the ones to take them, to lull us into a deep sleep despite the crying going on in the small space we inhabited, because the tablets were about as effective as feeding her pure sugar.

The next morning, after another night of insomnia, we walked to town as a family. I cracked a smile watching Maya run through small flocks of birds feeding on crumbs by the docks, as orange boats bobbed in the gentle waters of French Bay. We treated ourselves to a restaurant breakfast with ample coffee, then walked around the tiny bayside village, where every house looked like a cottage and even doorway mail slots had charm. With the sun still shining when we got back to the holiday park, we decided to give driving another go.

We would, after all, be driving for a few hours each day for the next month, so what was one more excursion?

We set our sights on Little Akaloa Bay, on the other side of the peninsula, and managed an enjoyable drive with plenty of rice cakes being passed to the back seat. The sun was high in the sky, casting warm light on the grass next to the bay. Water sparkled in the basin lined by rolling hillsides, shrubs clinging to the otherwise barren, yellowing grass. A small gap at the end of the bay revealed the expanse of ocean that lay beyond, just out of view.

There, we played. We breathed more deeply than we had in days. And there we learned that the best antidote to our tiredness and restlessness, and where Maya was at her best, was out in the fresh air, out where we could feel expansive and she could crawl where she wanted to.

* * *

THAT NIGHT WE MANAGED to get Maya to sleep by the time nighttime fell. She wouldn't sleep very long, but at least we had some quiet to gather our thoughts. As we prepared to go to bed ourselves, I slid the glass door of our cabin open as quietly as I could and slipped out into the darkness. I would make less noise brushing my teeth and changing my clothes in the camp kitchen, far from the sleeping baby. It was late February and the air was cool – cold enough to make me pick up my pace, arms folded in to keep the body warm. But I was stopped in my tracks on my way to the communal kitchen when I looked up, enamoured by the sea of stars that twinkled overhead.

The beauty of it was astonishing, and the peacefulness of the moment a much-needed pause. Stars have had a grounding effect on me on many occasions, as they did staring up at Nupste in Nepal. When I'm away from home or across the globe, they remind me that some things are always there, that the stars I see from my back porch are the same I can gaze up at from the other side of the planet. That night, I stopped, gazed at the stars and let out a laugh. Orion, an otherwise well-known friend, was hanging upside-down, his sword pointing upwards toward his feet. This was my first time in the southern hemisphere, and I hadn't considered how the stars might be different, but, of course, they were. So far, everything in New Zealand felt upside-down or off-kilter: my sleep, my knowledge of how to travel, my confidence in what was to come for the next ten weeks. If we were really looking for a friendly place to take a baby, we should have stayed closer to our time zone.

For a year now I had been navigating the shoreline that is parenthood. For many years longer, I had been navigating the shoreline that is a life I never thought I'd be living. But even with land in sight, mariners face a danger: get too close and you'll crash. Sailing along a coastline requires a delicate balance of remaining close enough to familiar features and keeping a safe distance from the comforts. Because you can't have adventure without setting out to sea in the first place.

Now we were out at sea and everything looked unfamiliar, even the constellations.

✳ ✳ ✳

THE NEXT REGION WE PLANNED TO VISIT was Aoraki/Mount Cook National Park, a protected landscape that boasts 23 peaks over 3000 metres high, including the park's namesake mountain. For the Ngāi Tahu (the primary Indigenous People of New Zealand's South Island), Aoraki, which translates to "cloud piercer," represents their most sacred ancestor. Now called Aoraki/Mount Cook, the mountain is the physical manifestation of Aoraki and links the natural with the supernatural.

The "Mount Cook" half of the peak was named after Captain James Cook, who in 1770 completed the first recorded circumnavigation of New Zealand on one of his three major voyages to the South Pacific. Captain Jon Lort Stokes, who disregarded the Indigenous name that was already in use, named it in Cook's honour in 1851. In 1998, a settlement between the Ngāi Tahu and the Crown saw the original Māori name rightfully returned to the mountain.

Cook sailed under the British flag, so his methods were infused with the colonial mentality that pervaded many centuries of exploration. The presence of his ships would forever change the course of history, including that of the Māori people of New Zealand. Yet his contributions to the advancement of science and knowledge of new geography are hard to ignore, as is the vastness of the coasts he charted.

I have long held a fascination for the ways that humans, like Cook, have navigated on both land and sea, especially without the use of maps and the advent of global positioning systems we have today. It captured my imagination as a child who grew up with paper maps strewn across the dashboard on family road trips and hours spent poring over a *National Geographic* atlas on the living room floor. Over time I came to recognize that *how* each of these travellers found their way is an intriguing history, perhaps as compelling as what they discovered at the end of their journeys.

By the time Captain James Cook set sail for the South Pacific, among many tools he had the use of a sextant, which measured the angular distance between two objects. He had the *Nautical Almanac*, which catalogued the positions of celestial bodies for the purposes of celestial navigation. Longitudinal readings, which relied on a timekeeping device, were relatively new in the practice of navigation, but Cook began to employ them as part of his techniques. As with many navigational systems, it was the combination of various readings and cues that helped a traveller get from A to B.

With no familiar landmarks to go by, and a sky filled with upside-down stars, moving on from the Akaroa Peninsula felt like setting off on the vast ocean with an endless horizon. As a mother I felt like I was out of my league, searching for some semblance of stability while the waves rocked the boat. I could sense that my efforts to navigate my outer world were mirrored by efforts to navigate my internal landscape. I currently lacked the tools to do either.

* * *

Twizel, a small town about 45 minutes from Aoraki/Mount Cook, was the next stop on our itinerary. I felt excitement that our family was finally moving on from Akaroa, but that bubble had burst by nightfall when we discovered that the holiday park we had booked did not have a crib available. Prior to leaving Canada, for some reason I had envisioned (hoped) that Maya would transition to co-sleeping with us. Why, I'm not sure, because she never had before. In my wishful thinking, I left the travel crib at home. In Twizel, another horrible, sleepless night ensued as we tried to settle the baby without the comforts and confines of four walls. Paul ended up driving around with Maya in the middle of the night, while I lay in bed staring at the top bunk, wondering what the heck we were going to do.

Maybe this was all wishful thinking, focusing on the way I wanted to believe our family could travel together. Maya had been a tough baby for us, and in all of our inexperience we didn't know if we should just try harder. Were we doing something wrong? Talking to other moms made it clear they didn't share many of the challenges we were dealing with: frequent protests and whining, constant wiggling and alertness, trouble settling for sleep, even in the car. It felt like we never got a break. So my choice to leave the travel crib at home was a symptom of a greater issue. It was as though by planning the trip I thought it would transform our baby into a more adaptable and easy-going child who slept like a champ. I could prove to myself – and others – that having a baby would not hold us back from the things we loved.

Just five days into the trip I already felt foolish.

The next morning, though we were very tired, we set off for Aoraki/Mount Cook, where we stumbled, eyes half-closed, through the Sir Edmund Hillary Alpine Centre, drank coffee, and stared out the window at the glacier-clad peak. Then, instead of returning to Twizel, we sent a message to a friend in Wānaka named Lisa, who had invited us to stay at her place. It would be the first of many changes we'd make to our itinerary.

Perhaps navigation sometimes involves changing courses altogether.

"Do you mind if we come early?" I asked, explaining what had happened in Twizel.

"No problem!" Lisa responded. "I'll have a crib waiting for you." Lisa had a little boy the same age as Maya and I could sense she could sympathize with our predicament.

Our time in Wānaka gave us respite, like a cold glass of water on a blistering hot day. For a few days we were back on our feet. Lisa helped me track down a used travel crib for Maya to bring with us on the rest of the trip. It was well loved and required some repair – mesh that required sewing and a floorboard that was cracked in half – but it was a hand-me-down we'd make good use of.

During our four-day stay, we slept deeply in between wakings when the baby couldn't settle herself back down. Our conversations with Lisa, an outdoorsy mother herself, reminded us we could find kindred spirits in other parents who sought to inject more adventure into a life with kids, even if it felt ambitious. With her, I could also commiserate: travelling with a baby was hard. Heck, parenting was hard.

In Wānaka, our travels finally began to resemble what we had hoped they would. We walked downtown and treated ourselves each day to coffee and breakfast at a cafe that welcomed kids with toys to play with and tiny chairs to sit on. We took in live music at a farmers' market that was set up in a park not far from the famous "Wānaka Tree," a willow tree so perfectly crooked that each year its sideways-hanging status brings throngs of photographers to its perch in Roys Bay. We drove to Queenstown as a day trip, where we walked by Lake Wakatipu, danced with Maya as buskers strummed their tunes near the harbour and grabbed lunch at a local pub. And we hiked the 250 metres of elevation to the top of Mount Iron, not a difficult trek but one that gave us 360-degree views and a glimpse of the route we'd be driving to Haast, our next stopping point. As I handed bite-sized snacks to the baby riding on my back, I diverted my gaze from my feet to the view of distant snow-capped mountains of Mount Aspiring National Park. The cerulean water of lakes

Wānaka and Hāwea pooled in elongated basins between strings of rugged peaks.

Doing *anything* felt good, but hiking as a family felt divine.

We found our stride and so did Maya, but in a more literal sense. Just before we left Canada, she began to stand up on her own and take a step or two forward, a look of satisfaction sweeping across her face just before her balance gave way. Lisa was in the middle of moving homes and her living room was empty, leaving a runway of carpet for the baby to experiment on. Paul and I knelt a few feet from each other, gradually widening the distance as Maya took one, two, three, four steps between us. Then, in one moment of shock amongst the adults, she took 12 steps in a row, straight across the room before collapsing into Paul's welcoming arms.

She was only 11 months old and it was the end of crawling. We'd be chasing her more than ever now, but it was certainly not a bad thing that she'd no longer be dragging her knees around. From clay-floored airports to beaches littered with dog poop, in the weeks to come we'd avoid some filthy situations so long as she could stay upright.

✳ ✳ ✳

WE DEPARTED WĀNAKA in early March, feeling more optimistic about the rest of the trip. During our layover there, I changed our reservations at each of the holiday parks to reserve cabins instead of campsites. Abandoning the camping plans, even though our preferred style was to rough it under the stars, brought a great sense of relief that we wouldn't have to compromise our sleep more than we already were. I also cancelled a few reservations to give us more time in each location, though it meant longer drives in between.

The two-hour drive from Wānaka to Haast skirted around Mount Burke on the west side of Lake Hāwea before hopping to the east side of Lake Wānaka. From there, it began to parallel the lake's headwaters: the Makarora River. We drove the highway, gobsmacked by the scenery unfolding at every turn as we followed the lower contours of treeless peaks, an open view to the lakes and river

ever present on at least one side of the car. As usual, the baby pro-
tested and we steeled our ears against the barrage of noise coming
from the back seat. We couldn't make much by way of conversation,
but as we passed the confluence of the Wilkin and Makarora rivers,
I knew precisely what Paul was referring to when he said, "I crossed
the river right over there."

The Makarora River originates near Haast Pass, on the eastern
flanks of the Southern Alps in Mount Aspiring National Park, and
flows south before emptying into Lake Wānaka. Trampers, as hikers
in New Zealand are called, know the river to be extremely dangerous,
especially after heavy rain. When Paul arrived at the banks of the river on his solo trek across the South Island in 2007, it had rained hard
and the water was treacherously high – a brisk-moving, frothing and
white-capped flow he'd be risking his life to cross on foot.

"I could see Makarora about half a kilometre away, on the other
side of the river," he told me over the phone. I was seated on the
floor with my back pressed against my bed while a rowdy group of
partiers hollered from a nearby campus parking lot. "After several
days in the wilderness, I was so wet and tired and kind of looking
forward to the upsides of civilization, you know? But one glance at
the brown water with debris floating past me...I knew it was a clear
'no go.'"

Due to the ongoing dangers, park rangers had put a radio nearby
where one could call for a boat if it was unsafe to cross. A ranger
Paul had met previously on the trail had cautioned him to use it and
not to fool around.

"I could have tried to cross when the water levels lowered," Paul
said. "I still had food. But I was really looking forward to getting to
Makarora to restock and get a meal. Dry out my gear. Plus, I didn't
know how long it would take for the water to settle down. So I put
in a call on the radio and the operator told me they were coming."

Paul cleared his throat. "Hours went by and I started to wonder
if they were coming at all. I wasn't sure if I should call again. Then,
finally, a jet boat came by. "Sorry," the driver said, "but we've just
picked up a body."

Paul's voice wavered and I could hear he was choking up. "Another hiker had made the choice to cross, but he forgot to unclip his backpack," he said. "His pack was sucked under the water and he couldn't free himself. They picked up his body downstream."

"Oh my goodness," I said, picking a pause in the conversation to express my sympathy. "That's horrible."

Paul continued: "The next morning, I was picking up some groceries when I saw the ranger I'd met on the trail. He said, 'Thank God, you're alive! I'm taking you for breakfast!' He had been convinced the body was mine."

When Paul called me to tell me about the incident, I could tell the situation was still raw for him. It left me feeling tearful and shaken as well. The realization of *what could have been* settled in, mixed with the sorrow that a fellow hiker had made the choice he hadn't. For all of the decisions Paul had made throughout his adventures, and a generally conservative approach to risk, this was one situation presented in black and white, of the difference between choosing to go for it or heeding to a greater, if even less-preferred, sense of caution. How many times had we taken chances in our climbing or other adventurous pursuits? Failed to recognize the danger at a seemingly benign fork in the road? Or recognized the risks but made a calculated decision that we could handle it?

Seeing the fragility of those choices first-hand at the Makarora River had a lasting impression on us as a couple.

Driving by the site of the incident with Maya in the back seat added new context to the river saga. Should something happen on a climbing trip or expedition, it wasn't just a partner left behind but now also a child. My thoughts grew murky with the same questions I'd been asking since before we became parents: *Should our tolerance for risk change when we become parents? Can a person pursue risky activities and also be a responsible parent? Are we not better parents if we pursue the things we love to do?*

I'd yet to get back into alpine climbing or anything categorically high-risk since Maya was born. But Paul had. I supported his climbing endeavours, but I wasn't yet ready to venture into exposed terrain or to embark on mountaineering pursuits of any kind. I wasn't ready to be away from the baby. It surprised me how little jealousy or yearning I felt for the days he had out in the mountains. Was it the tiredness? Postpartum recovery? Less tolerance for risk? All of it. I didn't have the desire, especially while my daughter was so young.

As a new dad, Paul didn't take long to ease back into mountaineering, still keenly aware that he needed to pay attention to his thoughts and feelings along the way. It was certainly on his mind the previous August as he departed for his first attempt to scale the highest peak in the Canadian Rockies.

"This trip could very well be about more than just climbing Mount Robson," he said. "I'll see how I feel about being disconnected from my wee family up there."

On that trip, his team was turned back high on the mountain due to snow softening across the bergschrund – a large crevasse feature – on the Kain Face, a 250-metre-high slope of 45-degree snow and ice en route to the summit ridge. It left him hungering for more, aware that his mountaineering pursuits were like soul food, essential to his happiness and sense of purpose as a human. In the weeks after the Robson attempt, he climbed mounts Quadra, Chephren, Chimney and Hungabee. I trusted his judgment, even if I couldn't trust that bad luck wouldn't befall him: the slip of a foot, a handhold coming loose, a rock barrelling down from above.

And though he had gotten back into climbing, our lives as adventure-seeking parents barely resembled the pre-kid version. Things were not the same when I was finding muddy crampons next to the pail of dirty baby clothes in the shower, or when Paul lay in his sleeping bag, high on a mountain, scrolling through photos of his round-cheeked wonder. And things were certainly no longer the same when one parent was staying back when it used to be something we did together. That first year as parents was about doing whatever was required to stay sane, and granting each other freedom to "escape" when we needed it. For Paul, that meant having the chance to head off into the alpine. For me, it meant keeping things as safe and simple as possible, though I relished any chance to get out into the gentler terrain of the mountains on familiar trails.

No one had stayed home for this adventure, though. Travelling with a baby for 70 days through New Zealand and the South Pacific, island-hopping like a bunch of backpackers...this was a test of endurance I was grateful to be sharing with my husband. We had made a great team as parents through the first 11 months of Maya's life so far. We'd actually grown closer, even though we barely had the chance to connect just the two of us.

We would need to lean into that partnership like never before.

* * *

OUR DRIVE TO HAAST opened my eyes to New Zealand's geographical diversity, as if the island's topography was being crammed into a children's pop-up book. In just two hours, we drove through lake country and forests, past braided rivers and glaciated peaks that faded quickly to flatter terrain and a glimpse of the Tasman Sea. On our first night after leaving Wānaka, we slept very little as the baby adjusted to yet another new place. But we weren't stopping for long, with plans to depart the next day to drive the coastline and stop for a few nights in Franz Josef. From there we'd follow the water all the way to Charleston before heading inland, up to Nelson, then across to Picton to board the ferry for the North Island.

In the days that followed, no amount of driving would familiarize the baby with the process of getting from A to B, or eventually put her at ease in the back seat. And two or three nights in a place wasn't enough for her to overcome her apprehension about new environments, especially new places to sleep in. We grew tired and weary. I alternated between feeling despair and deciding it would just take more time. Night after night we struggled, and a lack of sleep made Maya more volatile during the daytime. She'd shift from happy, joyful playing to all-out meltdown on a dime.

"She needs to learn how to fall asleep on her own," Paul said on our way from Haast to Franz Josef as intermittent sounds of protest blared from behind. We cranked the radio louder to tune it out.

I knew that, but I wondered if there was something else going on. Without having the vocabulary to speak, Maya left us in the dark about why exactly she was protesting. We figured out much later that, as a young child, she detested the feeling of being constrained. She wouldn't even hug or cuddle until she was 3. So, while she was overtired and struggling to calm down to sleep, the few hours of car rides per day also meant she couldn't move freely and she was persistent in letting us know.

"Maybe she'll outgrow it," I said, hardly believing it for myself.

We rolled along with the baby wailing. I almost wondered if people in the cars around us could hear her, she was so loud. Then a snicker flashed across my face as I stared out the window, thinking about our conversation with the guests at Skoki Lodge. Travel certainly wasn't the same. And though we *could* do it, right now I wasn't sure if it was worth it.

* * *

THE SCENERY CONTINUED TO UNFOLD around us like a storybook. As we drove through farmer's fields, not far from Gillespies Beach, the mountains of Aoraki/Mount Cook National Park rose beside us, with glaciers crumbling downwards, almost into the trees. Occasionally, we were treated to a baby quietly napping in the back seat; more often than not, we needed to stop, and gladly so. Fresh air was always the best antidote when the confines of the car began to wear us out. At Gillespies we stopped for a memorable play on the rocky beach, where Maya discovered sand and shovelled so much in her mouth that we later found the evidence in her diaper. At Franz Josef we walked to the base of the glacier that had receded out of reach, the baby taking a short nap on my back as we plodded along in terrain that reminded us of home.

Kilometre after winding kilometre, New Zealand continued to astonish us. The road from Franz Josef to Punakaiki wove us between imposing cliffs on one side and the rising tide on the other. Sea stacks stood like soldiers guarding the coastline, braving the crashing waves as they rolled through. Like all roads in New Zealand, it took us longer to get there than we anticipated. We stopped to explore the Pancake Rocks and blowholes of Paparoa National Park and let these wonders of nature fill our batteries before we resumed the drive to Punakaiki Beach Camp. As Paul unpacked the car, I played with Maya in the shade beside our cabin.

She stumbled around, climbing over tree roots and crushing dried leaves between her tiny fingers. I tried to be present with her, but my thoughts pulled me out of the moment. Pre-parenthood, travel usually offered me a time to be introspective, a break from everyday demands that allowed me to do some reflecting on my life. Travel used to offer a parallel, inward journey – a voyage through my thoughts, peppered with conversations with my travel mates when the timing was right. But I had brought my everyday demands with me to the South Pacific in the form of a small human who relied on me 24/7, her needs taking up space in even the furthest corners of my mind. I had so little time to pause and reflect. Our travels so far were forcing me not only to bend around my responsibilities as a parent but also accept that I'd need to ignore my own yearnings.

That sense of longing felt like an itch that couldn't be scratched. And it wasn't just the baby pulling me away from it. In that first year of motherhood, I had lost sight of where I ended and where Maya began. Her needs trumped my own, or I allowed them to, even when she would have survived just fine without me. Most of the time, I didn't mind being by her side. I got used to staying back or missing out. Part of me enjoyed the excuse. With our closest family living a ten-hour drive away, often the biggest break I got was when a friend would come take her for a half-hour walk, or when Paul would have freedom from work responsibilities to send me out of the house, baby-free.

As Paul lugged our bags to our cabin and rearranged the car, I continued to watch Maya toddle around. But a sudden, desperate need for solitude descended, rather unexpectedly, on me. It was a need, a sensation of *get me out now*, that I hadn't yet felt as a mother. Panic arose within me like a scream that wouldn't come out. Like I was trapped in the trunk of a car and no one could hear me. It was as though my inner voice, the one that spoke *to* me as the mother and wife, was shouting for attention. I could have told Paul I needed a moment to myself, to stop unpacking for a while so I could take a step away, but it would be years before I could confidently state my needs. I was plagued with feelings of guilt if I inconvenienced someone or asked them to give more in my place. The good girl had followed me into motherhood. In this moment, I saw that clear as day.

As I fixed up our dinner that evening, my yearning to escape slipped out of me in a simple phrase.

"I need a break," I said to Paul as I flipped grilled cheese in a pan. The statement was as general to my life as it was to this specific moment. Motherhood had been all-consuming. I'd been going for so long without taking time to catch my breath.

"Why don't you go down to the beach tonight," Paul said. He had also picked up on my restlessness.

"I'll think about it," I replied.

It was all so simple. The beach was less than 100 metres away. Yet for nearly a year I'd been the one staying back and I'd grown attached to that identity. It was easier to just stick with that narrative about myself. If I took off, certainly I'd pay for it later when the baby woke up and I wasn't there, and without me to nurse her she'd get riled up and we'd have to start the whole bedtime process again. I was sure this was going to happen.

When Maya was finally asleep, Paul gave me the gentle nudge I needed.

"Just go down to the beach for a few minutes," he said. "You don't need to stay long if you don't want to."

I gently nodded with a silent "yes" and put on my flip-flops.

I slipped out of the cabin and walked the short path to the ocean, a salty breeze meeting me well before I got to the water. I stood there watching the sun descend as small waves gently lapped on shore. I kicked off my sandals. In just a few minutes I could feel the scream dissipating, like it was slowly leaking out of me without a sound. I felt more peaceful, yet I was keenly aware of the voice in the back of my head telling me not to push my luck. Was it worth being here if Maya woke up and I wasn't there to nurse her back to sleep?

I felt pulled in two directions. I longed to watch the sun go all the way down, to see the sky change colours then darken into night. For a moment, I wanted to forget all responsibility and sit in the sand until *I* felt like going back. I should have gifted myself a few extra minutes, but I didn't. I wish I'd known then that I'd be setting a better example for my child by honouring my needs as much as hers, by reclaiming my identity. Instead, in that moment I reminded myself that the level of dependence Maya had on us was for a short season of life. And our time abroad would get easier, right? I'd go back soon, before the sun hit the horizon, even though I didn't want to. The good girl was winning, yet again.

As I watched the glowing ball dip a little lower, new realizations sank in like my toes in the sand. As much time as I'd spent with Maya that year, and thought I knew her inside and out, this trip overseas had exposed new parts of her personality. Home was predictable, but here, on the other side of the world, our circumstances were changing every day, sometimes every minute. Maya was surprising me with her resilience; that, despite our lack of sleep, she could be happy and engaged. Her eagerness to explore was inspiring.

I was parenting in uncharted territory. Routine and familiarity were as far away as Canada. I began to see Maya as her own person, separate from me – each of us doing our best to deal with an ever-changing situation and an evolving relationship between mother and daughter. I learned to tune into her in new ways, turning the dial ever so slightly for new frequencies when static – uncertainty – filled the air.

As I left Punakaiki Beach, I picked up a smooth black stone and, a few feet later, a white one. I didn't understand their significance at the time but later saw them as a metaphor for the separation I was beginning to feel, the *me* and the *her*. Paul and I often spoke about how, amidst all our moving around, *we* were Maya's home. And though we were the only constant in her life while we were travelling, we were, in actuality, three individuals, three separate entities on a journey together. My entanglement with her had begun to loosen.

Those rocks joined others I have collected on our travels and, still today, they are nestled in a Tibetan singing bowl on a shelf in my bedroom. They are a physical manifestation of my growth as a mother, as is the child who can now verbalize her opinions and describe her feelings instead of crying without explanation. In my own moments of vulnerability, she demonstrates a depth of compassion and empathy I never considered she might one day possess, certainly not on that evening of reflection as I watched the sun set at Punakaiki Beach.

* * *

FROM PUNAKAIKI, we continued our road trip to Nelson and across the Cook Straight to the North Island. For that first week on the North Island, I had a week-long migraine and wondered what would happen if I didn't get better. *We can't keep going like this.* The migraine finally relented in Rotorua when a cyclone touched down and released the barometric pressure with buckets of rain. We ended our New Zealand forays with a trip to the Coromandel Peninsula, then onward to Auckland where we stayed in our first hotel since we'd left Canada after many weeks at guest houses, hostels and holiday parks.

Auckland offered us a reset button. There was a coffee shop nearby where Paul and I took turns checking in on the home front, contacting family and seeing if there were any important work-related emails. We had managed to keep work to a minimum during our two months away, which allowed us to focus on gathering photographs and stories from the destinations we were visiting. I had secured a few freelance articles, mostly travel pieces for magazines. I was otherwise relying on my self-employed maternity leave.

Another reset was the chance to purge our belongings. We were headed into tropical temperatures and wouldn't be camping at all, so we could shed the warm layers, tent and any other gear that had proved useless. I packed it all in a large duffel bag and sent it back to a friend in Canada.

By the time we left New Zealand, we had driven 2500 kilometres across the South and North islands. The trip so far was Type 2 Fun on steroids. And ahead lay the "off the beaten track" portion of our family tour through the South Pacific: the island of Niue and the archipelagoes of French Polynesia. So far, Paul and I had shouldered the load together: the early morning wake-ups, the cutting of grapes into quarters, the frequent objections, the diaper changes on the back seat of the car. We stuck it out only by spelling each other off whenever we could.

Our shared memories would later help us to salvage the happier memories of a trip that left us feeling discouraged and dangerously sleep-deprived. Together, Paul and I could reminisce and hold the moments of ease and beauty close to our hearts. Time would eventually help us to loosen our grip on the more vexing situations, knowing the only alternative to our decision to keep travelling with our dear daughter was to point the compass toward Canada and go back home.

8
A World of Prospects

We had heard of a hidden beach, encircled by cliffs and large coral boulders that resembled a pirate's lair. It was hidden but not a secret. Togo Chasm is one of the more popular attractions on the island of Niue. Still, the idea of it tickled my imagination, as I glanced at the tourist brochure for the island. The child in me could see treasure chests and stolen loot half-buried in perfect sand. For a moment I wished Maya were older so she could appreciate and indulge in my fantasy with me. For that matter, I wished I knew what she was thinking most of the time. She was still a year away from having the words to express herself.

We drove the main road around the island to the other side, to the Huvalu Forest Conservation Area. This large tropical rainforest encompasses a large part of Niue and is bordered on one side by water. To get to Togo Chasm we hiked through parts of the forest toward the coastline. With Maya strapped to my back in the carrier, I trod carefully across slippery roots. The forest quickly gave way to a field of dark grey-coloured coral pinnacles, like a vast lava field that dripped straight upwards before solidifying. The path was quite flat and hard packed, but I was aware of the extremely tough, rigid terrain sitting all around me and I continued to walk cautiously, knowing that if I fell, Maya would fall too.

Suddenly, the path ended at the top of a 27-rung wooden ladder that descended rather precipitously toward the beach below – the base of the chasm.

"I don't feel comfortable going down that ladder with Maya on my back," I said to Paul.

I thought back to our hike down to the waterfall at Ravine Cyrique on Dominica. I didn't feel that the ladder itself was dangerous, but the idea of falling made me nervous. The island brochure guide called the chasm "a must-see but not for the faint-hearted." I usually found brochure descriptions to be too conservative, but this ladder made my stomach flutter. A squirmy 1-year-old affixed to my back wasn't helping the situation.

Perhaps I was overthinking it, but this was not a place to take a baby. I'd often thought about what we would do in the case of an accident or medical emergency, being so far from home on a remote island in the Pacific. We had travel medical insurance, but were we making a poor choice by taking our child somewhere so far off the beaten path?

What if something bad happened?

"Let's take our turns then," Paul suggested, snapping me out of my downward spiral of fearful thinking.

"You go first," I replied, "and when you come back up we can switch her to your back."

I walked back and forth on the coral trail, snapping photos of the seascape, until Paul returned about 15 minutes later, his eyes wide with wonder. I wandered over to the top of the ladder to meet him.

"It's amazing down there!" he explained. "I wish we could spend more time exploring; there's so much to look at!"

"I'm excited to see it!" I said as I unclipped the chest strap of our baby carrier.

"Take your time. It's magical."

With Maya safely off my back, I swung around to face into the ladder and gingerly made my first few moves to begin my descent toward the sandy beach below. The steep ladder had worn, slippery rungs that made my heart beat, double-time. I took them one step at a time and moved slowly and deliberately. Halfway down, I was confident I had made the right decision to leave Maya at the top.

When I reached the bottom, I exhaled with a sense of relief and took in my surroundings. It was exactly as I thought it would be, minus the actual treasure. Huge, pocketed walls of coral rose on both sides. A small, unlikely grove of coconut trees grew out of the beach. At the other end of the gorge sat a small lagoon, filled with lime-green moss and ferns. I stood for a moment, absorbing stories that echoed off the walls. Aware that this was perhaps a rare moment to myself, I stole a few extra minutes to enjoy the peace and quiet.

I suppose we wouldn't do anything if we weren't willing to accept any risks, I thought, as if to answer my earlier question. But were we being selfish? We were on an island Maya would never remember, so the adventure was more for us than for her. Or was it? Might this experience prepare her for the next one? I'd read that children do form memories, they just don't carry them for as long – something known as "infantile amnesia." Anna had alluded to that, years before, on the island of Tortola. So perhaps each adventure was like a rung on that ladder; string them together and one can lead to the next. Rung by rung, Maya could acquaint herself with the ideas of travel and adventure, of the discomfort that comes with being in new places and meeting new people, of the unique ways these experiences could prepare her for adversity and uncertainties down the road. At least, I hoped she would.

I also hoped she'd learn we were privileged to travel and to be *choosing* to face the hardships that arrived with the unfamiliar.

My heart was beating quickly again as I ascended the ladder back to my family. Paul had begun hiking back slowly – likely to get a head start before Maya grew impatient in a place where we couldn't put her down. Her pink hat bounced along behind him, an unlikely splotch of vibrant colour amidst the maze of coral pinnacles.

* * *

Before we flew to French Polynesia, we had hopped from New Zealand to the island of Niue for a quick week of exploring. Though self-governing, Niue is technically a part of New Zealand after it was annexed in 1901. To get to this remote island we flew 2400 kilometres northeast of Auckland, back across the International Date Line.

As chance would have it, Maya turned 1 year old the day we flew to Niue, on March 22, 2014. So, when she woke up the next morning, she turned 1 again. A month prior, I had missed my 30th birthday entirely. We'd left Canada to fly to New Zealand the day before my birthday. En route, we crossed the International Date Line and skipped ahead to the day after my birthday. As a mother, the circumstances were fitting, laughably so, with my child doubling her attention around her birthday and me missing mine entirely.

Niue is an upraised coral atoll, one of the world's largest – a wild place unlike anything I'd seen before. Trekking through the rainforest, we stumbled upon piles of coral, scattered like boulders. The coastal waters were clear as can be, with sea arches that hung overhead and living corals sheltered in peaceful coves. Captain James Cook named the island "Savage Island," when, in 1774, the locals refused his attempts to land not once but three times (apparently, due to a fear of disease, and rightly so).

Today, Niue welcomes tourists and the dollars they bring. The island's economy is otherwise heavily dependent on receiving aid from New Zealand. The locals we met were friendly and welcoming, and they particularly loved that we had brought a baby. While Paul and I shooed flies off our breakfast at a local hotel, Niuean women scooped Maya from her high chair and took her for a walk, rocking her to the tunes of songs I didn't recognize and hymns I was familiar with. She'd return with a hibiscus tucked behind her ear.

Flights landed and departed from Niue's small, clay-floored airport on Saturdays, with one planeload of people arriving and another departing on the same aircraft. That meant we had a week there and, after a month spent changing locations every few days, we enjoyed the slower pace. A week also allowed Maya to become comfortable with her surroundings and she began to sleep better. We noticed the pattern but dared not point it out because of what it meant for the upcoming weeks. We had more island-hopping planned, with just a few days in each place. We were beginning to realize it would be somewhat torturous for all three of us.

With a bit more sleep, we felt more refreshed to explore, hiking down to dramatic sea arches and natural formations like the Togo Chasm. We swam in crystal-clear water, visited with locals at the nearby grocery store and endured sudden rainstorms that left us dripping from head to toe. We had a good laugh when we drove into the jungle to an "official" viewpoint only to find the road narrowed and became rather grown in, forcing me to do an 18-point turn in a low-clearance rental car, between tightly placed rocks and trees.

We enjoyed the adventure and obscurity of the island. As with Saba or Dominica, no one that we knew had been there. I felt grateful to be visiting, also knowing how threatened the culture of Niue is. To give context to our experience, and any travel articles I might write, I spent time asking questions to locals and taking notes from various materials I found in print and on the web. I learned that, due to the annexation, Niueans have dual citizenship with New Zealand. Many are leaving the coral island to pursue other opportunities, especially after Cyclone Heta left 200 residents homeless in 2004. Many chose not to rebuild. Like many of the islands we would visit in the South Pacific, as much as they looked like paradise to us, they were unappealing to those who felt that living there would result in a lack of prospects.

Thinking about the frigid temperatures and snow back home, it was hard to imagine how life in Polynesia might be unappealing. But calling a place "home," especially one you didn't choose, could take the novelty out of it. I had the privilege to choose where I wanted to be, and I had chosen Banff. It never grew dull for me. As we travelled over to French Polynesia and saw the juxtaposition of those who *chose* it versus those who wanted more from life and couldn't have it, I became ever more grateful to have the freedom to be visiting *and* have a place I loved to call home.

✳ ✳ ✳

FRENCH POLYNESIA is made up of 118 islands and atolls (ring-shaped coral reefs). The country is known more popularly as "Tahiti," which is also the name of its main island. An airline pass permitted us to hop from one island to another, so long as we didn't retrace our steps. Our planned trajectory, therefore, would take us to Tahiti, Mo'orea, Huahine, Maupiti, Bora Bora, Tikehau and Fakarava.

As we said goodbye to Niue, we said goodbye to the stability that a week in one place had offered us. From then on, island-hopping began to feel like island-slamming, where we'd land face first on the next coral uplift and barely peel ourselves off before jet-setting or ferry-riding again. Of course, it was all by our own silly design.

When we arrived on Mo'orea, a rookie mistake we made as parents caused Maya to land face first – literally.

As parents of a young child, we had a sixth sense for dangers when we arrived at new accommodations. We put small objects away, identified areas where Maya might trip or fall and took sharp kitchen implements out of reachable drawers and placed them up high. It was an almost subconscious process. So, when we arrived at our condo on Mo'orea, we did an inventory of the dangers and slid a couch in front of some stairs that went down from the patio outside our condo.

When Paul went to ask the proprietor for some cooking supplies, I casually went about, figuring out the air conditioning (a luxury!) while Maya wandered outside. I didn't think anything of it, knowing the stairs were blocked, until two minutes later when Paul shrieked at me as he breezed through the door.

"She fell!" he hollered. Tears were running down his face as he rushed in, baby in his arms. "She crashed down the wooden stairs. She hit the concrete slab at the bottom with her head."

He could barely catch his breath between gasps.

I was frightened but also confused. Why had she fallen? Then it dawned on me. He hadn't put the couch back in front of the stairs when he left and, naturally, he assumed I'd be supervising her.

"I thought the couch was there!" I fumed.

Immediately, my instinct was to nurse to help soothe and comfort her. With her head perched on my elbow, I was able to scan for a significant injury. An obvious goose egg was forming, but she calmed down quickly. The guilt I felt was horrendous. When she calmed down enough, I used the spotty WiFi to search Google for the symptoms of concussion or head injury.

Paul was still reeling and understandably angry that I hadn't been watching. I felt angry that he hadn't put the couch back in front of the stairs. We had both made assumptions. In that moment I knew I needed to shove aside my tendency to keep digging for answers and focus on what to do next. The blame game wasn't going to help.

"It says here we should watch for signs, like vomiting, which are more obvious to see in babies than other signs," I said, relaying the information as I scanned my computer.

I was calm, though I hadn't witnessed the incident myself. Paul was still struggling to calm down after seeing Maya's tiny body flying down the stairs the way it did.

"And we should wake her or prod her every 30 minutes tonight to make sure she stirs," I added, aware this would entail a truly sleepless night. I would do whatever it took to make sure my daughter was well.

Keeping an eye on Maya was our only option aside from tracking down a doctor, if there even was one. Some Polynesian islands only have clinics run by nurses. A significant injury or illness might result in a helicopter ride to a larger island, usually Tahiti. (A local woman on Fakarava, an atoll we later visited, told me most pregnant women move to the main island a month before giving birth.)

The fleeting thoughts I'd had at the Togo Chasm about risk and remoteness were now landing firmly on my consciousness.

Maya seemed okay, happy even. She stirred with every finger poke all night long. Confident she wasn't facing a serious injury, we chose to proceed. But the incident put us on edge for the rest of our time on Mo'orea.

That could have been the end of the trip, I thought. For a moment, I realized it might have been a good idea to end the trip anyway.

Between the roosters crowing and dogs barking all night long, we had reached new levels of exhaustion. We weren't having much fun. Maybe our little family wasn't cut out for this. Whatever I'd felt way back on Tortola watching Mila running bare-bummed into the sea, that glimmer of possibility that we could venture off the beaten track with our kid...it felt like it was being extinguished.

It would take time for Paul and me to get over how frightened Maya's fall had made us. As a parent, I occasionally wandered down that dark hallway of the worst possible outcome – of the thought of losing a child – and that was one of them. I couldn't dwell there.

Yet for all the challenges we were facing, French Polynesia had granted us some treasures. After Mo'orea, we had a few days on Huahine, where we enjoyed a pool on our guest house property, bicycle rides and delicious pizza from the local food trucks called *roulottes*. And our next stop would be one we'd never forget.

* * *

MAUPITI DIDN'T MAGICALLY grant us more sleep, but it felt like a soothing balm to our weary hearts. In many ways, it was like a dream. It began with our landing on an unlikely airstrip built straight out of the ocean. It formed a diagonal line like the cross of a "*t*" through a short strip of land that wouldn't otherwise be large enough for a runway. From there we were greeted by one of our guest lodge proprietors, a heavy-set Polynesian man named Kalani, who adorned us with flowers (we'd leave with shell necklaces, as is the tradition). He wore sunglasses, a ratty T-shirt, board shorts and sandals. He led us to a small boat and I clipped Maya into her infant life jacket for the ride. Kalani then ferried us across the lagoon that makes up the interior space between the various islands of Maupiti to Motu Tiapaa, one of the smaller islands where we'd be staying. The water was so clear that from the surface I could see individual grains of the white-sanded bottom. Looking outwards it was a perfect pool of aqua-blue salt water. We glided across in a dinghy as the sun shone down and I longed to climb into the water. Maya sat in my lap, chatting incomprehensibly over the *put put* of the engine as it sputtered tiny clouds of exhaust behind us. Soon enough, we were pulling up to a small dock outside the pension, our home for the next five nights.

We were promptly greeted in joyful and fast French by Cecile, whose uniform was a black bikini top with bathing suit bottoms covered in a loose *pareo* (a wrap-around skirt). She was barefoot, hair pulled into a loose bun, with skin seamlessly tanned from head to toe. She enthusiastically showed us to our lodging, a rustic *faré* (cabin), outfitted with mosquito nets and a double bed. It didn't take long to notice that the air inside was completely still. No wind would pass through it throughout our entire stay. There was no fan and nowhere to plug in a fan anyway. The shade cut some of the heat, but the enclosure trapped the humidity. It would be like sleeping in yet another sauna, but at this point we didn't have a choice.

How you react to the challenges will determine your experience, I reminded myself, staring at the small spot next to the wall where I'd be installing the travel bed. *You chose this. You chose not to go home.*

We enjoyed the property immensely. It hosted a bathroom, a shower building and an outdoor vanity that faced the sea so that the mirror reflected the tropical scene when I was facing it, like a mirage in the glass. A dining area was used for meals and cooking our lunches. Breakfast and dinner were provided for us, and that is where we fell in love with Polynesian cuisine.

French Polynesia comprises a unique blend of various cultures, which were all expressed in the food laid on the table before us: Polynesian, of course, as well as French and Chinese. The archipelago became a French colony in 1880 and is now an overseas collectivity with semi-autonomous status. With that, the baguette has become the mainstay of breakfasts in Tahiti, served with butter and jam. Locals could be seen biking through towns with their warm baguettes, a daily tradition we adopted on a number of islands when we needed to forage three meals a day. Many French people, like Cecile, have relocated to French Polynesia in search of sun and business opportunities, or a place to retire.

I was never a fish lover until I was introduced to *poisson cru en lait de coco* or *'Ota 'ika*, the Tahitian dish consisting of raw fish marinated in citrus juice and coconut milk. The Chinese, who arrived in the 1860s (mainly to work on plantations), put their own spin on the *poisson cru*. In this rendition, the raw tuna is marinated in vinegar, ginger and oil and a variety of complementary flavours, such as lime, garlic and onion. Both were melt-in-your-mouth divine.

Every day in Maupiti meant a fresh catch and dinner consisted of two courses of fish. We watched with intrigue as Kalani tore fish from the bone with just two teeth remaining in his otherwise toothless mouth, expertly chewing and spitting out smaller bones that came off with the flesh. I was feeling well oiled after eating my equivalent to a year's worth of fish when Cecile handed me a bowl of fresh coconut oil one day and encouraged me to slab it all over my body.

"*La crème hydratante de Dame Nature,*" she said. (Mother Nature's moisturizer.)

My skin had bronzed after weeks in the sun, but it was also dry and itchy. The pure coconut oil felt soothing. Her thoughtfulness alone felt like a breath of fresh air.

* * *

PAUL AND I BEGAN to take turns watching Maya, which we realized was the key to our sanity and actually doing anything in the places we'd travelled so far to visit. One day Paul went to Maupiti's main island to photograph from the top of Mount Te'urafa'atiu, the highest point in the area. When it was my turn, I wanted to sleep but went out in the kayak instead, gliding across the water that glistened clear and blue. Another time I sat under a palm tree and typed the first words of what would later become a full-length book. On yet another, I lay in the hammock and closed my eyes. I was so tense from weeks of physical and mental demands that I needed to take a moment to breathe and be still. *You may never come back here*, I reminded myself. *You can wallow in the struggle that this trip has been so far, or you can enjoy this moment.*

Our *faré* on Maupiti was close to the water and Maya required an even higher level of supervision than we had so far experienced. She stumbled like a drunk around the property and along the lagoon, navigating the sand that shifted with every step. In the shade lay another hazard: stray, though docile, dogs we couldn't trust not to bite. But having the freedom to roam made Maya happy, so we stayed close by, ready to scoop her up. On Maupiti she had her own version of a uniform – a T-shirt over a saggy diaper (we waited a long time between changes in order to ration them). She hadn't worn shoes or sandals all week. The sight of her made me giggle.

And in the evenings, when the air cooled, we gathered on the beach to watch the sunset. I remember the low, honey-tinged sun hitting Maya's face, which revealed an impish smile and wild eyes, as if the world was opening up to her. And then she took off. By now, she had mastered the sand and soon we were chasing her past sea cucumbers and crabs as her giggles echoed across the lagoon.

There is a photo from one of those evenings. I was holding Maya in my arms and I happened to glance up at the camera, unaware that Paul was ready to take a picture. The look captured on my face is one of contradiction: eyes so tired they're ringed with dark circles, but my mouth subtly curling into a genuine, contented smile. And as the sunset faded to darkness, we could step just outside the door of our cabin, the sand still warm from the heat of the day, and look up. That Orion was upside-down no longer caught me off guard. Though my internal compass was still spinning, when I looked up, I knew where I was.

* * *

A WEEK LATER, we arrived on the snake-shaped atoll Fakarava after a few days spent on Bora Bora and a lesser-known island called Tikehau. This would be our final destination before retracing our steps to Tahiti and starting the journey home. We had six nights booked at Pension Poerava on Fakarava, the largest of the Polynesian islands we were visiting. Our original plan was to camp on the property until our experience in New Zealand suggested it would be the worst idea yet. We booked a *faré* instead, a mint-green-coloured cabin with a small front porch that looked out on a grove of trees, the ocean crashing just beyond.

As we settled in with our belongings, I turned to Paul: "Perhaps being in one place for nearly a week will help Maya sleep better." It was probably wishful thinking, but I was still hoping I'd get a bit more sleep.

"Maybe. There's a bit more of a breeze through this place," Paul said.

That was true. The windows were situated in such a way that the air passed through the cabin. Even if I couldn't sleep, at least I wouldn't be sweltering at night.

Just a few days into our stay on Fakarava, we realized we'd made the same mistake that we had in the Caribbean, thinking the larger the land mass, the more time we should allocate to explore it. The issue was that we didn't have a car. We could explore by bike, but some destinations were too far away to reach on two wheels, especially under the searing hot sun.

So when we set our sights on a local's snorkelling sport about ten kilometres one-way, we paid a driver to take us there. The road was so potholed it took nearly an hour to reach the secluded beach in a van with little clearance. For the final few kilometres we didn't see any other vehicles. Our driver dropped us off and agreed to come back by 11:00 a.m., before the sun got too hot.

Paul and I took turns snorkelling, and that underwater world was like a dream. Fish more colourful than I'd ever seen before swam in patterns, seemingly unaware of my presence. Their world felt abundant and healthy, and in that water I felt a buoyancy in my spirit that I would try to keep intact when I was back on land, supervising Maya as she poked around in the shade. By this point in the trip, I felt a constant tug-of-war between feeling disappointed that our travels weren't what we'd hoped they'd be and trying to make the most of things, no matter what.

When it was time to go, we gathered our belongings and walked back to the spot where the driver had left us. There we waited. Eleven o'clock rolled around and there was no sight of him. After 20 minutes, I began to worry.

"Paul, we have no way of contacting him to see if he is even coming," I said. The sun was becoming unbearable and there was no shade by the dirt road.

Paul shook his head. "It feels like we can't get a whole lot on our side on this trip," he said. His tone indicated a rising frustration. "Let's wait a bit longer."

An hour went by. Maya fell asleep in the baby carrier on my chest.

"If he doesn't come in the next minute, we need to find some shade," Paul said. "Worse comes to worst, we can walk back to town at nightfall."

I breathed in, fighting off tears. It was an insane idea but much better than waiting any longer in the sun with a baby. We were going to run out of water soon.

We stretched one more minute to five, hoping the driver would come. Finally, we heard a vehicle approaching and the van reappeared.

"Finally," I said, exhaling the words.

The driver made no mention of his lateness as Paul slid into the passenger seat and I climbed into the back with Maya to clip her into her seat. No matter, it was behind us now. There was shade in the car, the air was blasting and we'd get a breeze once we started driving.

Once the doors were closed, the car crawled along, bumping through potholes. We were finally on our way back. I breathed a deep sigh of relief. Then, curious to know the time, I cranked my head to look between the front seats at the clock on the dashboard. It read 12:31 p.m. And that's when I saw something else: the driver was holding a beer in his hand as he drove. Actually, not only one beer but two. He had one in each hand, leaving him with his index fingers and thumbs to grip the steering wheel.

I turned to Paul and the look of alarm on my face said what I didn't want to say out loud. It didn't feel safe, but it was either that or we walk the hot, dusty road. Without water, we would be in a truly life-threatening situation. What were we supposed to do? Perhaps Paul could drive instead? Would the driver even understand our concern?

I decided the car was moving so slowly that, if I needed to, I could open the door and escape with Maya even while the vehicle was moving. For now, I sat there, my body rocking with the massive potholes, and considered the strangeness of the situation – that adventure took many forms, that we were making the safer decision by staying *in* the car with a potentially drunk driver, that risk taking isn't so black and white as making a good decision when you're forced between two evils.

We arrived back at Pension Poerava without incident but decided from then on to cycle to our destinations.

* * *

TO MY DISMAY, Maya didn't sleep better on Fakarava. Every night she awoke, every 45 minutes. I'd nurse her back to sleep and carefully put her in the bed. And just as I fell asleep again she'd wake up and the whole process would start over. Paul would barely rest but, being so tired, he managed to sleep through some of the crying. He'd rouse when she did at 5:00 a.m. and take her out into the cool morning breeze before the sun came up. Looking out the open front door of our *faré*, sometimes I could see him pacing back and forth in nothing but his underwear while she wore nothing but a diaper. I could hear him singing to her. The silhouette of her in his arms, father and daughter, against the deep blue sky of dawn is one that stood out to me from that trip. She was calm and quiet in his arms as they paced under palm trees that blew in the breeze coming off the ocean.

Watching Paul in those moments made me think about the man I met and the man I knew now. On our first international trip together, backpacking in the Caribbean, I had pondered how his determination could take him to places no one else could imagine. I didn't know then, when Paul first expressed interest in photography, that what he actually possessed was a rare kind of artistic ability. The landscape and adventure images he began to create were entirely unique and the world took notice. His images required as much visioning, patience and technical skill as they did immense physical output. To get the shots, Paul put up with discomforts that few were willing to withstand: wading into glacier-fed lakes, climbing with a pack loaded with camera gear, losing countless nights of sleep to photograph the aurora borealis. His ideas and sense of determination seemed to go hand in hand. The images required tremendous effort, yet the pursuit of such images also fulfilled Paul's desire to explore. After nearly a decade with him, I had seen just how innate that drive was. It was a part of who he was, as vital to him as water and air.

As his wife, I had witnessed first-hand how often Paul ignored his insatiable thirst for creativity and adventure for the sake of his responsibilities as a father. I didn't take this for granted. I knew similar creative and curious souls for whom this was a struggle, and family came second. In the greater mountain community, I had heard stories of absent fathers, sometimes mothers, who prioritized their passions and independence. Some had walked out altogether. But I knew Paul was dedicated to his family; we both saw his work as the income that sustained us, even if it took him away sometimes. I recognized that, for someone with his degree of ambition, for someone whose gift to the world required him to be *out there*, I admired him for the ways he contributed to the family. What mattered to me was that when he was *here* he was present, loving, helpful and attentive. He was that, and more. Over the years with him I had learned to "free" him when I had a good handle on things because he might otherwise hesitate to even ask. And the moment he had an open window, when I said, "You go," he was up a mountain, out into the wilderness, photographing through the night.

He would always come back even more happy and ready to dive into family life.

I wouldn't often go back to sleep after watching Paul and Maya through the doorway of the *faré*. But the chance to just lie there was a gift. And, despite those long, sleepless nights, the heat and the ever-changing plans, Maya would smile as we played later in the day, when we filled a basin with fresh water and let her splash, when we walked by the ocean in the cooler evening air, when we biked by the shoreline where sharks could be seen swimming just under the surface and ominous storm clouds built up over the ocean. When she smiled, I knew she was okay, that she wasn't being damaged for eternity, no matter how taxing our nights were.

We'd been travelling as a trio for two months now, and as exhausted as we were we found a bit more of a groove on Fakarava. We spent our days balancing time as a family and taking turns with Maya, and our evenings working on our laptops on the front porch of the *faré*. Occasionally, Paul slung his photo bag on his back and biked to a location to take images under the stars.

Perhaps it was knowing the trip was almost over, but we had also developed a thicker skin for the challenges we encountered. Some we found to be quite surprising, like how the island was devoid of food since it had been three weeks since a shipment had come. Breakfast was the most reliable meal of the day. Each morning, I set off by bike, with Maya behind me in the baby seat, to buy a warm baguette from a local bakery. Otherwise, the grocery store shelves were lacking even staples and there was no fresh fruit available (even that was imported). We'd brought packaged food and some fruit pouches so we were able to keep Maya well nourished. But one day another traveller tipped me off about a papaya he'd seen at a grocery store and I went off in search of it like it was the Holy Grail. Another day, a Swiss couple staying in the *faré* next to us made dinner for all the guests staying at the pension. They made potato rosti, the perfect choice seeing as the grocery store only sold potatoes and onions in large Costco-sized sacks. They were on Fakarava to celebrate their "empty-nest-hood" by learning to scuba dive. They took pity on us, perhaps with some fondness, as they watched us at the beginning of the parenting journey.

We were certainly struggling, but we would be okay. Soon we would fly home to Canada and could get back on our feet. But in those last few days on Fakarava I got thinking about this place we'd travelled so far to visit. I wondered if what *looked* like paradise *felt* like paradise to those who lived there.

One afternoon I had the chance to ask that very question to the proprietor at Pension Poerava, a French expat named Pierre who employed the local people and seemed to have his finger on the pulse – even though he, too, came from elsewhere.

"The people here are lacking prospects," he responded plainly, in French. He didn't sugar-coat the truth. "We have high rates of depression, substance abuse and suicide because, unless people leave the island, there is little for them to do with their lives."

I thought of our driver with beer bottles in his hands, and why he might have been turning to booze. About a quarter of Polynesians lived in poverty and many struggled to make ends meet. Tourism was the country's main economic activity. Thanks to our low-end budget, we were often staying with born-and-raised Polynesians, or expats who hired them, and we hoped our tourism dollars were going to people who needed the money. Still, after talking with Pierre, I felt conflicted about my own woes from travelling with a baby. By most measures, I had little to complain about. I was enduring hardships that had come because of my choice to travel and spend my savings on those experiences. And while it wasn't easy to brush off the extreme fatigue I was feeling, back in Canada a whole world of prospects was available to me.

My daughter held all those possibilities in her tiny hand.

I hoped to raise Maya in such a way that she would come to recognize this privilege: that she would have the ability to choose what she did for a living, where she wanted to go and how she wanted to live her life. For me this required popping the bubble I grew up in. Would our travels with her early on in her life help to expose her to different ways of life? Might they broaden her world view? I pondered how we might also instill these values in her at home.

On our last day, we cycled the main road lined with coconut trees as the sun set over the sea. The wind kissed our faces and rustled our sweaty shirts, cooling us down after another blazing hot day. I passed snacks to Maya, who sat on the back seat of the bike; it had proved to be a solid whining-prevention strategy, though snacking in transit would be a habit we would eventually need to break. As we rolled along, I experienced a moment of bliss. The tiredness couldn't reach me there. It was peace and contentment on two wheels, an idyllic moment that would stay with me forever. After a few minutes of quiet pedalling, I initiated an exercise with Paul that might help us remember the trip differently.

"While we ride, I want us to take turns saying something we're grateful for from this trip," I said, raising my voice above the breeze. "Or it can be a happy memory."

"Sure, babe!" Paul said. It was one of his standard answers that indicated either genuine enthusiasm or a suggestion that he was willing to play along with me. I couldn't know for sure, so I went ahead anyways.

"I'll go first," I said. "I am grateful for all the fresh fish we have eaten."

"Those pizzas on Huahine were pretty amazing," he added.

Clearly, we'd eaten well, aside from the shortage of fresh food on Fakarava.

"I appreciate how we've worked as a team," I said. "Without a co-parent, I don't think we would have pulled it off."

"That's for sure." Paul turned his pedals a few more times before speaking again. "The snorkelling has been outstanding."

"Yes, it has. And Maupiti – that beach. I wish I could go back already."

I smiled as we rallied our ideas back and forth. It was a bitter-sweet dialogue – like adding sugar to cough medicine to try to make it taste better. Yet the more sugar we added, the less bitter we were about the experiences that had nearly crushed us.

* * *

SIX METRES was all that lay between us and the million-dollar view outside our resort window on Tahiti, our last stop before starting the journey home. But we were sitting on the bathroom floor, the only place available for us to eat our pizza from the nearby *roulotte*, and we couldn't see the colours of sunset over the ocean. Instead, our entourage consisted of a toilet paper roll, a jet tub we didn't have time to use and fluorescent lights so bright we considered eating in the dark.

Under normal circumstances, I'd have felt gutted. But our expectations after nine weeks travelling with Maya were beyond rock bottom.

Here on Tahiti, the juxtaposition was more funny than cruel: After weeks of sleeping on decades-old mattresses in rustic seaside bungalows that reached hellish temperatures at night, we were finally being treated to total luxury, a four-star resort. This was the Tahitian tourism bureau's thank you for some freelance work we'd done for magazines during our island-hopping. They'd arranged a two-night stay, with breakfast and a taxi ride back to the airport included. We did our best to take advantage of it, sipping endless cappuccinos at breakfast after a month of instant coffee (France's renowned cafe culture never quite infiltrated French Polynesia), splashing around in the resort's pamphlet-worthy infinity swimming pool and enjoying views that spilled straight into a cyan-coloured lagoon. But mostly we deprived ourselves of the hotel's amenities and restaurant, all part of a plan to make our transit back home at least somewhat tolerable.

Our goal was to let the baby sleep enough before we caught our 11:00 p.m. flight out of Tahiti's Fa'a'ā International Airport to Honolulu. That meant putting Maya to bed at 6:00 p.m. and waking her two hours later to grab a taxi to the airport. The problem was her travel crib sat by the beds, between the entrance to the room and the balcony. If we could levitate and walk through walls, we'd make it there, but for fear of waking her, we didn't dare cross the room and slide open the patio door. We didn't dare poke the bear just to feel the soothing breeze coming in off the water, sweet and salty like kettle corn. We were already facing a sleepless night in transit; a sleep-deprived baby might be enough to push me off the deep end.

So while I put the baby to bed in yet another strange home away from home, Paul ran out to the closest food truck, braving narrow roads where you hold your breath in as vehicles pass closely beside you. When he arrived back at the room, he knew to quietly open the door and close it without the slightest click. A sudden noise of any volume could wake the baby. We looked at each other, wondering where we were even going to eat the darn thing.

"In the hallway?" I whispered. We might get locked out.

"The entryway?" Too small.

The next best option was the rather spacious bathroom, complete with swan-shaped towels.

We ate in silence and I stared longingly at the whirlpool bath.

When it was time to leave, I had to muster some courage. Waking a sleeping baby was strongly classified in my list of things I least liked to do. But somehow she was bright-eyed and bushy-tailed within 30 seconds. After a quick diaper change, we packed a few final items in the suitcase. Folding up the crib one more time, we decided to bring it with us, even though there was no use for it anymore; another one awaited us for our three nights in Hawaii – a quick stopover on our way back to Canada.

After hauling our bags to the elevator, I took a final glance at the room and, as is the ritual, walked back one more time to check under the bed. A deep, audible sigh fell out of me as I considered the idea of moving one more time. One part of my brain had started on the next task, but another was still processing our weeks of travel in one of the most spectacular places on the planet. *What the heck were we thinking bringing a baby here?* We'd just spent four weeks in Polynesia and watched the world go by with eyes half-closed. To this day, I can still taste both the cough syrup and the sugar. Time hasn't healed the experience, but we certainly learned from it and never travelled that way ever again.

The taxi ride to Tahiti's airport went smoothly. Paul chit-chatted with the driver while Maya and I sat in the back seat and watched the city lights zip by. Shortly after pulling up in front of the terminal and disembarking the vehicle, Paul began to unload our bags.

"I'll get a head start checking in," Paul said. From the look of the crowd through the terminal windows, it looked like our overnight flight to Honolulu would be quite full.

"Sounds like a good idea," I said.

A short moment later, I saw that Maya was already running through the airport door. Paul carried our heavier pieces of luggage and struggled to keep up behind her. Quickly, I began to unload the rest of our belongings, sliding the diaper bag messenger-style across my chest and taking a carry-on on each arm.

After I pulled the travel crib out of the taxi I paused.

"Do you know of anyone who might use a travel crib?" I asked the driver. "It needs a new board to support the mattress, but otherwise it does the job."

For a travel crib that was purchased second-hand back in Wanaka, New Zealand, and had since been on ten flights, umpteen ferries, in taxis, buses and countless hotels, guest houses and shacks by the sea, I was amazed it still had four walls and could be used safely.

His reply surprised me. "I'll take it," he said. "My wife and I are expecting a baby this month!"

"Really? It's settled then!" I said, sliding the bed back into the trunk. "I'm glad you have a use for it!"

I chuckled at the irony and wished him well.

Paul and Maya were out of sight now, but I wasn't too far behind. I walked unhurriedly toward the terminal, excitement rising in my chest. From this point forward, every step was a step closer to home.

9
Growing Pains

Dying leaves fluttered to a cold, hardened earth and stacked in crisp piles of yellow and brown. Winter was creeping in after a short summer and an even shorter autumn, but that's how it goes in the Rockies. The smell of fall filling the air was usually a cue for Paul and me to have our annual conversation about our next family trip.

"I just want to go somewhere warm," I said, putting my laptop aside so I could grab a cup of tea.

This was our usual evening routine when Maya was sleeping. When the day was winding to a close, Paul and I spent time hanging out on the couch, watching television and catching up with each other. The late-day hours were also prime for trip planning.

"Warm but without any insane travel days, at least while Maya is still young," I continued, cupping my hands around the hot mug.

"Maybe South America?" Paul replied.

I knew that, in his logic, he was trying to keep things within our time zone. But the sheer length of transit to South America would be too much, I thought.

"Without insane travel days," I said, half-smiling. "Can we keep individual flights under five hours? I don't mind doing more than one if there's a break in-between."

"Well, we're kind of limited then," Paul said, shrugging his shoulders. If there was something I'd learned about Paul, it was that he didn't like to be limited. Over the years I had also learned to respect that about him, even if what seemed "limiting" to him would be someone else's dream vacation.

"I know, but it's just for a few more years," I said. I, too, wanted to speed time up in that regard, but I had a more realistic approach. "How about we go back to Hawaii?"

It wasn't the first time I'd suggested it. Now that I was living out west, Hawaii was closer and I had been wanting to spend time there. During our visit to Oahu on our way home from Polynesia, we primarily used our days to refuel and recuperate before finishing our journey. Going back to any one of the Hawaiian Islands would still give Paul, Maya and me the chance to explore somewhere new.

Paul was pensive and quiet and I could sense his hesitation. He paused to take a sip of his tea. It seemed he didn't want to say it out loud, but his lack of enthusiasm was enough to tell me he didn't really want to go to Hawaii. It wasn't far enough off the beaten track.

"I don't know," he said. "If we spend our hard-earned money to go somewhere, I don't want to feel like I'm in North America. It's got some beautiful areas, but Hawaii seems so commercialized."

I could relate to his wanting more of an adventure. Beyond the excitement of getting out of our comfort zones, travel could be an opportunity for all of us to experience different cultures, learn how to problem solve in tricky situations and gain a greater appreciation for our lives in Canada. For the moment, though, I just wanted a family vacation.

We'd taken to heart the tough lessons our "adventure" in the South Pacific had taught us. So much so that the next year we travelled to Belize, where we rented an apartment for three weeks on the tiny island of Caye Caulker. Having the same place for a few weeks made for a better sleeping routine, even if Maya started her day at 5:30 a.m. (A pair of noise-cancelling headphones also allowed one parent to sleep in.) With more sleep in our bodies, we had energy and better moods to actually enjoy the destination. We had plenty of time the three of us, but when one parent needed to work, the other could take Maya for a dip in the pool, out on bike rides around the car-free island in search of freshly squeezed juice or to play on a small beach by one of Caye Caulker's only resorts. On my 31st birthday, I even went for a massage and took some solo time sipping a bellini by the water.

Compared to what we had experienced in the South Pacific, Belize was so easy that I felt inclined to recreate it somewhere else. This time, I didn't give in to Paul's usual push to "up" the adventure quotient.

"I'd still like to consider one of the Hawaiian Islands. People seem to love it," I said. I scrolled through some web pages while I waited for Paul to answer.

"Okay, maybe the Big Island then," Paul responded. "There is some good photo potential there."

A compromise. Was this the key now? A destination for a family trip didn't necessarily need to be remote; it at least needed to fuel Paul's creativity.

I booked a three-week stay at an apartment in Kailua-Kona, and we set our sights on Hawaii for our next family trip.

✳ ✳ ✳

MAYA TURNED 3 ON THE BIG ISLAND. With her growing maturity, our day-to-day experience, whether it was at home or on a trip, was getting easier. We brought my mom along with us – the first of many times she'd join us on trips – and inviting her to come along was like a secret weapon. Now we had businesses to run and more responsibilities that we couldn't afford to ignore for the weeks we were away.

Paul's photography business had grown to the point where we'd hired a full-time assistant to help us carry the load. In addition to coffee table books and limited edition prints, Paul was selling images to magazines, advertisers, tourism organizations and large corporations. He was a sought-after educator and ran popular photo workshops with another photographer named Dave Brosha, who had become a good friend over the years. They were hatching plans to host more photography workshops abroad. So, while we were on the Big Island, we were putting the bones in place for a new company called OFFBEAT, which would host photo experiences in far-flung places around the world, as well as an online community.

As for me, the year prior I had co-founded a new mountain culture media company that would publish a magazine called the *Canadian Rockies Annual.* On top of that, I was assisting Paul with his business and working on freelance articles and marketing materials for various clients. Paul and I had also pitched a paid media visit to the tourism bureau for the Big Island, which it accepted, so we had photography, social media and blogging deliverables we needed to complete during the trip. It was a fun way to make money, but still required our time.

It was clear that a family "vacation" now depended on us being able to work from the road. Adding an extra adult to the mix meant we didn't need to be passing the baton – i.e., Maya – between only the two of us. It meant more family time together, playing in the sand, snorkelling, hiking and eating coconut shrimp. It meant building memories, including those between a granddaughter and her grandmother who otherwise lived on opposite sides of the country.

It was a great relief to know my daughter was well taken care of when Paul and I needed computer time. On one of my half-days of work, I sat in Kona's Daylight Mind cafe, sipped some of the best coffee I've ever had and reviewed the first design drafts of the magazine. I checked my emails and wrote back to a few clients. And when I looked up I wasn't staring out at Banff Avenue or a mountain. I felt the salty ocean air on my face, looked out at palm trees blowing in the breeze and I smiled.

These moments, where I realized I could do my job from almost anywhere, were some of the sweetest for me. Paul and I had worked hard to get our freelance careers up and running but still felt so fortunate to be able to do what we loved for work. We weren't free of stress, yet having the option to work from the road was a blessing and a privilege.

After I finished my work session and closed my computer, I took a few minutes to be with my thoughts. I looked out at the waves rolling in from the Pacific and pondered the year that was about to roll in on our family. In the upcoming 12 months, Paul would be teaching throughout the Rockies, in Whitehorse, the Torngat Mountains of Labrador, Greenland and Antarctica, where he'd be floating aboard a ship for six weeks. I needed to take time in Hawaii, both physically and mentally, to prepare for it.

There would be a lot of comings and goings and, for the most part, Paul would be gone and I'd be home alone with Maya. My previous stints of solo parenting had left me wrecked, mainly because Maya was a toddler and required so much of me. In general, she seemed to require more energy than other children her age. Looking at Paul's travel schedule felt like looking at a severe storm coming my way with dark clouds swirling in the distance. It was hard to navigate in those conditions. Knowing there would be so many more of them in the year ahead – weeks on end with Paul off the grid – in my mind and heart I could feel myself barricading the windows and building up walls of sandbags to avoid getting flooded.

In the coming weeks, before he left, a pattern dictated that I would harden myself so I'd be tougher to break. I would conserve my precious energy by reducing social time and plans of all kinds.

Outwardly, I'm not sure others noticed the boundaries I put into place when I was parenting alone. Some might have seen me disappear altogether as I learned to keep my most meaningful relationships close. For those in my inner circle, I tried not to let my boundaries affect my interactions. But those closest to me perhaps might have noticed I was more withdrawn when Paul was out of town. If they asked about it, they might hear that some days were smooth sailing and, on others, I was hanging on by a thread.

The truth was I dreaded the idea of holding down the fort, over and over again. Often it felt like getting the short end of the stick, though I knew it was necessary – a feeling that had become a point of conflict between Paul and me. I was genuinely happy for him and this exciting life he was pursuing. At the same time, his job flying all over the world doing cool stuff seemed like a better deal. For him, the pressure of guiding big groups and being "on" all the time made it feel like work, though, of course, he loved it.

"If you want to work, I can stay home," he said, more than once. I wasn't sure how serious he was, or whether he'd really thought it through.

I didn't think it was that simple. Sure, I could make up for the income. But his career was his passion and purpose, as was travelling and fully expressing his desire for exploration. To take that away would extinguish the flame in him. His talent for photography and teaching were meant to be out in the world, I thought. Moreover, at the time, I only wanted to work part-time so I could spend more time with Maya.

So, if Paul's career were going to carry our family forward financially, at least for a few more years, I would need to let him fly and photograph as much as possible. I could wallow in self-pity or acknowledge that I had the power to say no if I had actually wanted him to take a different direction with his work.

I had chosen to say yes to him, to us, to this life.

For now, we were on Hawaiian time with Hawaiian perks: beach, fish, gelato, volcanoes and Kona coffee, with some work in-between. We would spend a few hours on the computers in the morning, then hit up a coffee factory for cappuccinos on the way out to our chosen beach. We were elated to discover that, after our years of dealing with a child who detested the car, Maya could now endure 20- to 40-minute drives. That meant we could explore farther as long as Grammy wasn't tired of entertaining her in the back seat.

Our days were filled with sandcastle building, reading and delicious meals by the water. It was yet another trip that we *enjoyed*, and I went home feeling like my battery was full.

* * *

FAST-FORWARD FOUR MONTHS to July and there was a backpacking trip in Mount Robson Provincial Park on the calendar with *my* name on it. When it was my turn to go, I struggled to remember how to pack for the backcountry. For many years the process had been second nature. I sang "Head, Shoulders, Knees and Toes" in my head while I scanned my gear to make sure I'd covered my bases, and off I went. But now I was working off a mental list in an already foggy brain. Did I have everything?

I had also forgotten how to be on my own without Maya. For months, we'd been back in the Rockies and I'd been flip-flopping between solo parenting and living as a family of three, with a calendar meticulously documenting everything that needed to happen to make life run smoothly. I was always busy, *doing*. This backcountry trip with a few friends would be a chance to hit pause on the constant barrage of questions that comes from a small child and just be with my own thoughts. If it was like any of my other backcountry trips without Maya (there had only been a handful), I'd be oscillating between awkwardly navigating the world of adult conversation and suppressing my desire to talk about my kid. I yearned to be back on the trail and trusted I'd find my rhythm once my boots hit the dirt.

Later, as I unpacked at the Berg Lake campground, I pulled out my one-person tent and sighed with contentment. I was with friends: Doug, Karen, Dee and Tony. Two couples. I was the fifth wheel and had been lamenting the fact that Paul couldn't join us. It was his turn to stay back with Maya – something he did very graciously knowing it was usually me waving goodbye from the house. But once I lay down to test my sleeping mat, I didn't mind being alone. I had a bit of space all to myself and I didn't need to share it with *anyone*. This was a rarity and I would savour it.

It was my first time in the vicinity of Mount Robson. At 3954 metres high, it is the Rockies' highest peak and arguably the most beautiful in the range. Everything else I'd seen before in the Rockies paled in comparison. As we hiked up toward the Hargreaves Glacier on our first day camping at Berg Lake, we took turns exclaiming how beautiful and impressive Robson was as it rose behind us. It sits like a throne on the landscape, with broad armrests and crumbling glaciers that cascade down like mantles before melting into teal-coloured lakes. If ever the word "majestic" should be reserved for a single mountain, it should be this one.

It may have been my first time visiting Mount Robson, but I still had a history with the mountain. The year before, I remained at home while Paul returned to Robson with a friend to try the Kain Face again. They were a strong, capable team and this time they had favourable conditions. The night before their bid for the summit, Paul sent me a message on his satellite device to tell me their rough plan. They would leave for the top in the early morning hours so they could ascend and descend the Kain Face while the air was cold and the snow was supportive.

The next day, around midday, I waited for a text to say they'd made it back down safely. Five hours went by and no such text came through. Then I waited another hour. I'd been through this many times before – the waiting – and usually didn't worry until Paul was more than eight hours overdue. But Robson had claimed a number of lives over the years. The dangers of this peak weren't easy to ignore.

Not wanting to give in to any worst-case-scenario thinking, I tried to rationalize. I called a friend, an alpine guide who had been up Robson before, to ask his opinion.

"Sometimes people wait on the summit ridge until nightfall and then descend as the snow hardens again," he said.

That gave me one possibility to hang onto.

Another two hours went by – hours I spent playing on the floor with Maya, making our dinner and letting her watch a television show so I could get a mental break. But once eight hours had passed since I had expected a check-in from Paul, I called the superintendent of BC Parks, an acquaintance of ours, to see if he'd heard from the pair. He'd been tracking their climb too.

"I haven't heard anything, Meghan. But I'll call you the moment I do," he said. "I'm sure they're okay. It's hard to know what's happening up there."

I wasn't feeling very reassured.

As nighttime fell once more, my worrying escalated. This was unusual. Paul and I always discussed his plans before departing, and I was usually informed if something changed, or if he'd be longer than expected. Maya was only 2 years old, not able to understand what was happening, but I could sense from her behaviour that she was picking up on my anxiety. Naturally, I was preoccupied; she wanted my full attention. When I couldn't give it, she threw tantrums – and objects. My patience was worn to shreds, but I managed to get her upstairs and into bed without any further episodes.

As we sat on her tiny bed, reading books together and cuddling, my mind was elsewhere.

After she fell asleep, I walked quietly to her door and closed it behind me. With Maya no longer requiring my attention, I prepared to make the call I had hoped I'd never have to make. I walked down the creaky stairs to the kitchen of the log cabin home we were renting and leaned on the counter. I breathed in and out to try to calm my thundering heart. Then I used my phone to find the correct number for search and rescue in Jasper, which serviced the Robson area, and dialled.

The phone rang just once. "Parks Mountain Safety," said a male voice on the other end.

"Hi, yes." I cleared my throat. "I have two climbers overdue on Mount Robson," I said. "Based on the information that was provided to me, they should have checked in from their high camp by midday today."

Fighting back tears, I explained which route they were on and the possibility that they were waiting to descend.

"We'll prepare to do a flyover in the morning if you haven't heard anything," the rescuer said. "Can you tell us what colour jackets they are wearing?"

I wasn't completely sure, but Paul always wore something colourful in the mountains.

"I think Paul's jacket is red. I'm not sure about his friend," I said.

"All right, thanks. We'll touch base in the morning. If you hear anything, please give us a call."

"Thank you," I said and tapped the phone's screen to end the call.

Morning felt like an eternity away. I figured that if I could fall asleep, time might pass more quickly. So I got ready for bed and slid into the sheets. I placed my phone nearby with the notifications on so I'd hear a text from Paul if it came in.

Sleep did not come easily. I stared at the ceiling and stewed over the possibility that Paul was gone. The thought had stood on the periphery of my mind many times before. *What if he doesn't come home?* I imagined taking Maya aside and sitting her on the bed to tell her he wasn't coming back. Ever. I had to shake myself out of it sometimes, this dark spiralling of thoughts as I imagined the worst. Maybe it was healthy and reasonable to acknowledge the possibility, as long as I didn't dwell on it. We had purchased a special policy in addition to our life insurance in case anything should happen while we were out climbing or skiing in the mountains. There was always that possibility, so long as we partook in activities that involved some risk.

But now things were real, not only a concept captured in a string of letters and words on an insurance policy I'd printed out and put in a file – tucked away hopefully forever.

Hours later there was still no message from Paul. My thoughts kept me awake. I knew it wasn't helping to think about it all, but I couldn't control it. Everything kept playing like a movie trailer on repeat: the events of the day, the phone calls, the scary possibilities. I just didn't know the ending.

At least now I knew the wheels were in motion and the rescuers were ready to fly out the next morning.

I was in a half-awake state when, at 11:30 p.m., my phone buzzed with a text message. It was Paul: "Back at the tent. Incredible day."

I let out a long, audible breath, billowing my cheeks as the air released. *Thank goodness.* I felt relieved and also frustrated. Did he know that I had been worrying?

Though it was very late, I called the superintendent at home to let him know they had safely returned to the tent. I also called off the rescue helicopter. I didn't have any answers as to why they were so late, but I decided not to ask by text in order to avoid further miscommunications. Instead, I sent a simple response: "Great work! Keep me posted on descent."

At least I went to sleep knowing they were safe.

Upon his return, Paul filled me in on what had transpired. It turned out he and his climbing partner decided to leave for their objective much later than they'd planned. But, due to logistics and the satellite device taking too long to queue up enough satellites to send out a message, Paul hadn't sent an update. While I wallowed in fear back home, they were blissfully unaware of my concern as they climbed their way up the Kain Face to the summit of Mount Robson and back down to their high camp.

It was a highlight of Paul's life. As for me, I felt self-conscious that perhaps I'd blown things out of proportion.

"You did the right thing," Paul reassured me, after I told him all the steps I'd taken when I thought they were overdue.

I'm still reassured that Paul carries a satellite device. But now I keep even more space in the back of my mind for the possibility that no news isn't necessarily bad news. All the same, if it happened again, I'd be picking up that phone and putting wheels in motion.

On the third day of our trip into Robson, my friends and I ascended the trail up to Snowbird Pass on what would be a 22-kilometre, round-trip hike from our campsite. From there, we could see the north side of the mountain and the challenging terrain it poses to climbers.

As I hiked up the switchbacks, I thought about how, somewhere along my journey as a mother, I had gotten my mountain legs back. I felt strong, fit and capable – and happy to be back at it. And when I got my first views of Paul's route up the Kain Face, it confirmed for me just how big and serious Robson was. I marvelled at Paul's abilities, stamina and strength. And I was ever more grateful that he came back from his climb.

* * *

THE REST OF THAT YEAR felt like the world's most spectacular juggling act. There were many moments of enjoyment, but my sanity largely depended on whether or not we could get some help with Maya, especially when Paul was out of town. To keep my head above water, Paul and I began to coordinate a visit from a grandparent when he'd be away for more than two weeks. And, during the weeks when it was just me and Maya, I found that a solid routine and a breezy schedule were crucial. Our relationship as mother and daughter swung wildly from one extreme to the other. We had special moments bonding just the two of us: watching cartoons in bed and eating Cheerios, visiting the community centre or going on nature walks. Then full-on screaming matches over something so simple as putting pants on (hers). My fuse was often short, and I knew it.

One summer day I planned to take Maya to nearby Johnson Lake, one of Banff's only beaches with a lake that warms just enough for swimming. I packed everything in the car, put Maya in her car seat and drove to a coffee shop in town to pick up some lunch and treats. When we left the coffee shop, I realized the car was parked on the other side of the street and my hands were full with a paper bag looped over my wrist, my wallet in one hand and a latte in the other.

"I can't hold your hand, so stay close to me, please," I said to Maya. She had a tendency to act on impulses, like the time she ran straight from the grocery store into a parking lot, so I was aware she might do the same here.

I waited for some cars to go by and then we started across the street. She stayed close. *Good job, Maya.* Then, just as we reached the centre line, she sat down, right in the middle of the road.

"Maya, what are you doing? Please stand up," I implored, looking down at her. "We need to keep moving."

She refused to budge.

"I'm serious, Maya! We need to go!"

"No!" she yelled, with as much defiance as she could muster.

I could see cars approaching the stop sign at the end of the block.

"Come on!" I yelled. "Get moving!"

"Humph!" Arms crossed. Legs crossed. Not moving.

I switched my coffee into my left hand, somehow holding both the sloshing caffeine and my wallet in the same palm. Then I bent over to take Maya by the wrist. As I did, she jerked away from me and my coffee spilled all down the front of a brand new tank top I was wearing.

"SHIT!" I yelled, even louder. A few people sitting outside the coffee shop turned to look at me. I never swore — I still couldn't shake the good girl from my lips — so I surprised even myself. Now covered in coffee, I had nothing to lose. Feeling completely infuriated and embarrassed, I bent over, picked up Maya like a football and carried her to the car.

We eventually got to the lake, but not before I drove back home to change and left Maya in her car seat to wait for me. Somehow she got the idea we weren't going to the lake anymore, and I gave it just enough time to give her the illusion of a consequence. Because the reality was *I* needed a day at the lake. Parenting was easier outdoors, with the sand and water to play in.

The day would start like this but end with us eating chicken fingers and giggling and cuddling on the couch and saying sweet goodnights as I tucked her into bed. Those were the ebbs and flows. And then we'd start again the next day.

* * *

MAYA AND I eventually found our groove. But when Paul came home, the transitions were taxing. Often he wasn't in the rhythm Maya and I had established while he was away, as syncopated as it was. He would be jet-lagged and behind with work. I'd be desperate for a break. Our conversations whenever he got back from a trip felt like déjà vu.

"Did you sleep on the plane?" I'd ask, already knowing the answer.

"No, I caught up on editing," Paul would say. He wouldn't have slept in 24, sometimes 48, hours.

Upon his arrival, I could feel my adrenaline seeping out of me, as though his coming home had forced my barricades down.

"Well, I'll get up with Maya tomorrow," I would say. The truth was I wanted a break. I wanted to sleep in. But Paul was on a different time zone and needed to catch up.

When Maya was in bed, we'd unpack his bags, get his photo gear into his office and put the dirty laundry in the washer.

"How was it?" I'd ask.

"It went really well. One of our best workshops to date. The group was great," he'd say. That was about as far as some of our recaps went.

"How were things here?" he would ask. Sometimes the question came in a dull monotone, like he already knew the answer. Was it better for me to be honest or to fake positivity? Solo parenting was hard, but was it supposed to be *this* hard?

"It was all right," I'd say. "Some fun times, some rough times. It's been pretty full-on."

"It's been full-on for me too."

"I'm tired," I'd say. "So when you feel up to it, I'd like to take some time for myself."

"I'll just work tonight when you're all in bed, then," he'd say.

I thought that was being unreasonable.

"You need to catch up on sleep, though!" I was becoming worried about just how little sleep he got.

"Well, there's only 24 hours in a day. I can't do it all."

And on and on we'd go, in circles until we'd eventually find common ground, like two parallel lines – two parallel lives – finally crossing over. We learned later that he should spend his first night or two at a local hotel, so he could decompress, catch up on sleep and work before walking into the house.

The result of our lifestyle was that Paul and I couldn't fathom how people had more than one child. We watched in astonishment whenever a family with four or five children sat at a neighbouring table at a restaurant, as though they were a rare species.

"That's insane," we'd take turns saying.

I once sat next to a man at an airport gate who saw me travelling alone with Maya and told me how he looked back on those years with fondness. I asked him how old his kid was now.

"Kids," he responded. "We have two sets of twins, now ages 16 and 18."

I was speechless.

It was clear to Paul and me that the idea of even just one more child was off the table, at least for a few years. Since we had Maya, we'd met many more couples who sought to keep their passions alive as they transitioned to parenthood. But we'd also seen how couples could drift apart with just one child in the mix. We were doing fine – not thriving, but fine. Life was filled with fun and exciting experiences; things that made people on the outside say, "You're living my dream life." Media visits into backcountry lodges, a flexible schedule that allowed us to bend our desk hours around adventures, taking our turns going up mountains or into the backcountry, and bringing Maya along when we could. But we were often feeling strung out and tired. Another baby at this point could break us. It wasn't the time to go back to night feedings and taking care of the all-encompassing needs of a newborn.

The question of whether or not we should have another kid nagged at us, especially when well-intentioned but nosy people would tell us the benefits of a sibling or the downsides of having an only child. It became a source of ongoing uncertainty, and one we didn't know how to navigate. How do you decide when to have another kid, if ever?

Neither of us really brought up the conversation beyond saying things like, "Can you imagine having a baby around right now?" We weren't ready to even put the option on the table.

It wasn't just that we were ambitious people. Maya was a particularly intense and perceptive child. That was made clear talking to other parents who didn't deal with the same challenges, and perhaps explained why solo parenting was so hard. She was sensitive to cold, to hot, to the tag on her shirt rubbing on her back. She often freaked out about things rather than just telling us calmly. She met transitions with resistance, whether it was leaving the house for the dayhome or ending an activity to eat dinner. Her tantrums sometimes resulted in us sitting on the stairs with her, holding her arms crossed from behind her so she wouldn't hit others or hurt herself. With time, we figured out how to prevent her from reaching what we called the "red zone." We also learned that offering a hug could calm the storm.

It was around this time I discovered there is a term for children who are more sensitive, perceptive and intense: *spirited*. She was one of them. At the time, I could not imagine the bright, sparkly and mature child she would grow into by grade school.

Sometimes I just didn't feel cut out for the job. Parenting, even when Paul was home to share the load, left me feeling exasperated. Maya wouldn't take no for an answer without a battle, so parenting became a creative challenge. Our attempts to do what we thought were basic things outdoors, like biking or camping, resulted in meltdowns on her part, frustration on ours. When she didn't like something, we couldn't convince her otherwise. We once packed up a campsite at 3:30 a.m. when she wouldn't stop screaming in the tent. No matter that we brought her blanket, pillow, stuffed animals, a lantern...all the comforts we could think of. She didn't want to be there, and made it so we didn't want to be either.

At times, it felt like negotiating with a tiny terrorist. Until I remembered that I was perhaps as equally spirited as a child. Now the tables had turned.

"You've got to break the will without breaking the spirit!" my mom would say when I talked about my relationship with Maya. She was obviously speaking from experience.

Having Maya in my life helped me understand why my parents rarely interfered with or suppressed my ideas. My parents often had to find ways of saying yes to me. If I wanted to do something, I'd find a way – a skill that has served me well into adulthood.

The daily battles with Maya were overwhelming at times, but I could mitigate them in advance if I was mindful enough. And if I didn't take care of myself when Paul was away, I was like a volcano ready to blow. I did what I could to keep some balance: hiking up local peaks, going to the gym, meeting a friend for coffee or ending my work days early.

Fortunately, my work was fulfilling. I spent half my time making sure Paul's business was running smoothly while he was off-grid. It was our family business now and I felt purposeful in my contributions to marketing and product development. We'd also been commissioned by our publisher to produce four photo books catered to the tourism market in the Rockies and they were due later that year. It was our first chance to collaborate on book projects that combined Paul's images with my writing. I also enjoyed researching, writing and editing – much of it for the magazine I was co-publishing (which also meant I was bookkeeping and selling advertising). Occasionally, I freelanced for other publications, including an anthology about travelling with babies titled *You Won't Remember This*. My chapter was about our arrival to the Akaroa Peninsula in New Zealand.

Life was busy, and I thrived on feeling like I was creating something meaningful. I fought the idea that, as much as I loved my spirited daughter with all my heart, I wouldn't let motherhood overtake my other passions. I knew I was firing all cylinders but didn't know how to slow down. When I did, if I took a step back, I dealt with feelings of restlessness and unworthiness. I recognized I'd been like this since I was a child and didn't yet have the mechanisms to deal with it.

Life was go, go, go.

With Paul, it was turbo speed. Being married to him felt like running a marathon every day.

"Sleeping is such a waste of time," he'd say. "I can sleep when I'm dead."

In August he was scouting a photography workshop in the Torngat Mountains, in eastern Canada, when my whole plan to valiantly hold my head above water came crashing down.

* * *

THE TORNGAT MOUNTAINS of Labrador on the far northeastern coast of Canada are about as remote as Antarctica. The Inuit-run reserve is equally complicated to get to, and few people get to witness its grandeur. Torngat means "Place of Spirits" in Inuktitut, and indeed the place feels sacred. Deep fjords are fringed by a continuous stretch of brown, rugged peaks that slope toward the water. Glaciers high up melt into rivers and creeks, with cascading waterfalls that cut through some of the oldest rock on the planet. Icebergs bob in the ocean offshore, while polar bears roam the land. There are so many of them that authorities have stringent rules about where and how one can explore. The Torngat Mountains Base Camp & Research Station offers the only accommodation, where Inuit guides, national park staff, tourists and various researchers – naturalists, geologists, archeologists – stay when they visit. Due to its remoteness, the only means of communicating with the outside world is through a satellite device. And no one can step outside the base camp's electrified fence alone. Not without a guide, gun in hand.

The problem with the Torngats is that it can take a few days or more than a week to get there (or back home). The weather is infamously stormy, with bouts of fog that linger for days on end, making it too hazardous to fly. A traveller might get stranded on any of the three or more flights required to access the region. The journey within Labrador begins from the small Goose Bay airport. From there, it's a flight to the province's northernmost town of Nain, then a flight one more hour north to the outpost of Saglek Bay. Paul got stranded in Goose Bay for four days trying to get into the park. But, fortunately, he was travelling without paying the thousands of dollars it normally costs to go. We'd promised the tourism authorities we would bring a group back the following year for a photography workshop if they could cover his scouting trip.

Meanwhile, it was still summer in the Rockies, about five weeks after my backcountry trip to Mount Robson. To mix things up for Maya, I planned a short road trip to Radium Hot Springs, British Columbia. It's only an hour and a half from Banff but would get us into lake country. For a few days we would get out of our usual stomping grounds and do a bit of exploring and sandcastle building, just the two of us.

That week, prior to leaving for Radium, I had begun to feel odd yet familiar sensations. I was more tired than usual. I felt cramping and fluttering in my abdomen. My period was late. I felt emotional. I felt undeniably pregnant.

The symptoms only grew stronger with each passing day. The night before departing for Radium, I came to the surprising conclusion that I was excited about the prospect of another baby, even if it had been somewhat forced on us. Actually, I was elated. It was perhaps partially a hormone-induced reaction – nature's way of infusing a mother with a nurturing, protective disposition from the get-go. I tried to control my thoughts, which were fleeting in all manner of directions, usually into the future. *Were we always meant to be a family of four?*

We hadn't been planning for this and I wasn't sure how I'd tell Paul the news. *Hey, honey, so I know our lives are a little bit crazy these days, but good news! It's about to get crazier!* It was too early to take a pregnancy test, so I planned to tell him about the possibility when he was home from the Torngats at the end of the week.

I couldn't yet confirm the pregnancy but knew deep down this was *exactly* the way I had felt with Maya. Never before, never after, until now. So, while Paul roamed the wilderness, disconnected from life as he knew it, I was deeply entrenched in a different reality. I teetered on the border between not wanting to get my hopes up (I hadn't wanted this before now, anyway) and preparing myself for the possibility that two blue lines would appear on a pregnancy test.

The next morning, something felt off, but I was busy packing the car while Maya watched cartoons. I had the car fully loaded with our overnight duffle bags, groceries, beach toys and snacks, which I organized on the front seat to hand back at regular intervals. I often felt sick to my stomach anticipating a trip, no matter how short. But this day I felt downright awful.

We set off, and as we drove the winding highway through the mountain national parks, I felt cramps in my abdomen. Maya was completely unaware as she sat in the back seat, singing her Raffi tunes and bopping her head. The sense of dread I felt couldn't have been more opposed. I didn't want to believe what was happening, but I knew.

The intensely painful cramping continued as we turned onto the 93 South. We weaved through Kootenay National Park, past mountains and small glaciers and burnt forests that had been engulfed in enormous wildfires in previous years. The pain was almost too much to be driving, so I kept my eyes out for roadside pullouts where I could make a quick stop if needed. But we managed to get all the way to the hot springs, where I had planned to take Maya on our way to our vacation rental. Not wanting to let on that anything was wrong, I stuck with the plan, which ended up being a blessing in disguise. We grabbed our swimming gear and I tossed some menstrual pads into my bag, not sure what was about to transpire exactly. We crossed the bridge that leads to the hot springs and made our way to the ladies changing room.

I *just* managed to get into a bathroom stall when the bleeding began. I could see Maya's feet dangling from the bench just outside the stall and kept my eyes fixated on them.

"Don't go anywhere, please, Maya!" I called to her in as motherly and calm a voice as I could maintain.

Inside that stall, I felt crushed, confused, sad. The bleeding wouldn't stop. My practical mind kicked in and I knew I just needed to pretend everything was okay for my daughter, even though I was crumbling to pieces. I considered calling for a stranger to help watch my child, but Maya was being an obedient little girl. I could still see her feet kicking, and she was yapping away in the kind of babble only a 3-year-old can produce.

Just as I thought I might need to go to the hospital, the bleeding finally stopped. I waited a few more minutes before I slipped into my bikini top, pulled up my shorts and underwear lined with a pad, just in case the bleeding started again, and stepped out of the stall. I only went into the pool up to my thighs, but Maya didn't notice. We splashed and she laughed and the water from the hot springs camouflaged my tears as I played along.

Once we were at our vacation rental, I unpacked and told Maya we could go to the beach, even though I didn't feel like it. I wanted things to be fun for her. Really, I felt like crawling under the covers and letting the tears flow. It turned out the highway to the beaches in Invermere was closed because of an accident, so we turned around and I bought Maya some ice cream. We spent the rest of the day back at our place, playing games, watching cartoons and colouring. The owner of the apartment had been thoughtful to leave some construction paper and craft supplies for me, knowing I was bringing a small child along.

When I finally got Maya into bed, I went into the bathroom and the heavy bleeding continued. I texted Paul, a world away, on his satellite device to tell him what had happened, about the high likelihood of a pregnancy *and* a miscarriage all in a flurry of words. I felt badly that I had infiltrated Paul's remote position on the planet with news I couldn't even be certain of. But I couldn't wait. The physical distance between us was distressing to me.

My messages arrived in the Torngats completely out of order, and the first message I got back from him a few hours later was: "So, are you or are you not?" I responded as concisely as I could to avoid more mixed messages.

I needed to talk, so I called my mom back in Ottawa. I called my sisters, who were having a visit together in Vancouver. I talked and I cried; I never felt so alone. When I hung up the phone, I burrowed my body into the comforter of the bed. I felt myself sinking, unable to keep my head above the water anymore.

It was one of a handful of particularly trying times I learned that, in this life that Paul and I were pursuing together, I would need to develop a "switch on/switch off" kind of independence. It wasn't his fault he wasn't home when it all happened, nor would it be the next time I faced challenging circumstances on my own. It was *our* choice to have our income partially dependent on him being away – not just away but entirely off the grid.

And what kind of a life would it be if we always stayed home or nearby each other in case something bad happened?

I can't remember how the conversation went when Paul finally returned home from the Torngats. He was on a high from an opportunity to photograph one of Canada's most spectacular landscapes.

But I pretended I was more okay than I felt. The experience had shaken me. The sense of powerlessness and lonesomeness had been accentuated by the fact that my one companion at the time was a small child. When I returned to Banff, I told some friends but felt like only a few of them took my sadness seriously. I saw a doctor who said it was entirely possible I'd miscarried – my only validation that my experience was perhaps as true as it felt.

Why had the experience rocked me so violently from my foundation? Had there been a baby, I would have only been a few weeks along. All the same, I felt a weakness developing in my foundation, an awareness that this life of firing on all cylinders wouldn't hold up much longer at this rate. Perhaps the pregnancy failed because of the stressors in my life, I thought.

Despite my feelings of sadness, of isolation, something had shifted. I now had a sense that maybe another child *was* in the cards for us. Not right now, but sometime in the next year. And I now knew that the key to sailing through the solo-parenting stints was to know how, and when, to be more self-reliant.

I needed to learn how to protect myself from the storms without building up walls around my heart.

* * *

AS THE YEAR DREW TO A CLOSE, our family got into a better rhythm. Life was good. It excited us daily and felt full of potential. A big part of that was my learning to accept things as they were. I could waste my energy in the struggle and paddle upstream, or I could ride the whitewater.

I had become accustomed to Paul's whimsical ways: how he'd track northern lights data while we were watching television, how often I'd wake up in the morning and he hadn't returned home from photographing, how I'd find just one rubber boot in the front hallway (he'd tell me later the other one was stuck somewhere in a muddy lake). I joked that his mistress was named Lady Aurora.

"Where's Dad?" Maya would sometimes ask, with a quick follow-up: "On a mountain?"

We knew from the photos he posted the next day where he'd been all night: chasing dancing lights and shooting photographs under a wondrous, star-filled sky – usually on his own.

Opportunities kept coming his way on the work front and we weren't fretting over finances anymore, at least not as much. The photography workshops run by OFFBEAT proved to be successful and a reliable source of income. Paul's upcoming trip to Antarctica for a photography symposium at the beginning of 2017 wouldn't necessarily pay top dollar, but it was an all-expenses-paid trip and the experience of a lifetime. It also meant he would be away for six weeks, with very little contact, even by email. It would be our longest stint apart and I'd need to step it up with the business, and with Maya. I felt capable and in control, but only *just so*.

The growing pains were real, but we were working as a team to figure it out. Still, I danced that fine line between feeling burnout and loving it all at the same time. That was the yin and yang of the life we had created.

I needed to be careful not to let a busy, passion-filled life pass me by, like I was watching a movie rather than living it. I wanted to remain present and soak up the moments, rather than setting my sights on the next exciting thing. And I wanted to watch my daughter grow and learn, not realize only down the road that she had changed.

I wanted us to leave a legacy for Maya that she would be proud of. I wanted her to know, beyond a shadow of a doubt, that in the process of being parents we hadn't abandoned our passions.

Before us lay a challenge. How could we create the life of our dreams without simultaneously creating a nightmare?

part three

THREE BECOMES FOUR

Life isn't about finding yourself.
Life is about creating yourself.

—GEORGE BERNARD SHAW

10

Two Ships in the Night

"Paul? Can you hear me?" I yelled into the satellite phone.

Nothing. I was in the trees, boughs of pine casting shadows over the trail. I looked for a clearing, hoping the satellites hurtling through space thousands of miles away would eventually connect us. A ray of sunshine shone into the forest like a spotlight, so I followed it to its source. There I found a small open area that would do the trick. Looking once again to the skies, as if that might somehow boost the connection, I redialled.

Dial tones, emptiness.

"Paul, can you hear me?"

I'd been trekking for two days in a forgotten valley of Banff National Park, not knowing if Paul had made his flight out of the Torngat Mountains after his second trip to the remote park. We had four provinces and over 3000 kilometres stretching the distance between us. But it wasn't the distance that was bothering me. Also floating in limbo was our daughter, then 4 years old, whom I'd dropped off at daycare the day before, hoping Paul would land in time to pick her up as planned. My call from the tree-lined trail, 20 kilometres from the road, was to see if she had ended up with a friend of mine overnight, signifying it was time for me to make a quick exit from the backcountry. Or, if Paul had indeed returned in time, all was well.

Up until that point, I couldn't shed the feeling that, with every step away from the road, I was failing at my responsibilities as a mother. We're supposed to disconnect in the wilderness, but all I wanted to hear was a voice on the other end of the line telling me my daughter had landed in the loving arms of her dad.

* * *

SOMETIMES A BACKCOUNTRY TRIP blocked off on the calendar is enough to fulfill my longing to get into the wild, weeks before I actually depart. It exists in my mind 20 times longer than on the actual trail. When the daily grind starts to wear me down, my thoughts turn to the path, the quiet, the tent, the simple task of putting one foot in front of the other. Like a lighthouse, words scribbled across squares on a calendar – *MOLAR PASS TRIP* – show me there is a safe landing waiting for me ashore, whether the seas are tumultuous with the stressors of daily life or flat with the humdrum of keeping things afloat: emptying the dishwasher one more time, booking appointments, packing snacks, answering an email as five more pop into my inbox. As long as that lighthouse is there, I can see the light blinking in the distance as it scans the seas, reminding me I'll soon land on solid ground.

So it was with a two-night trip I had planned with Carolyn. Both moms, we'd been raising our kids together since they were born, five weeks apart. The previous summer she joined me on a trek through Banff's famous Skoki area, camping at Hidden Lake for two nights and doing one long day trip past the azure blue water of Zigadenus and Myosotis lakes, to the front porch of Skoki Lodge, and back to our campsite. While the husbands minded the girls, Carolyn and I fought off vicious mosquitoes, a human-sized porcupine and wildfire smoke, and loved every minute of it.

An escape from motherhood, no matter how brief, felt a bit like breaking the law and getting away with it. The need to sterilize sippy

cups and book swimming lessons was no longer listed in the catalogue of daily tasks. Instead, I could pump glacier-fed water and
turn the rhythmic motion into a creekside meditation. Snuggled in
my sleeping bag, I could read, uninterrupted, for as long as my eyes
could stay open.

The rare experience of having personal time (and space) in the
quietness of the wild fostered a kind of tent-bound utopia. Knowing
it was a brief escape from reality made it that much sweeter. Motherhood, I had discovered, was one of life's great juxtapositions, with
moments so joy-filled I could barely handle it, and others so taxing
I wanted to slide under my covers and never emerge. I escaped to
the wilderness as a convalescence from life's injuries. And, simultaneously, it gave me the distance I needed, literally and figuratively,
to appreciate home and the sweetness of a 4-year-old's endless
requests for snacks.

For our next trip, Carolyn and I planned a three-day, two-night
circuit through an area of Banff National Park I'd visited ten years
prior: the North and South Molar passes. On my previous journey,
Paul, Rachel and I tackled the 50-kilometre trek in just two days,
camping at Fish Lakes before marching the remaining 35 kilometres
through the willow-choked Pipestone River Valley, around to South
Molar Pass, and back out through Mosquito Creek. Either somehow
we'd forgotten to bring enough food for the second day, or Rachel
and I were blindly following Paul's lead and had no idea of the distance we'd be doing, but we trudged through the entire second day
on a pack of Starburst candy, split three ways. Fortunately, we had a
camp knife so we could share the flavours.

Back then, Paul did the navigating, but I remember the trail being
pleasant, even though portions of it were deep with mud and horse
manure. Hiking through the Pipestone Valley meant placing one
foot precisely in front of the other, as seldom-visited trails are often
deep and narrow. Remembering it was beautiful, and likely not busy,
I suggested to Carolyn we book at Fish Lakes Campground and then
at Molar Creek. Starburst meals or not, the second day with Paul

and Rachel had been too long, so breaking it up would make for a more enjoyable hike.

With Carolyn on board, I blocked the dates off on my calendar and built a lighthouse that would guide me through the next few weeks of day-to-day living.

* * *

TRIP LOGISTICS were enough to take over my life for a few days prior to departure, with stints of packing snuck into the precious evening hours when Maya was asleep. On previous backcountry trips, I'd seen her pulling items out of my backpack and learned to leave my camping gear out of sight, spreading meal ingredients out on the kitchen table when she wasn't awake to mess with them. In the days prior to the Molar Pass trip, I was well prepared as packing goes but faced a conundrum when Paul hadn't returned home from Labrador to take over for me.

July and August of 2017 consisted of a delicately planned matrix of trips and childcare swapping, more complex than any we'd ever created as a family. Our calendar brought me back to my stage management days through university, coordinating 12 actors entering and exiting the stage, with lighting, props, sound effects and costume changes thrown in to complicate things further.

Just prior to the planned Molar Pass trip, I was in Ottawa visiting family with Maya. Meanwhile, Paul flew separately to Labrador for his photography workshop. I flew back to Alberta a few days before Carolyn and I were scheduled to depart from the trailhead at Mosquito Creek. If everything went according to plan, Paul would fly home two days before my departure, giving us one full day of crossover and life as a family of three. Meanwhile, a French filmmaker, Mathieu Le Lay, was arriving for two weeks to gather footage for *In the Starlight*, a documentary film about Paul and our family. The day after my return from Molar Pass, Paul would join Mathieu, his filming assistant and two climbers in Mount Robson Provincial Park to ascend Whitehorn Mountain.

These were just the comings and goings; piled on top of them were doctor appointments, groceries, birthday parties, financial management, buying clothes, car repairs, estate planning and our various workloads – all requiring time, care and attention. And, as at any time of year, our family rhythm was often determined by what was happening in the sky. If a comet had made its way past Earth, or the northern lights were due to appear, I knew it was a "drop everything, grab the camera" kind of occasion. Paul would be out the door, vibrating with excitement.

With so much planned, there was barely any room to budge; certainly no room for wrenches to be thrown our way. With no family living nearby, we had no built-in back-up plan when things went wrong, and instead needed to rely on a network of friends to help us stay on track.

So, when Paul's flight home from Labrador didn't take off, I began to worry. I knew that poor weather would prevent any aircraft from leaving the Torngat Mountains base camp, and Paul still needed to make numerous connections. I wouldn't have worried except I knew from the year before that he could be held up for days. With every passing hour, I could see my trip with Carolyn slipping through the cracks. The beacon of my lighthouse was fading away, disappearing into blackness. I was unwilling to give up and began to work on Plans B and C.

Paul's flight finally took off, but he wasn't scheduled to arrive back in Banff until after I'd left for my trip. That would mean dropping Maya off at the dayhome and departing for the backcountry, assuming Paul would arrive in time to pick her up. I felt uncomfortable with this idea, like I was abandoning my kid for the sake of my own happiness.

Yet, as guilty as I felt, it didn't hold me back from committing to my plans. I compensated by putting various back-up plans in place. I rented a satellite device (Paul had ours with him) so I'd be able to check in and hike out as needed. I had friends arranged to pick Maya up from daycare, others to keep her for the night, just in case.

After I dropped Maya off at the dayhome that morning, Carolyn's husband Marty drove us to the trailhead. We set off on our hike and I thought of that black stone and white stone at Punakaiki Beach. There, I had struggled to walk 100 metres to the beach. Now I was about to take a full day's walk into the wilderness.

∗ ∗ ∗

WE SPENT THE FIRST NIGHT at the Fish Lakes campground, and all the while I wondered if Maya had slept in her bed or at a friend's house. The next morning, we had hiked for a few hours when I decided to give Paul a call, just to be sure he'd arrived back in Banff. When the satellite phone wouldn't connect, I almost gave up. But before I left the clearing to join Carolyn back on the trail, I redialled one more time. The phone crackled a bit. Then, from what felt like the other side of the universe, I finally heard his voice: "Meg?"

"Oh good, I got you! It's me, yeah. Just checking to see where you are?" I asked.

"I'm home. I got back just in time to pick up Maya yesterday."

"Sweet. I'm glad to hear you're home. I wasn't looking forward to hoofing it back to the highway."

"No, all good," Paul said. "How's it going back there?"

"Mosquitoes are bad, but we're in good spirits. I love this area," I said.

"I'm glad, babe. You two have fun."

"We will. Thanks for holding the fort. Love you."

"Love you too."

We hadn't spoken since he'd left for the Torngats, but we kept our conversation short. We could catch up upon my return. And with that I took my last-resort plans off the table. I wouldn't need to hike back out. I could enjoy the hiking without worries dominating the experience. I could concentrate on what I was doing. And as we turned the corner toward the next valley, I would need that concentration to negotiate the terrain that was to come.

* * *

I DON'T GET IT, Carolyn," I said, dumbfounded. "I was here ten years ago and there was an obvious trail!"

We had left Fish Lakes on a well-worn path, which petered out shortly after we took a hard right into the Pipestone River Valley. After a few hundred metres, the trail had disappeared entirely beneath a forest of willows nearly as tall as me. Water overflowed from the river and seeped into any depressions in the terrain.

I took my turn in the lead as we stumbled over roots and circled around large shrubs in search of the trail. It was easy to get caught looking down for too long and unknowingly steering off course. It wasn't a matter of being lost; I knew where we were, but a trail would be easier to walk on.

"It must be under water," Carolyn said.

"Maybe," I responded, scanning the terrain. "Either that or it's hiding under these shrubs. But I don't see how this vegetation could have grown so much in a decade."

The willow shrubs required a full-body motion to push them aside, and adequate distance between Carolyn and me so we wouldn't whack the person walking behind. Unable to see more than a few feet in front of us, we called for bears in a semi-hysterical fashion, begging them to stay away more than letting them know we were coming.

"Look!" Carolyn said, pointing up ahead.

After many kilometres searching for what now appeared to be a decommissioned trail, we had come upon a sign pointing toward South Molar Pass. Relief! We were at least in the right place. But when we looked for a trail leading away from the sign, all we could see was a wall of willows that grew taller than our heads.

Carolyn and I looked at each other and simultaneously laughed out loud before shrugging our shoulders. With a resounding "Hey, bear!" Carolyn began crashing through the wall and I followed behind. The forest went on for an eternity, but I just stared straight ahead, pushed my way through, and hoped above all that we would not come across a bear.

When we reached Molar Creek, we knew we were meant to follow it. The creek soon turned to bog and for more than a kilometre I opted to hike barefoot, sloshing though moss that compressed with each step. Eventually, I put my boots back on, but the ground was wet, with creeks braiding through the bottom of the valley.

"The campground is supposed to be just up ahead," Carolyn said. "But the ground is far too wet. It doesn't make sense."

I checked the map once more and, indeed, the campground was nearby. I was becoming disheartened, but I wasn't afraid. As we walked, I kept my eyes on the darkening skies.

"We'll need to find dry ground before nightfall," I said.

After another hundred metres of trudging, Carolyn noticed two men wildly waving at us from the other side of the valley. They were the first people we'd seen all day.

"I bet the campground is over there," she said.

"I can't see any other reason why they're trying to get our attention," I said.

We crossed the valley, which required removing our footwear to ford Molar Creek, and stumbled into the campsite. It would seem it was incorrectly marked on our paper map. When we finally arrived, the men told us they'd used a GPS application to find it.

By the time we pitched our tent the mosquitoes had found us. We hurried up our eating and slid into the tent for some reading. But, first, I wanted to survey the damage. I felt like I'd run the gauntlet, with willows attacking from both sides for the better part of the day. I examined the scrapes on my arms and legs and felt a hint of pride for what we'd endured.

The next day posed more difficulties finding the trail up to South Molar Pass, but when we finally reunited with it, it carried us up and over exquisite terrain, past fields of wildflowers and erratic boulders. We descended until the trail met up with our entry route and pounded out the last few kilometres to meet Marty at the trailhead.

These two moms still had it. How was a branch brushing my leg for the millionth time any different from a kid asking me their millionth question of the day? Or a watery bog any different from stepping in spilt water on the floor that was never cleaned up? Or the wall of willows any different from the wall of uncertainty I faced as a parent because children don't come with a guidebook or instruction manual?

After a few days recalibrating in the wilderness, I was ready to face the chaotic schedule back home. That trip through the Pipestone Valley had taken mental tenacity, but perhaps life with small children had prepared us for it. And I hadn't thought about Maya or worried about her after I finally spoke to Paul. Instead, I assumed the rhythm I had previously found on the trail, pre-motherhood. It took four years, but I was back in the game, like I was back in my skin.

On the flip side, I felt like maybe, just maybe, I was ready to move on to our next stage as a family.

* * *

A FEW WEEKS LATER, when Paul had returned from his trip with Mathieu, I built up the courage to bring up the conversation I knew we needed to have. It had been easy to keep putting it off because the concept of having another child had never come naturally to us. But I was ovulating, and I knew that meant we were on a tight timeline.

The filmmakers for *In the Starlight* were living with us, as were my parents who were visiting. Paul and I had an upcoming backcountry trip, and others planned that summer, and he was off to Greenland again in September. If we wanted to get pregnant, we had to fit sex into a narrow window in the calendar and cross our fingers that it worked. More than that, we hadn't fully decided if we wanted to go ahead with the whole thing. If we were going to, we wanted to do it soon, before the age gap with Maya grew too great and we were forced to start over with another baby. We needed to make that decision, and make love, in the two-day window we had available to us.

"Can we have a quick chat?" I asked Paul, not too long after he had arrived back from his climb.

"Sure, babe. What's up?"

The house was empty at the time, so we sat in the kitchen, sitting on chairs facing each other, his backpack still filled with unwashed clothing from his trip to Whitehorn resting between us, propped against his knee.

"I just wanted to talk about whether or not we should try again," I said.

"Wow, yeah. Okay," Paul said. I could tell I had caught him off guard as he was switching gears from filmmaking on a mountainside to being back home.

"It's just that I don't want to look back on this crossroads 10, 15 years from now and regret that we didn't have a second kid when we could have. Just the fact that I am even wondering whether or not we should have another kid tells me that we should."

In my heart, I knew I wanted it, as hard as it might be to start over.

"I know what you mean," Paul said. "We've been toiling with this for so long."

He took a pause and ran his hand through his black hair. Age had given him a few greys.

"If we have a second, you'll have to be prepared to be a really hands-on mother," Paul added.

It wasn't a jab so much as reality. With his travel schedule, it was true. I'd have to assume even more responsibility, especially when he was away.

"Yes, that's my main worry," I said. "But with Maya starting kindergarten, maybe it will be all right."

There would never be a perfect time.

"Well, how about we try and see what happens," Paul said.

I slowly nodded. "Okay." Oddly, our conversation sounded more like a discussion about buying a car instead of a heart-warming moment between husband and wife. But, underneath it all, we both seemed excited about the idea. For me, the decision felt like the right one.

"Well, I guess that's that," I said, with a smirk of a smile. I rose up from my chair. "I can get a load of laundry started if you guys throw your dirty clothes in a pile."

A week after that pivotal conversation, Paul and I were off in the backcountry for a trip, just the two of us. Our objective was to climb Lychnis Mountain – a peak that met my personal criteria for an experience that would be enjoyable but not scary. It turned out I was glad to be on a mountain that kept me within my comfort zone. As we approached the peak, I had that familiar flutter in my belly – the overwhelming sense I was pregnant. *Already?* Our climb up the final ridge to the summit confirmed it for me. My balance was off and this was my telltale sign, even early in pregnancy. We ascended and descended safely, but I knew that would be it for alpine climbs for a while.

Just before Paul left for Greenland, as he was scanning glacial lakes on his computer, I went down to his office in the basement and officially told him the news. I handed him the pregnancy test.

"Here we go!" I said.

"I can't believe it!" Paul responded. "So soon! I honestly didn't think it would happen *this* fast." He got up from his chair to give me a hug. We melted into each other for a sweet moment.

Life was about to change again. This time I felt ready.

Mathieu had been working on his film for a few years by that point, and we couldn't extend the process much further. Yet it already seemed odd to feature Paul, Maya and me without a mention of that little seed of a family member. From the get-go, that baby was as much a part of our family as the rest of us.

In the Starlight came out in February 2018. It captured Paul's spirit and his relationship with his photography so perfectly. It captured my being his number one fan. It captured Maya's precociousness and enthusiasm. And it captured the stars that have forever bonded us all together.

* * *

THEY SAY THE BODY REMEMBERS. Like muscle memory when tying a figure-eight knot when you haven't in a while. If you disengage the thinking mind and let the body do what it has either been designed to do, or taught through repetition, the process will be easier in the end.

It was May 2018, and after days of prodromal labour – what feels like early labour without leading to anything – I was overdue again with my second baby. Then, on the evening of May 4, the cramps turned from random to rhythmic, and I *knew*. At midnight, I got out of bed and texted Paul, who was working in his office, that I suspected something was happening. He met me in the kitchen while I was making a cup of tea, and, moments later, my water broke.

Fortunately, Paul's parents had arrived the day before to help us watch Maya and hold the fort in the first weeks with a new baby. The hospital required us to check in when the water broke. So Paul told his parents we were off to the Canmore hospital and out the door we went.

It took many hours to get officially checked. Though I was in a lot of pain when the contractions came, by 8:00 a.m. I'd barely dilated. We were told to leave the hospital and come back at 2:00 p.m. At our doula's guidance, we went for breakfast to build up some energy then checked into a hotel nearby so I could labour in peace and quiet.

At the designated time, we returned to the hospital and my body was being jolted at regular intervals, the contractions bearing down through my abdomen in textbook fashion. This was another 20-plus-hour labour, with pain as intense as it comes.

Just before 7:00 p.m., on May 5, 2018, our second baby girl was born. We named her Léa Claire Zizka, Léa meaning meadow (but mostly just a name we loved), and Claire after Paul's mom. We were hopelessly in love with her, and it wasn't until hours later that I snapped back to the realization that I had another child at home, waiting to meet her sister. One with the same brown-coloured hair and eyes as her.

This baby, for me, was a miracle, like all babies, but also because of the years we wondered if we'd ever have a second child. But, more than any other milestone in my life, more than any achievement or acquisition, this made my life feel complete. I was relieved of wondering if we should expand our trio to four, any apprehension evaporating in an instant as I held this new little wonder and stroked her tiny nose.

I marvelled at her, and also at my own resilience. The birth had been entirely natural, aside from the pitocin meant to increase contractions, not alleviate pain. In moments of weakness in the years to come, when I think I just don't have it in me, I don't think of reaching a mountain summit or enduring the cold of the Arctic. I think back to that display of strength, back to the day I became the mother of two.

* * *

THE WEEK THAT WE HAD PLANNED our first-ever backcountry trip with kids, the Rockies saw some of the worst wildfire action in years. My visits to the local farmers' market were cut short when the heat of the day would combine with the smoky skies and become unbearably hot, like we were living in a sauna. The smoke burned my lungs and I worried about being outdoors with our 2-month-old. During our routine checkup at the family doctor, I inquired about whether or not the smoke would be a hazard to my children's health if we indeed embarked on our three-day trip.

"They're probably not feeling it much worse than you are," she said. "At least, you aren't causing long-term health issues."

"That's reassuring," I said. "I guess I'll see how the conditions are when we're heading out."

The smoke subsided a bit in the days prior to our trip, so we decided to go for it. We'd have our satellite device to call for help if we really needed it. And we'd never be *too* far from the car.

The packing job made it look like we were leaving for three months, not three days. But being joined by two kids, who couldn't carry anything, we somehow needed to get all of our gear into two

80-litre packs. I'd be carrying the baby on my front in a soft carrier. I was perfectly aware of how difficult it might be to lug our gear in, but the strain was worth it if I could spend some time in the backcountry and introduce my children to the experience. Léa was a much better sleeper than Maya was as a baby, and I was confident that with some nursing overnight she'd cope well in the tent. After a trial run at a nearby campsite we were confident that Léa would handle the night just fine as long as her mama was right by her side.

Our itinerary would cover roughly 25 kilometres. After a lift up a gondola from Sunshine Village into Sunshine Meadows, we would descend through Simpson Pass to Healy Creek campground. Our second day would take us up to Healy Pass and back to the campground to rest before a 5.5-kilometre hike back out to the Sunshine Village parking lot the next morning.

Our first day was riddled with accidents and near misses. It started with Maya tripping on a rock within the first 200 metres of the hike and face planting into a mud puddle. After she spit the pebbles and mud out, I checked her teeth (that could have been an end to the trip right there). With some water to wash away the grime, everything looked fine so we proceeded. A while later, when we reached the signpost for Simpson Pass, we realized our paper map had been incorrect and it would be an extra two and a half kilometres to our campsite. That was no stress for the adults. But it made for a 12.5-kilometre hike for Maya, the longest she'd ever hiked at one time. The wildfire smoke was ever present, yet, despite its heaviness in our chests, it seemed tolerable.

Maya stayed with Paul while I trudged on ahead. I often stopped to drop my pack and sit on it to nurse the baby (my rain jacket hung over my head to protect me from the mosquitoes), and the rest of the gang would catch up. It was probably good they didn't see me wipe out on the trail a few times. I couldn't see my feet past the baby in the carrier and at one point stepped right off the trail and into the bush, which fell a foot away from the height of the slope my other foot was standing on. I went crashing down with my big pack, twisting my ankle, doing everything I could to protect the baby (who came out totally unscathed) and letting out a *yelp!* that no one heard. I felt flustered with the shock of the fall but still happily plodded along. I reached the site about an hour before the rest and set up a tent, where I promptly lay the baby down to free her of the crowd of mosquitoes landing on her face. Paul eventually arrived with Maya, who was utterly exhausted. He later showed me a video of her hiking, her precious blanket in hand, French braids swinging with her steps, but not so much hiking as stumbling like she was drunk. I was so proud of her for what she'd accomplished. I was impressed that she was still in good spirits.

Later that day, after we set up the tents and ate dinner, I looked under Maya's hat and discovered that her forehead displayed no fewer than 40 mosquito bites. *If it gets really bad, we can hike back out tomorrow,* I thought. No one was complaining, though, so I took that as a sign that the hardships hadn't done anyone in – yet.

As we tucked in for the night, I lay Léa down beside me and zipped her into my down jacket, a makeshift sleeping bag. I felt happy. After a few years of struggling to do things outdoors with Maya, we'd turned over a new leaf. *We're finally doing this*, I thought. *We're finally doing the trips I always wanted to do with my kids.*

Overnight, the air cooled off and it began to rain, clearing the wildfire smoke and making it more comfortable in the tent. My expectations for a good sleep were low, but Léa had a decent night. She stirred several times, but I could nurse her back to sleep without her fully waking. I didn't sleep much, but I was content. I had my baby snoozing next to me and my other family members in the tent next door. I was here in the backcountry with the pitter-patter of rain hitting the tent. This was my idea of bliss.

* * *

IN THE MORNING, I found Paul hanging up Maya's sleeping bag after an accident in the night left it rather wet. Maya's face looked like she had a vicious case of chicken pox. I took a motherly inventory of the state of each family member and, to my satisfaction, everyone was smiling, even Léa, who was lying helplessly in a backcountry camping chair. The cool morning air kept the mosquitoes at bay and we downed some hot drinks and oatmeal while we weighed our options. We'd been eaten by bugs, hiked through air that felt like breathing in a pack of cigarettes and covered more ground than we anticipated. But the greatest determining factor, Maya, was still eager to go wildflower hunting. So off we went in search of paintbrushes and those funny flowers (*Anemone occidentalis*) we called both "Tina Turners" and "Hippies on a Stick."

Hiking was slow, but I didn't mind, except when the bugs came back out with a vengeance. As we cleared the treeline, we came upon fields of wildflowers in Healy Meadows. Swarms of buzzing, biting mosquitoes made it impossible to stand still.

"I want to see how many flowers I can identify right here!" Maya said, sitting on the trail and cracking open the wildflower guidebook I'd brought for her.

We stood, patiently waiting, while she scanned the earth and looked inside her book. A few minutes later, she was so enthralled by her search that she didn't notice Paul and I had started a funny dance, shaking our legs and swatting our arms to keep the bugs off of us. Completely unfazed by the tiny, blood-sucking villains, Maya announced every discovery and, as kids do, turned to us for validation. Admittedly, I was only half paying attention as I worked to fight off the mosquitoes and keep them from biting Léa.

Unsure of what Maya had actually said, I tossed out a few words of encouragement: "Nice work, you found it!"

Paul seemed more attentive: "Wow, that's an unusual colour for a paintbrush!"

She finally got up and I breathed a sigh of relief. Then, 50 metres later, she stopped again. By now the mosquitoes were following us, so it didn't take long for them to start diving in like we were idle targets. I didn't want to burst Maya's little bubble of discovery, but the bugs were becoming unbearable (apparently, only to the adults).

"Maya, can we please keep hiking?" I asked. "We can look for more flowers at Healy Pass."

"Okay, Mom," she said, reluctant to interrupt her game.

We reached Healy Pass after some bribery with "trail gummies," as we called them. A light breeze picked up and prevented the mosquitoes from attacking us. And there we stopped, a family of four, and asked a stranger to take a photo. Because we hadn't only reached Healy Pass – a feat in itself. We had also come full circle. My daughter, that shadow of a bump following me on the trail years before, now standing beside me. And another child snuggled into my chest, unaware what her crazy family had been through to stand in this spot. Paul and I had endured a lot to get to this point and I felt like we had earned this moment of elation.

Assiniboine stood in the distance, shrouded by wildfire smoke.

About ten kilometres down the trail, after another night spent at camp, we eventually emerged back at the car, our first-ever back-country trip with two kids brought to completion. We were dirty, tired and riddled with mosquito bites.

But we were still smiling.

11

My Back to the Sea

A few passengers began to clap when the airplane's wheels touched down on the landing strip. Soon the whole cabin was clapping and cheering. I grabbed Léa's tiny hands between my palms and joined in the celebration. After more than four hours and over 3000 kilometres, flying across nothing but the wide open water of the South Pacific, we had reached our final destination: Rapa Nui or, as it is perhaps better known, Easter Island. Everyone was just so damn excited to be there.

I had numerous reasons to be happy. For one, yes, we had landed safely. I didn't want to think too much about the consequences of flying across that expanse of water with nowhere to land for thousands of kilometres. When we hit terra firma, I breathed out a sigh of relief I didn't know I was holding in. We had also survived, even enjoyed, yet another plane ride with our two young children after travelling from Banff to Calgary to Los Angeles to Santiago, and then on to Easter Island. Paul and I had chosen a more remote, off-the-beaten-track location for a family trip when we saw how Léa was a rather easygoing baby and Maya's spiritedness had mostly evolved into enthusiasm and pure energy. We were confident we wouldn't replicate the South Pacific experience. There would certainly be bumps along the way, but we were prepared to tackle them head-on.

Finally, my heart was full because this was a place I'd dreamed about for many years. I couldn't put my finger on when I first heard about the mysterious "heads" of Rapa Nui. It's hard to know precisely when these monolithic statues entered my consciousness, when they had also made their way into the mainstream through commercials, funny birthday cards and school textbooks. With me being a history buff, these heads, the *moai*, had gotten my childlike sense of wonder exploding inside. It was the same for Paul. Now we were here to see them for ourselves.

We descended from the plane onto the tarmac, where the re-cycled, stuffy air of the plane's cabin was instantly replaced by a wave of heat. It was the first time I noticed that this kind of runway heat had a particular smell, one that evoked nostalgia from previous trips to the tropics. It was the smell of fuel and asphalt cooking in the sun, but somehow it was pleasant when it meant we were escaping the bone-chilling temperatures of a Canadian winter.

It was also a welcome feeling when it marked the end of transit. This journey had been our longest with two kids. Our usual approach was to push through without added stopovers, opting to deal with potential meltdowns from overtiredness and constant motion once we'd reached the end of our transportation. But this time we decided to stop over in Santiago. It turned out to be a hassle to leave the airport, find a taxi to our apartment and live out of suitcases, which we ended up emptying to find important items. As adults, it would have been straightforward enough. Despite our tiredness, we were tasked with entertaining two young children in a tiny, stuffy apartment in a high-rise overlooking the smog-filled city and distant hills.

Stopping in Santiago didn't prevent a meltdown, it triggered one for the youngest member of our crew, whose easygoingness suddenly evaporated into the humid Chilean air.

"Shh, shh. Please stop crying," I begged the tiny screaming baby tucked into the soft carrier on my chest as I paced around the courtyard outside our apartment building. The air was cooler down below, but when she wouldn't stop crying I went back up to our unit to try something different.

Hours into consoling Léa late into the night, my own resulting sobs somehow, surprisingly, calmed her. Perhaps it was the soothing feeling of my chest heaving with loud, unrestrained gasps.

Whatever the reason, Léa suddenly stopped wailing. Surrendering to exhaustion, we piled onto the bed, the fan blowing on us at maximum strength. With Léa tucked safely beside my body, I fell into a deep sleep – ironically, my longest stretch of uninterrupted slumber in the nine months since she was born.

All that was behind us now. Hopefully, that was the end of inconsolable crying on this trip. As my eyes adjusted to the bright sun of Rapa Nui, I absorbed the world around me: the light breeze teasing the grass that lined the airstrip, a small replica *moai* greeting visitors at the entrance to the airport. I glanced back and Paul was holding 5-year-old Maya's hand as she bounced toward the airport terminal. She had ants in her pants from sitting on the plane so long, but her excitement was genuine.

"I love travelling!" she announced, a smile spanning from ear to ear.

Little Léa was smiling too, but hadn't a clue that she had just landed on a speck of land more isolated than nearly any other on the planet.

∗ ∗ ∗

THE REMOTENESS of Easter Island is startling. The nearest inhabited land, Pitcairn Island, is just over 2000 kilometres away. From Rapa Nui, you need to journey 3512 kilometres to central Chile to reach the nearest continental point. Until the 1960s, when propliner flights began to service the island from mainland Chile, the island could only be reached by boat.

Rapa Nui's first recorded visitor was the Dutch explorer Jacob Roggeveen, who came across the island on April 5, 1722, Easter Sunday, and thus named it Easter Island. Its official Spanish name, it being part of Chile, is a direct translation: Isla de Pascua. Rapa Nui is both a name for the island and the name for the descendants of the early Polynesian inhabitants. The island's various names give us clues about the people who have laid claim to the land over the course of millennia.

What has resulted from this history is a Spanish-speaking culture with Polynesian roots, petroglyphs and abandoned seaside villages that confirm the presence of a past. There are a thousand *moai* scattered around the island, which were once symbols of political and sacred power and now tantalize tourists as artifacts in a large, open-air museum. I was gobsmacked when I saw one of these enormous statues for the first time, especially with a baby in the foreground providing an even more mind-blowing sense of their size. And though I was aware of the *moai* prior to visiting, what I wasn't aware of is how astonishingly beautiful the island is, with a rugged coast that crumbles into turquoise seas, vast craters defining the tops of volcanoes that rise straight out of the water and wild horses that run in herds along dirt roads in the island's interior. For an island only 164 square kilometres in size, Rapa Nui sure packs a punch.

No one knows for certain how the *moai*, on average four metres tall and weighing 12.5 tonnes, ended up at their final resting places atop platforms called *ahu*. Some *moai* stand 17 kilometres from where they were carved. Numerous theories exist: that they were rolled on logs like a conveyor belt, shifted with a crane-like contraption or "walked" upright by having their weight shifted sideways and forward using ropes. But the definitive answer cannot be proven. It was lost in a gap in oral history, and no archeological evidence can prove anything with absolute certainty. I joked with Paul that maybe the descendants of the Rapa Nui have known all along and have sworn themselves to secrecy.

On our first days on the island, we settled into the place we'd rented and toured around to get a lay of the land. It turned out that *anything* to get us away from our accommodations was a welcome escape from a place we'd forked out good money for, but turned out to be in a state of total decrepitude: broken curtain rods, ripped window screens, a couch cover popping staples from where it had been "repaired," general uncleanliness and cockroach and ant infestations. All this with a baby learning to crawl, and who'd pollinate the floor with sweet potato puffs and later collect them to eat if we didn't clean them up first.

Early on during our stay, we had nothing but rain in the forecast, so we hit the road, driving most of the island in the span of a day. The rain let up briefly at Ahu Akivi, an archeological site hosting seven small *moai* perched in a perfect line on a large plot of grass. It was enough to whet our palates for what the island had to offer. Though we could see little out the windows as the rain pelted down, we drove to get a sense of distances. Paul would be returning to the sites a year later to run a photography workshop for OFFBEAT, and needed to scout things out.

As we approached one of the island's most famous sites, Ahu Tongariki, Maya's gaze was fixated on the iPad, which we'd permitted her to play on as we drove without much by way of visibility. As the most famous of Rapa Nui's *moai* came into sight, I made sure to tell Maya, who perhaps couldn't see them from the back seat.

"Maya, look. *Moai!*"

"I know, Mom," she said rather casually, not lifting her eyes from the screen.

Immediately, I got annoyed. Here we were, in the middle of the Pacific Ocean exploring a new place and she was playing a game she could play at home. *Was I being a bad mother for entertaining her with a screen?* No such option existed when I was a kid driving for hours on end with my family, in all kinds of conditions.

"Maya, honestly, take your eyes off the iPad! Check out those statues!" I repeated.

"Mom, I see them!" she responded, again not looking up.

I was now more confused than annoyed, but it wasn't until I looked at the iPad that I saw it. The characters she was interacting with had randomly arrived on the shores of Rapa Nui and cartoon *moai* stared back at me from the screen. The timing was uncanny.

At least it's an educational game, I thought to myself. But now, here they were, the real deal, right in front of us. She looked up from the iPad to see them for herself, the 15 *moai* standing by the sea, and we all laughed at the irony. Because *this* was part of why we travelled with our kids. We could read about something in a book or see it on a computer, but nothing could replace the opportunity to see it with our own eyes.

We couldn't get out of the car that day; the rain only increased in intensity and the baby had fallen into a deep sleep. But we returned a few times to Ahu Tongariki to feel the ocean breeze floating past our skin, play in the grass that surrounded the *ahu* and stand face to face with a historical marvel we dared not touch for the sake of respecting their archeological integrity. But, oh, if only we could have.

* * *

HISTORIANS CAN'T AGREE on when the Polynesians first arrived on Rapa Nui – somewhere between AD 300 and AD 1200 – but the general consensus is that the first settlers came from the Marquesas Islands, from the west. To find distant islands like Rapa Nui, Polynesians had developed remarkable navigational skills, which they passed down to future generations without the written word. Instead, they communicated their seafaring techniques through stories, song and even stick models.

Much knowledge was lost when the Polynesians came into contact with Europeans. Fortunately, there were exceptions. Micronesian navigator Pius "Mau" Piailug, who passed away in 2010, was a student of the oral tradition and became a master navigator at the age of 18, just as the first American missionaries landed on his home island of Satawal. With the hopes of preserving his wayfinding knowledge, Piailug shared it with the Polynesian Voyaging Society (PVS), based in Honolulu. In 1976, he assisted the PVS with sailing 3862 kilometres from Hawaii to Tahiti aboard a double-hulled Hawaiian voyaging canoe called the *Hōkūlea* – without the use of instruments. Today, Piailug's legacy and wisdom live on through the PVS, which continues to mentor new wayfinders.[1]

The Polynesians' sophisticated wayfinding techniques rely on the combination of several detailed observations. A complex system using the declination of stars can be used to guide a voyage. Distant islands interact with ocean swells, and the sea activity can provide clues as to where an island might be located. Clouds frequently form over islands, giving away the presence of even lower-lying islands when land reflects on the underside of the cloud formation. Bird migrations and behaviour provide significant proof that land can be found hundreds or thousands of kilometres away.

Clue by clue, sign by sign, wayfinding is all about keeping the big picture in mind. Where you've come from, where you're going.

* * *

THE MORE TIME we spent on Rapa Nui, the more we saw evidence that this was a place where cultures and ideas have intermixed and conflicted for centuries, where various influences made their mark and complicated history, leaving behind a tangled web. It was difficult to separate one element from the others, or imagine the place as it once was. Thousand-year-old relics remained by the sea while cappuccinos were served in the island's only town. One could walk the tourist trail and meet Spanish-speaking Polynesians selling tiny replica *moai* on keychains or, as Paul discovered, stumble upon an ancient spearhead, carved out of obsidian, while on a foray to photograph a seldom-visited coastline. The island possessed a striking

---

1   The Polynesian Voyaging Society is doing fascinating work to keep wayfinding practices alive, which includes embarking on other great voyages aboard the *Hōkūlea* and her sister ship, the *Hikianalia*. Traditionally, only men could be certified as deep-sea navigators through a sacred ceremony called the *pwo*. But, before he died, Piailug granted his successors the choice of whether or not to include women in the *pwo*. Today, the PVS trains and certifies both men and women. To learn more about the Polynesian Voyaging Society, go to hokulea.com.

blend of old and new, of layers piling one on top of the other and unsolved mysteries that suggested some things may be lost forever.

As a mother, I was once more beginning to feel like *I* was lost forever. Like I'd set off on a grand voyage and been caught in an unending storm. That feeling of separation I'd felt with Maya in New Zealand was one I had yet to feel with Léa. She was still so small; our life as a family of four was still a novelty. Maya had started kindergarten and didn't need me to tie her shoes anymore, but her newfound emotions required a new level of support from her parents.

Rapa Nui had amplified my sense of disorientation. I suppose it was because travel offered me a comparison of my life at various stages, in various places. I thought back to the independence I had in Costa Rica, when I could go where I wanted, when I wanted, with no one but myself to be responsible for. Or the feelings of freedom in Nepal and the ability to take months off from "normal life" and go trekking. On Rapa Nui, I could feel the entanglement as much as I observed it in the island's complex history. My six years of motherhood had woven me my own tangled web and my two beautiful children had wound themselves tightly around the outside. I never thought I'd be the kind of mother that would "lose herself." But on this trip I realized I'd been buried under the accumulation of parenting demands, life's logistics and the impulse that I would sacrifice anything for my kids. I had regained some sense of self before Léa was born. But now I felt like I, Meghan, was being buried again.

Occasionally, amidst the diaper changing and packing of snacks, Paul and I would crack an inside joke that took me back to pre-kid days. My emails from my publisher about a book project reminded me I had a professional career. But mostly I put my head down and just did what needed doing. I met others' needs before I even considered meeting my own. I struggled to speak "adult" anymore, to put two coherent thoughts together. Sleep deprivation was the norm at home. And there on Rapa Nui I was on parenting hyperdrive. I'm generally a relaxed kind of mom and a firm believer that being dirty and curious are important parts of childhood. But I needed to be abnormally protective of my kids when we travelled to foreign countries, where cars don't always follow the usual rules of the road, where stray dogs abound and where swallowing water while brushing teeth might mean days of tummy troubles. These kept me on high alert.

The only "time off" from parenting came at night. On Rapa Nui, when both kids were asleep, I'd sit on the couch and often end up staring off into space, too tired to go out. The sun would be setting over the sea, out of view. If I looked out the window, I could just barely see it – the cotton candy pinks in the air, the orange glow fading to blue.

Paul often went out to photograph or scout locations when the stars came out. I didn't mind the quiet and solitude. Perhaps, too, I had forgotten how magical a sunset could be. In my motherly duties, I'd sacrificed my own yearning to stay out late, to watch that golden ball hit the horizon. I had two little kids to keep watch over, and seeing the sun descend had become a memory largely preserved from my childless past. Partly by necessity, partly by choice. Even if it was Paul's turn to stay home at night and he insisted I go out, I often stayed back to spend time with him or catch up on work.

One rainy day he nudged me out the door.

"Go to a cafe, grab a coffee and write," he said.

"I guess I could," I said. "That would be really nice."

Nice didn't quite describe how I really felt inside: that the idea of sitting with a cup of coffee and writing was about as heavenly as things get for me. But Paul knew that. He also knew I needed some prompting.

"Take the opportunity, babe," he said.

"But it's raining. What are you going to do with the girls all day?"

"I'll figure something out," he said. "You go."

"Okay!" I said, my voice sounding more convinced than I was.

I packed my laptop in a backpack and grabbed the umbrella to walk to a nearby cafe, Tiare Coffee.

"*¿Un americano doble, por favor?*" I asked.

While the shop owner made my coffee, I parked my belongings at a table outside under a straw-covered shelter. After I retrieved my order, I opened my laptop and knew exactly what I wanted to work on: my new book project. I poured 1,500 words into my keyboard as the rain poured down outside. I sipped my americano slowly as if my writing session would be over when I could see the bottom of my mug. I updated my social media. There in my happy place I felt tranquility.

While I wrote, it turned out that Paul drove the whole island with the girls to find items for a scavenger hunt that he'd concocted. They looked for volcanoes, horses, grey-coloured cars and *moai*. I admired him for his creativity and stamina with the kids.

I returned to my family feeling a bit more refreshed. Yet a single outing felt like trying to cut down a sequoia with a kitchen knife. It would take many more outings to feel truly separate from my kids. Where I ended and my children began had become impossible to distinguish – again. I was somewhere in the centre of it all, the forgotten mass beneath the entanglement.

I felt a bit like a *moai*, a relic of times past, standing watch over the next generation, my back to the sea.

* * *

AFTER A WEEK ON RAPA NUI, a place where most people spend just a few days, the mysteries of the island still enthralled us. I didn't think that much could top Rano Raraku, the quarry on the interior of the island where most of the *moai* were carved. There, some remained in the rock bed, partially carved, including one that would have become the tallest, standing to a height of 21 metres had it been completed. A short hike through the quarry with one child on my back and another holding my hand was barely enough time to absorb the mind-boggling scale of the operation. Even archeologists who have been working on the site for decades are discovering new things each year.

What also continued to mystify us was the state of our accommodations. On one peculiar morning, Paul went to take out the garbage and bumped into the proprietor, who lived nearby. She casually handed him a bedsheet and explained in broken English and fast Spanish that we were meant to cover our counters and food because exterminators were coming to fumigate the place. *Control del dengue.*

We were all for reducing our risks of contracting dengue, not for having the *interior* of our cabin sprayed with toxic chemicals. I spent an hour on Google trying to figure out what they were proposing to do but couldn't discern exactly *what* they'd be using to do it. After some basic reading, I learned that, in general, all linens and surfaces – every single surface – needed to be washed after fumigation. It sounded nasty. We didn't have the means to do that kind of cleaning, or the desire. We had a 9-month-old baby with us who was putting everything in her mouth. Technically, we also shouldn't have been inhabiting the place for 24 to 48 hours after a fumigation, but we had nowhere else to go.

"We need to tell her we don't want them to fumigate, at least not inside the cabin," I said to Paul, my heart sinking into my stomach. I wasn't sure if fumigating outside was any better, considering none of our windows closed properly, but it was better than the alternative.

"What's fumigation?" Maya asked. I didn't want to concern her by talking about poison.

"Let's just say it could make us all very, very sick," I responded, as casually as possible. I didn't really know the consequences of fumigation, only that it was bad. The stress was getting the better of me as I considered everything we needed to do to avoid all of our belongings getting sprayed. Of Léa licking poison off the dining table.

Paul set off to explain our case to the proprietor as best he could, combining his English and Spanish with exaggerated hand signals. Meanwhile, I translated a handwritten sign that said, "¡*No hay fumigación en el interior!*" (No fumigation inside!) and hung it on the door. Not being sure if our messages had been successfully delivered, we packed all of our belongings into our suitcases and put them in the car, took the sheets off the beds and placed them in the cupboard, and packed the towels away, though they were still wet. We then set off for the village of Orongo, hoping we wouldn't come back to a place that had been showered with chemicals.

Orongo was yet another mystery of Easter Island that had captured my imagination. A part of Rapa Nui National Park (a UNESCO World Heritage Centre), the village is made up of 53 round, windowless homes constructed out of stone, with sod growing on top so that, if viewed from above, they'd blend into the surrounding grass. This design protects the structures from the prevailing winds that blast through the village.

Those winds clobbered us with unrelenting force as we walked toward the stone houses. I could hear Léa's hat flapping in the wind as she rode in the backpack and I wondered if the chinstrap would hold it in place. The attendant encouraged us to take Maya by the hand and I understood why as the village came into view and I saw the earth fall away from it on either side. Orongo sits on an exposed ridge on the southwestern tip of the island, on the rim of the Rano Kau crater. To one side, a 300-metre cliff drops to the ocean below. To the other, a steep slope drops into the heart of a freshwater-filled caldera. I wondered why anyone would want to live in such an extreme location.

Like most parts of Rapa Nui's history, the village had a bizarre past. It was the main hub of the Birdman Cult, which rose to prominence on the island in the 18th and mid-19th centuries. The cult held an annual race to the nearby island of Motu Nui to determine the next Birdman leader, or *Tangata manu*. The objective was to retrieve an unbroken egg of the sooty tern, swim back to Rapa Nui and scale the dangerous cliffs up to the village. Many died in the effort, and it was with little surprise: as I looked down from Orongo at the cliffs and the choppy, shark-infested seas, I thought it was a marvel that anyone returned in one piece.

My life suddenly looked pretty straightforward. More than straightforward, it was a joyful day travelling with our two girls. Travelling with kids usually meant surrendering to the idea that certain activities or locations would be more for them than for the adults. But, on occasion, both kids and parents enjoyed themselves. Those days were the diamonds in the rough. And on this day, we quickly forgot about the fumigation fiasco as we let ourselves be kids and explored the village of Orongo.

"People really lived here?" Maya asked, yelling to cut through the wind.

"They did," I responded. "We can see how they've left their mark even in the most implausible of locations. And they've left petroglyphs to tell their stories."

At the time I wasn't so sure she understood what I was saying, especially by using words like "implausible" and "petroglyphs," when the wind prevented us from hearing much of anything. I could explain later when she did her "homework." Since we'd pulled her out of school, we kept Maya engaged with a notebook and markers where she drew the history of the island, including a rather graphic illustration of the islanders coming down with smallpox.

We rounded the village and stopped at a platform overlooking the caldera. Together, we gazed out at the crater of Rano Kau, ringed by the deep blue of the ocean below. Wind swept our hair and the baby's hat flapped in the breeze as she sat in the pack on my back. I could see the look of awe on Maya's face. Whether she heard me or not, she understood just how incredible this place was. And for a kid who seems to never stop talking, this time she was speechless.

* * *

WHEN WE RETURNED TO OUR CABIN, we couldn't tell if it had been fumigated. No signs, no smell, so we figured it hadn't been sprayed, inside or out. I thought I was in the clear for new surprises until the next morning in the shower. When I accidentally sprayed the wall with the shower head, hundreds of tiny, panicking ants began to scramble out of holes I had blasted with the water, their micro-sized bodies spreading out in black patterns across the tiles. To my horror, many got trapped in the flow of liquid and followed it down the walls into the tub where they swirled in a whirlpool around my feet. Half-stunned and half-disgusted, I stood there, frozen. *Just when I thought this place couldn't get any worse.* I wanted to cry.

A few other things were making me feel more sensitive than usual. We had no fans, certainly no air conditioning and the broken screens made us hesitant to open the windows. At night, the room I shared with Léa turned into a sauna. Every few nights, around 9:30 p.m., a nearby venue would start a boisterous concert of drumming and dancing that we never got to see for ourselves. Drumming so loud I felt it in my body. It was a wonder that either of the kids slept through it. Later, Léa would wake up to nurse in the middle of the night and would often end up sleeping with me in the bed. But it was unbearably hot and sticky. I mostly lay there for hours at night and finally drifted off just before the baby woke me up. To make matters worse, I'd also picked up a stomach bug and for four days had barely eaten anything.

I emerged from the ant-infested bathroom.

"Paul, let's see if we can find a different apartment!" I exclaimed. "Just for the last few days. This place is disgusting."

I was done. It was rare for me to hit the wall, but I had hit it, literally, when the ants came spilling out like a horror film.

"Let's see what we can find," Paul said. "I'm with you. I'd spend a fair amount to get out of this place."

I was grateful we were now in a place where we could potentially afford to switch to a better set-up. But a search online with the spotty WiFi revealed it would be too complicated for us to move. A hotel with a single room and no kitchen would be less than ideal with two kids, and other apartment rentals were much too expensive for us. With no other options, we stuck it out. (When we got home, we would take satisfaction in leaving the worst review known to humankind on the platform where we'd booked our accommodations, hopefully saving others from the same disappointment.)

This time, however, we applied what we had learned over the years: that it was okay to pivot and change plans to make an experience more enjoyable. We had planned to cook most meals for ourselves but instead ate out more often and savoured the fresh fish and carpaccio by the sea each night when I was feeling better. By the end of the trip, we went out for breakfast and ordered our *americanos* and *huevos* in near-perfect Spanish (we like to think). Eating out allowed us to engage more with the residents, both Chileans and Rapa Nui.

Despite the repulsive living conditions, we'd fallen in love with Rapa Nui: its rugged coastline, gentle interior, wild horses and intriguing history. And amidst all the ups and downs, we'd fallen in love again with travelling as a family. I felt a bit lost as a person but found as a mother. For ten days on that foreign soil, we kept our kids safe and fed, hydrated and happy, without shielding them from discomforts. We watched our kids thrive in a place that barely resembled home. And we thrived as parents through the tiredness, language barriers and discovery of yet again more cockroaches when we moved furniture around.

Late one night, Paul had gone out to photograph. He had a special permit to photograph the *moai* at Ahu Tongariki at night, under the stars. Though I had aimed to go to bed early, I stayed up to edit the next volume of the *Canadian Rockies Annual*. I now also had a contract for my first full-length book, which I'd negotiated while we were on Rapa Nui, and I took some time to work on the outline. When I realized how late it was, I took a step outside. Darkness had fallen and the stars had come out in all their glory. Light pollution was no issue here in the middle of the Pacific Ocean. Paul would have perfect conditions for his images and I could picture him with a big smile on his face as he executed the compositions he had in mind.

I stood on the grass outside our cabin and looked to the sky. As I had in New Zealand, I observed how Orion was upside-down. I realized it was my first time in the southern hemisphere since that trip five years prior. And, as it turned out, I *had* learned to cling on, even when my world was flipped over, filled with the unfamiliar. But that was why we travelled too. It was to break us out of the ordinary, to show our kids that life could be lived differently. These experiences built resilience in all of us. Together, we solved problems. We found a way to stay positive and keep our hearts open to learning something new.

The stars twinkled, like each one had something to say. They told me they'd watched over this place for millennia. That they'd seen all the comings and goings, seen life unfold one chapter after another. They'd seen the *moai* raised up on the landscape and toppled toward the sea.

The next day would be my 35th birthday, and we would celebrate it – we would celebrate *me* – somehow. I would find a way to put myself at the centre of my life, if even for a short time. Motherhood wouldn't always be this intense, this entangling, I thought. My children wouldn't be this small forever. As the years passed, I could carve out more time for myself. Those young years were but a short phase in the grand scheme of things.

I felt lost as a person, but maybe I was looking for the wrong person to begin with. Motherhood had changed me. It wasn't like I'd tried on a shirt that I could take off again. Perhaps the Meghan beneath it all was someone entirely new, waiting to be discovered. I needed to stop wasting time feeling like I wanted to go back to something and instead dive into embracing the person I had become.

Here I was, just a small pinprick on a timeline – the duration of my life like a single sooty tern flying over the vast sea. Milestone to milestone, waypoint to waypoint. One day I'd be gone, but life would keep going. And the stories people would tell about me long after I'd left...well, perhaps only the stars would know them.

12

Moments of Awe

The Irish have an old saying: "If you can't see the hills, it is raining. If you can see the hills, it's not raining yet!" This is especially true in November and into the first months of winter, with more rain in the forecast than other times of the year. Clouds are a near constant. Sunny blue skies offer intermittent respite and a reminder that the sun shines beyond the ceiling of grey. The temperatures aren't freezing, but the wet-cold has a bone-chilling effect. And as for "The Emerald Isle," in autumn it fades to various shades of brown, deterring many tourists who prefer to see it covered in golf-course green.

For these reasons, the idea of visiting Ireland in November wasn't initially appealing to me. But Paul had put it on the table. Usually we went to warmer destinations in our winter months. In the past it had given me the break I needed, mentally and physically, from our abnormally long winters in the Rockies. It felt foolish, but I was having a hard time letting go of the chance to chase summer.

"You can't have it all," Paul said to me matter-of-factly during one of our evening trip researching sessions on the couch. It was the end of July and we were getting a head start on our autumn plans.

"Yeah...I know." I looked out our large living room window, thinking. The sun had set a while ago, but it was still light out. Aspens trembled in the breeze.

"We *could* go somewhere else," Paul said. "But I think Ireland will be great. You'll see."

Paul was usually right about these things, like going to places at a time of year when other people didn't. Many of his decisions were made in this way and I had admired him for that. As always, he could be relied on for spicing up the ordinary.

"And I was thinking: How about we split our time between Ireland and Malta?" Paul said. "There are direct flights to Malta from Dublin. It would give us the chance to experience two climates and two wildly different places."

I had only vaguely heard of Malta before.

"Where is Malta in relation to it?"

"It's in the Mediterranean, south of Italy."

"I like the sounds of that," I said. Malta wouldn't be tropical, but it wouldn't be cold either. "Plus, it's two places you've never been, which makes it more interesting for you. I haven't been anywhere in Europe, so it's all new to me. What should we start with first?"

Looking at Paul's computer screen, I could see he was already figuring out our flight path.

* * *

ADAPTING TO A NEW DESTINATION often makes me feel both anxious and excited, like I want to go home and never want to go home all at once. When I'm jet-lagged and hungry, the tasks involved with settling in feel much more arduous than they should. Yet I'm spurred on by the idea that the sooner I can get everything sorted, the sooner I can enjoy the place I'm in.

First up on my list in Ireland was food. As the meal planner of the family, I was tasked with the first grocery run while Paul hung out with the girls. That translated to the first walk around to get a bearing on what was around us, and, most importantly, a hunt for the best coffee.

Caffeine would be essential for our first day in Galway, Ireland. We'd flown long distances with the kids before, but it had been a long time – since our trip with Maya to the South Pacific five years prior – that we experienced significant jet lag. Ireland was seven hours ahead of our time zone in Canada. After landing in Dublin, we crossed the island on a two and a half hour drive that took us straight to our accommodations in Galway. We had yet to rest.

When Paul and I were researching Ireland, a friend raved about Galway's charm. The stars aligned when Paul saw that many of the locations he'd flagged for photography could be reached within a half-day's drive from Galway. Basing ourselves there would grant us the access we needed to explore various places on Ireland's west coast. Our vacation rental on Lower Salthill Road was a three-bedroom, newly renovated 1940s apartment with a complicated heating system. Baths required at least a one-hour heads-up so we could warm the water tank. We loved the quirkiness of the place and its location, just 15 minutes on foot from the old city.

Things started off on the right foot when I found a well-stocked grocery store and located what would become our favourite coffee shop. After dumping the groceries at our apartment, I told Paul to get some sleep (he'd done all the driving thus far). I walked with the girls on the seaside promenade, where sunshine and fresh air kept me awake, and found a playground where I could turn my brain off for a bit and let the girls play.

That evening, we took our first walk across the bridge over the River Corrib to Galway's famous Quay Street.

It was difficult to pick out other tourists, and that's because there weren't very many. But we stuck out like walking highlighters. The Irish like to dress in dark colours – black, navy, brown, earthy green – a stark contrast to the orange, turquoise, pink and red of our rain jackets. I was accustomed to dressing brightly for Paul's photos and it never occurred to me that the colour of my jacket might give away my tourist status. Had we dulled our colours we might have actually blended in, except for our accents giving away our country of origin.

On our way downtown we had passed an establishment called Wards Hotel and it got me thinking about different origins, that of my own ancestors. I've rarely met another Ward outside my family, so seeing the name on a sign made me stop. Here in Ireland I was about 500 kilometres from the land of my ancestors in the United Kingdom, at least the ones I knew about. The Ward line can be traced back to the Nottinghamshire region of Britain and Sherwood Forest – yes, *that* Sherwood Forest. Many Wards still dwell in the area. But I knew very little beyond that about other family lines and generations of the past. Maybe one day I could discover more about them. Maybe I'd find some kindred spirits in my family tree.

My thoughts were suddenly interrupted from my ancestry when we went to cross the street and cars were coming from the "wrong" direction. My tendency to look left for oncoming vehicles would be a difficult habit to break. Paul pushed Léa in the stroller. I grabbed Maya's hand and coached her as we crossed safely to the other side.

* * *

ORIGINALLY FOUNDED by Anglo-Norman settlers in the early 1200s, Galway has a complex 800-year history filled with feuds, sieges, plagues and upheavals. A valuable port opening toward the North Atlantic Ocean, it was once a walled city, which protected its citizens from outside attack. By the early 1400s, most of the town, an area of about 11 hectares, was enclosed in these walls. By the end of the 18th century, after centuries of rebuilding and reinforcements, these fortifications had fallen into disrepair and decay. Today, only two upstanding sections remain by the Spanish Arch and in the Eyre Square Shopping Centre. The modern city juxtaposes the ancient with the new with medieval structures converted into bustling pubs, live music venues, bookshops and jewellers. Look through a glass floor in the 16th-century building now home to the Aran Sweater Market on Quay Street and you'll see the preserved remains of walls from a 13th-century castle, the oldest of Galway's buildings so far to be uncovered.

The dread I had felt about Irish weather in November vanished the moment we began to walk down Quay Street. I laughed at myself for having even scoffed at the idea that travelling there in the fall would be less desirable. The magic of the place radiated from every door, lamp and window frame. As we started up the street, I held Maya's hand and walked in an astonished silence. A thought arose: *Who was I to turn my nose up at the idea of cold when my life now afforded me the opportunity to travel when I wanted to?* This was one of those times I wondered why I could be so short-sighted, why I couldn't see the golden opportunity – the gifts of privilege – staring me in the face.

Quay Street embodied the Europe I saw in my dreams, each step down the cobblestone a step back in history. A continuous stretch of pubs, cafes and specialty stores lined each side of the street as holiday decorations and twinkle lights criss-crossed overhead – a ceiling of glitter and stars. I gazed at store names and attempted to pronounce them, the Irish getting lost somewhere in the back of my throat with combinations of consonants I didn't recognize: *mh*, *dh*, *gh*. We walked slowly, wetness underfoot from a recent rainfall, with the wheels of the umbrella stroller thud-thud-thud-ding over each stone that made up the pedestrian-only street. I zipped my jacket up to my chin and breathed in the damp Irish air. Vapour came out as I exhaled and suspended in space until I walked through it.

I thought to myself how I wouldn't want it any other way. The dampness, the cold, with overhanging ribbons of lights warming my spirit.

* * *

THE FIRST FEW DAYS IN IRELAND were delightful yet also brought back faint memories of the Akaroa Peninsula. When dusk turned to darkness, Paul and I were desperate to get some sleep. But jet lag told the toddler it was five o'clock in the morning, nearly time to get up. This time we weren't all sharing a one-room cabin, though; we had three bedrooms to work with. We planned for one parent to be on bedtime duty – it could take hours for Léa to finally fall asleep –

and the other on the morning shift. Maya could put herself to bed when she was finally tired enough.

We had trouble regulating the temperature of the old apartment and, one night, the room where Léa was sleeping went from freezing cold to oppressively hot in a matter of hours. She threw up in her bed and we found her sweating through her pyjamas. After some rearranging, we got her back to sleep. But each night, for the first four or five days, she'd wake up for a party in the middle of the night and wondered why the sun wasn't coming up. Some nights I felt like I was just getting to sleep when Léa would wake up at 3:00 a.m. shouting, "Agi! Agi! Agi!" It wasn't until the third day that I realized she was telling us she was hungry. One of her first words! In the middle of the night, whichever parent was on toddler duty would crawl out of bed, put Léa in her travel high chair and put a bowl of Cheerios in front of her. If we were lucky, we might get her down for a morning nap but not before spending hours picking up markers off the floor and playing in the cold living room while the rest of Salthill Road soundly slept.

We were exhausted but, unlike New Zealand, the first week in Ireland didn't tie us into a knot. Paul and I knew to take our turns so we could catch up where we could, and one parent would sleep in as late as possible. And I knew we'd taken some strides in our family travel when I saw how Maya managed the jet lag and sleeping in new places. For years, every bedtime had been a battle. But now she could sleep nearly anywhere, including in that stuffy, dirty cabin on Rapa Nui on an uncomfortable mattress with a live drumming show clamouring next door. She may not have slept, but she didn't complain.

For the first few days in Ireland, Maya slept until 10:30 a.m, so we started our sightseeing after lunch. In the past we would have felt like we were missing out on half the day. Now we knew this was just how things had to be. Her transition to better sleeping had happened on its own as she grew up. It wasn't anything we did except for enduring many nights of crying and squirming until she was so fatigued she conked out. And hoping it would get better. Because sometimes hope is the only thing bridging us to a change we have no control over.

* * *

"ARE YOU KIDDING ME?" I exclaimed. I had never seen a bona fide castle before and this one was plucked straight out of a storybook. *"And* we can go inside it?"

"Looks like it!" Paul said, his eyes sparkling.

Ireland has many castles, long abandoned and many of them crumbling away brick by brick. Yet in the ruins you can see the home it once was. The doorways people walked through, the staircases that led to a now nonexistent upper floor, the cellars where they stored their food, wine, maybe treasures.

The 16th-century Menlo Castle was the first one we visited very early in the trip when we weren't venturing too far from Galway. We had parked at the end of a laneway where a chain-link fence suggested we needed to walk the rest of the way. With Léa on my back in the carrier, we had marched down the remains of a road that petered out and disappeared into drying grasses and low brush. Soon enough, the ruins of the castle appeared and my heart skipped a beat.

An obvious structure remained, gift wrapped in ivy, with small towers punctuating a grey, cloud-laden sky. Birds swooped overhead and my spine tingled. Nearby, a handful of large leafless trees stood watch as the River Corrib flowed lazily by. I glanced at Maya and saw her eyes sparkling with wonder and felt myself shrink to the ripe age of 6. Together, we stepped into the fairy tale.

If these walls could talk, I thought as I walked inside the remnants of a door, my hand gently brushing a moss-covered stone in the supporting wall. I hesitated at first, as if entering a sacred space, like a church or memorial. I trod gently and kept my voice to a whisper until a resounding "Mom, check this out!" echoed through the space. Maya had found a window frame she could sit in.

Léa and I explored every corner we could until she began to squirm and I knew it was time to let her run around. I left the castle in search of flat ground where she could move around safely. I let her out at the base of a prominent tree, which shouted its presence through a fan of bare branches that reached for the sky. It was home to several birds and, no doubt, many stories. How long had it been growing there watching the comings and goings of this castle?

Léa found her legs and took off in a flash. In the taller grasses, all that appeared was her little head topped with a tousle of brown hair, but I could also follow her by the sound of her squealing. Paul found us and took over supervising so I could keep exploring. Passing the baton had become second nature in our daily rhythm as a travelling family. It was the only way the adults could withstand the high degree of supervision that two young children require and actually *see* the places we were in. Paul and I had developed a mostly unspoken language around it, and often swapped roles without realizing we were doing it.

I walked down to the river, the one place I had avoided visiting with a toddler on the loose, and discovered a man-made harbour carved out of the riverbank. There, I could see things even more clearly: that for centuries this – Menlo Castle – was home to *someone*.[1] What had become of them? In those ruins were the rooms they had slept in, the dining room where they had gathered for meals.

---

[1] I found out later that Menlo Castle was the ancestral home of the Blake family and it was used from 1569 to 1910. In the early hours of July 26, 1910, a fire broke out while Sir Valentine Blake and Lady Blake were away in Dublin. The coachman was able to save himself and rallied help. Two servants were stuck on the roof and were prompted to jump 12 metres down onto piles of hay. One survived, but the other was killed upon impact. The Blake's disabled daughter, Eleanor, was never found and was presumed to have been cremated by the fire.

I didn't know that day that this fire had damaged the home. I might have felt differently, knowing the crumbling walls weren't only the remains of time past but all that remained from a massive fire that took lives and also many family heirlooms and valuable paintings. Looking back on my time there, I now see how this ivy-covered castle is a poignant reminder of how fragile life is.

This harbour was their personal access to the river where they could fish and swim, maybe float down the water toward Galway.

The impermanence of their lives struck me square in the face. *How was I any different?* My time on this planet is but a blip in the grand scheme of things. Someday, someone else would be living in my home. Perhaps it would even be torn down and rebuilt.

I asked myself again: *What kind of legacy was I leaving for my children?*

As I gazed back at the castle now succumbing to the overgrowth, my thoughts shifted again from future to past. I knew as much about my own ancestry as I did about what became of the people who once lived in Menlo Castle. I didn't even know where exactly most of my ancestors came from and when they'd come to Canada. For that matter, I didn't know the names of most of my great-grandparents.

I walked back toward my young family in silence as I considered something so simple, it should have been obvious, but wasn't until now: that the blood running through my veins had come from a long lineage. That my ancestry goes back and back and back and back and back forever. I came from somewhere, but I didn't know where. Suddenly, I was bothered by the blankness of my tree's upper branches, by my own ignorance.

When I got back into the car I turned to Paul.

"Here I am, guiding my children into their future and I don't know anything about my past," I said. Questions bubbled up inside me, but I had no answers.

"Maybe you can look into it more one day," Paul said. He knew I had a tendency to spread myself thin with projects and hobbies. Where would I even find time to look into that?

We left Menlo Castle with a hankering to see more of Ireland. So, instead of returning to Galway, just 15 minutes away, we drove north for a drive around the Lough Corrib. For kilometre after kilometre we ambled down the narrow roadway as the countryside unfolded. Vast fields of tall grasses and shrubs stretched as far as the eyes could see with properties demarcated by low stone walls. As we drove we saw the old mixed with the new: centuries-old structures speckled the landscape while brand-new homes stood in isolation at the end of long driveways.

Occasionally, we took a brief stop to give the girls a break from the car. At a gas station we found Keogh's potato chips flavoured like roast turkey and stuffing, and other unusual but delightful treats. We changed Léa's diaper in the trunk of the car and dug out more layers as the air cooled amidst an Irish drizzle.

In Cong, we took a longer stop. I'd seen the village on a "top day trips from Galway" listing, so we stopped to see what the fuss was all about. Our explorations took us through the grounds of a 13th-century monastery, along trails that follow the River Cong and picturesque bridges that crossed over it. We swooned over the narrow roadways lined with quaint boutiques and cafes and doorways painted with deep red, blue and green.

I thought about my parents and how much they'd enjoy the history, the ambiance, the symbols of faith punctuating the scene. The question of my own faith was still a pain point for me – one I'd not yet resolved with my parents, aside from largely avoiding the topic. A few years before I was forced to address it head-on when I saw how confusing things were becoming for Maya. Paul and I had made a choice not to raise our children to believe in a particular religion. We both felt that this was something our kids could explore when they could think more critically and make choices for themselves. Yet it was becoming clear to Maya that her grandparents represented two different belief systems. I didn't have the courage to speak to my parents about how to make it easier on her. The written word had always been my forte, so I wrote them by email to explain the situation and requested that they present their faith and belief in the Bible as a personal choice rather than the absolute truth.

Since then, it had been better, but for me the whole topic felt like an elephant in the room. I still couldn't stand the idea that I had disappointed my parents, nor could I face the awkward conversations that would arise if I were more transparent. All the same, I could appreciate how much a place like the Cong Abbey would mean to them.

Perhaps there were some roadblocks in life that were meant to be circumvented without fully dismantling them.

We got back late, well after darkness had fallen, and while I unpacked from our day Paul played shadow puppets with the girls using the flashlight of his smartphone. Sleep would still be hard to come by, but we felt better knowing there was a big day of exploration behind us.

Travelling as a family of four was tough. I often found myself holding my breath or bracing for the next meltdown. I still wondered at times if it was worth all the uprooting, the packing, the long days, the changes, the constant adaptation. But these big days out made it worth the challenges. They also helped to open Maya's eyes to the greater world. Even those of us who loved to explore needed to be kicked out the door at times. Maya loved to explore, hike and see new things, but at the age of 6 she could also be perfectly content staying in the apartment and doing the things she loved to do at home. She needed to learn how to sail the shoreline and keep familiarity close while also keeping a distance. Because why would we go all the way to Ireland to watch *PAW Patrol* or play with magnets?

While Maya was missing school we had her keep a journal that she drew in each day and explained what she was seeing. No matter how deep our desire to open her eyes to the world, her interpretation of the day's events would often leave us dumbfounded. We could spend a full day out in a foreign country, walking through ancient castles and driving scenic coastlines, and she'd finish the day drawing a hot chocolate with marshmallows: her afternoon treat. In that way, travel with kids is like an investment. There were days I saw a great return, when my child verbalized her appreciation for what she was experiencing. And there were days I wondered if my investment was getting me anywhere at all. In the long term, I hoped it would.

While I planned more of the logistics, bookings, food and cultural experiences, I was grateful for Paul's enthusiasm in choosing many of our sightseeing objectives. As a landscape photographer, he had an eye out for the best photo opportunities, which were simultaneously the kinds of places our family would want to visit anyway. Over the years, mixing kids and photography on our travels had been another juggling act. His photography took a back seat if the kids were with us, and I admired him for never complaining about it. I made sure he had some days, and nights, to head out alone to get the images he was after, but it was far from productive. Sometimes he rubbernecked as we drove past something – like clouds drifting over the water – and I knew in his mind he wished he could stop. It pained me too. But most kids come with built-in timers. We had to choose when to stop and when to keep going, to minimize the waiting and time sitting in the car. Occasionally, we pulled over when he saw something he liked, or I took the kids for a walk so he could photograph. I didn't mind. It was our livelihood. Plus, having a photographer along meant we came home from trips with spectacular images.

As I finished unpacking from Cong, Paul got the girls into their pyjamas and ready for bed, even though it was wishful thinking that anyone would go to sleep at a normal time. We brushed our teeth and read a few books to simulate a bedtime routine, then piled into the beds. Perhaps the energy we'd spent on our day of exploring could help us catch up to the time zone.

As we drifted off, I listened to Léa sucking her thumb and imagined voices in Menlo Castle echoing off the walls, telling the stories of the people who lived there. I wondered what happened to them and where their descendants are now. I thought of where I've been, where I came from and what kind of life I was creating for my children.

Most of all, I thought of family – past, present, future – and the inextricable links between us all.

* * *

WE CHOSE THE NICEST DAY of our stay for a visit to Connemara National Park so that perhaps we could hike without cold and rain – a tall order for Ireland in November. But the sunniest day landed early in the trip, and we'd been having a rough time with Léa. She cried a lot those first few days. We didn't know what bug she'd picked up on the plane or what else was bothering her. Her usual spunk and sweetness had taken a back seat to her plight. Without words, she couldn't explain, so we guessed it was all the changes.

The day we'd planned to go to Connemara, she woke up with red swollen eyes oozing discharge, the telltale symptoms of pink eye. I wiped them gently with a wet cloth several times that day, being careful to wash my hands each time.

"I think we need to see a doctor," I said to Paul. "We only have ten days here. I don't want this to ruin our trip."

Paul agreed. "If we can get an appointment this morning, we could head out to Connemara afterward."

I sought out a doctor who worked weekends, knowing it might have been asking too much. But a quick Google search found one not too far from where we were staying. I called the number.

"Dr. Maire MacInerney speaking!" said the voice on the other side, her thick Irish accent tickling my ear.

I fell in love with Ireland again right there. Her name, complete with rolling "R's," made me chuckle with endearment for her. It just sounded so *Irish*. So did her voice. I had often wondered what I sounded like to others when I was travelling. Her accent made mine seem dull.

I explained our situation and asked if she took out-of-country patients.

"I've got an appointment this morning," she said. "Come on over at 9 o'clock!"

Dr. MacInerney could have been Léa's grandmother, complete with nursery rhymes playing on her computer and a nutcracker that stood in as a model for her stethoscope before she slid it under Léa's shirt.

"Oh, the little pet! Oh, the little pudding!" she said, empathizing with Léa as I described her symptoms. These two phrases have joined our repertoire of family inside jokes since.

Dr. MacInerney confirmed my suspicion and gave me a prescription to fill only if Léa's eyes didn't get better on their own. Her kindness and sincerity filled my tank like a few hours of sleep, and when we stepped out of her clinic we were ready to face another day.

After seeing the doctor, we loaded the car with every kind of layer, footwear and snacks we could think of and loaded the iPhone with podcasts for Maya. We didn't know how long we'd be.

The drive from Galway to Connemara takes you northwest and straight toward the Atlantic coast. The narrow highway weaves through villages and countryside, past small loughs (lakes) and farms before the conically shaped peaks of Connemara rise from the landscape and gradually grow larger as you approach the park. We briefly diverted from our course to drive the Sky Road, skirting the edges of a peninsula to gawk at the sparkling water of the Atlantic before turning back inland toward Letterfrack, the gateway village to the national park. We'd set our sights on the Diamond Hill Trail, a trail actually made up of two loops that meet in the middle, allowing hikers to walk only the lower portion or connect with the higher, more strenuous path to the summit. We departed around 2:30 p.m. for the two- to three-hour round-trip hike and brought our headlamps in case our late start meant we'd return after sunset.

Unlike our hiking back in Banff National Park, where trails begin by switchbacking through a few hundred metres of forest, in Connemara the far-reaching views began to unfold shortly after we set off. From the bottom we could see the peak of Diamond Hill, like a pimple compared to the snow-capped peaks back home, but it would give us a fine vantage point of our surroundings. It didn't take much elevation to gain views toward the ocean of the peninsulas that reached like tentacles into the sea. We hiked on a road, then boardwalks, then a staircase made of stone. Without complicated terrain to navigate, we could look outward and absorb the vistas.

Léa was on my back, and as our family had become accustomed, I hiked ahead so we could increase our potential of us all having the chance to complete the trek. I fed Léa airline pretzels while Paul hiked with Maya, luring her ahead with trail gummies. She didn't need much for incentive though. She was only 6 but so comfortable in the outdoors. The rocks were wet and slick at times, but I watched as she scampered up them fearlessly, barely out of breath as she walked and talked. She had a talent for endless chatter while she hiked, on all subject matter imaginable.

"Did you know paleontologists wrap dinosaur fossils in toilet paper? That the sun is the largest object in our solar system? And it can take a Venus flytrap over a week to digest big bugs!"

So while I walked with Léa, Maya's voice gave away her location never too far behind. I hiked in relative silence while Paul listened to science facts. Bless his heart.

The blue sky of daytime began to fade into the yellow haze of late afternoon. The sun reached down and warmed our faces and we never felt a drop of rain. I reached the summit only an hour after departing the trailhead, and knew from experience I should wait for Paul. Léa was in good spirits, especially when I let her free on the broad summit trail, so there wasn't a rush to get down. Paul would want to take photos and I wanted some of the family. The light was magical, with a gradient sky now blending to white near the horizon. I had so rarely hiked in view of the ocean, any ocean, and breathing in sea air from the top of a peak felt invigorating even as the warmth of the day began to dissipate.

When the other two arrived, we took time for our pictures. Paul photographed from the summit, while the rest of us stood on a lower shoulder of the peak where our bodies could be silhouetted against the silver sea.

An hour later we were on our way back down and I felt Léa's body go heavy.

"I'm going to plod on ahead," I said to Paul. It was our usual plan when Léa was napping on the trail.

"Enjoy the quiet," he said, alluding to the fact I would be leaving him on his own to absorb the bombardment of facts that accompanied Maya wherever she went.

"See you down there," I said, and picked up my pace.

Léa was now fast asleep, soothed by the constant rocking as I walked down Diamond Hill. The sky turned to purple and the horizon glowed yellow and orange. Then the sun set and we hiked through dusk, past brown grasses and rocks made darker as the light dissolved with the day. Maya and Paul were well behind me now, but I could see his headlamp lighting their way. Any hint of light then faded to darkness and I clicked my headlamp on too.

Apart from my footsteps and breathing, I had total silence. I had satisfaction. And contentment. The most I'd had in a very long time. I no longer felt the total entanglement I had on Rapa Nui, where I could barely see myself anymore. I simply didn't care as much about who I was and who I was not, about trying to appear like I had it all together. And I didn't care anymore about proving that I hadn't lost anything to motherhood. That shift had happened naturally; the illusion was like a canyon, eroded over time. Eventually, the water broke through and flowed where it was meant to. Some of it came to heart matters and learning what was actually important to me. And some of it was in my head. Because, thinking logically, you can't add two children to your life without moving something out.

And there on Connemara any hint of struggle faded away to an hour of peace, all to myself, as my daughter slept and I walked us down from the bliss of an afternoon spent up high. In a rare moment on that trip I was left to my own thoughts without chatter or crying or interruption.

I wondered if Léa, the youngest of our clan, thought about home. *Does she wonder if she'll ever return?* As an adult I found it was easier to accept or adapt to my circumstances the more "knowns" I had available to me. I *knew* travel was temporary, so I accepted the discomforts and adjustments because it was just for a few days or weeks. I *knew* that eventually I'd go home where I had all my belongings, my house, my usual routines. I tried to live in the present because, otherwise, I'd miss out on the trip I was actually on.

But Léa seemed to respond more to the immediate as if nothing else existed. Whatever was in front of her became a fixation, fear or joy. At her age, she was a master of living in the present. She adjusted quickly as long as her basic needs were met and we weren't throwing too many curveballs her way at once. We, her family, were the familiarity she required to feel secure. And perhaps those cheese puffs she loved so much.

I envied Léa for her ability to stay in the present. In Ireland our pace had slowed down, but at home our lives were hectic. The work/life balance had shifted wildly out of control in recent months and things were so busy it felt like even the good stuff was blowing by without me noticing. All the businesses were flourishing: the photography, writing and magazine. But with only 24 hours in the day and Léa home part-time, Paul and I were often in coping or coasting mode. We had a mutual respect and several years of juggling experience, which got us through the tougher times when we could have easily slid into arguments and misunderstandings. But our conversations were dominated by practicalities and logistics.

These opportunities to travel allowed us to create new memories and bond as a family. But they were also vital to our ability to recalibrate and deal with the pressures back home.

In Ireland Paul and I didn't get much time as a couple, but we took what we could get. In the evenings, when the kids were finally asleep, we took it as a chance to catch up on work. And as unromantic as it may have seemed to others, we loved those opportunities to work side by side on the couch. To us, this represented a dream come to life: the chance to work while abroad and see the world while also keeping the businesses running. There was love flowing between us, even if there wasn't much conversation. I knew we needed to make some changes back home to slow the pace of life, but for now we didn't talk about that. We could figure that out when we got back to Canada.

An hour later, we all reunited at the trailhead and tucked into a local pub for dinner before the drive back to Galway. Around the table sat four tired and happy faces. Old photographs, fishing nets and vintage nautical equipment clung to the walls, and lobster cages hung from the low ceilings.

Over fish and chips we recounted that sunset on Diamond Hill, the way the golden light shimmered in the low grasses and how the ocean looked purple and silver all at once.

∗ ∗ ∗

IN THE WEEK AHEAD we visited more castles. We drove winding roads along loughs, listened to hours of children's podcasts and laughed at how poorly we pronounced the road signs. We revisited our favourite restaurants, toured the Galway Christmas Market and bought new chapter books for Maya. We hiked to what felt like the end of the earth at Keem Bay on Achill Island and looked down the towering Cliffs of Moher.

I wasn't quite ready to leave Ireland when I realized our last day had come. Tomorrow, we would fly to Malta for yet another adventure. While Léa napped, Paul and I allowed Maya to watch a television show so we could review our flight information for our next stop. We were glad we took the time to look things over in advance. It turned out that Ryanair offered near-opposite allowances to most airlines we'd travelled with: less luggage in the cargo and more allocated to carry-ons. This made for a complicated packing job. We already had 30 pounds of camera gear to spread out between various backpacks so we could safely carry it on board instead of shoving it in with the cargo. Now we needed to pack even more of our belongings in our carry-on bags. As for the suitcases, I'd need to estimate their weight and hope we didn't need to repack them at the airport.

"Why don't I take the girls out to the coffee shop while you sort things out?" Paul offered as we stared at the mound of luggage.

"That would be great," I said. "Give me at least an hour and I should be good to go."

By taking the kids out of the equation, I'd be able to get the job done with fewer distractions, hopefully saving us from any delays at the airport. This would help me pack efficiently, but the truth was that taking Paul up on his offer to "divide and conquer" would also allow me to hit the reset button.

They left and, in the silence, I gathered my thoughts as I gathered our belongings. As I sorted through clothing, toiletries, games and camera gear, I rebooted my system for the next leg of our trip. I thought through logistics and calmed my worries about settling into yet another new place. Everything would turn out just fine, but it would be much more enjoyable if I could stay positive along the way. If I was tired *and* feeling scattered, I was prone to snapping or escalating things if Paul and I started to bicker. An hour of peace and quiet was enough to put me on the right track.

Just as I zipped up the last suitcase, my family walked through the door.

Before we left Ireland, I had one more thing I wanted to do. That evening, I walked with Maya down to the Aran Sweater Market in Galway, which is famous for its hand-knit wool products. Together, we wandered the colourful aisles in search of a blanket for our home.

After several minutes scanning the patterns and colours, a grey and blue blanket caught my eye.

"What do you think of this one?" I asked, holding it up for Maya to see. "I think it's perfect," she said.

I purchased the blanket and requested to have it shipped so we could reunite with it back in Canada. There was no way it was going to fit into the luggage I'd so intricately packed.

I rarely buy souvenirs apart from functional pieces that can be used around the house – objects I can associate with happy memories from our trips. And this one from Ireland, a place that saw us thrive while we travelled as a family, is one I would cherish for a long, long time.

13
The Big Picture

"One...two...three...THIS ONE!" I yelled.

Paul cranked the wheel left and we pulled onto a new road. This one was dark, with few streetlights. The pavement was uneven from construction and Paul used it as an excuse to drive more slowly. As Paul weaved around traffic cones, I recentred our location on my phone app. Zooming out, I identified the next traffic circle, 200 metres away, before zooming back in to identify which exit we needed to take next.

"What's coming up next?" Paul said. His voice was sharp, his hands clutching the steering wheel like it was about to fall off.

"We've got another circle coming up. It looks like it's the fourth exit, but I can't tell which roads are roads and which are alleys."

"Okay...say when." He readjusted his grip.

As we approached the traffic circle, I counted again. "One, two, three, four...wait, no. Shoot, that was it!"

If Ireland was a slow-paced exploration of a laid-back culture, with wet weather to match, Malta was like holding on to a merry-go-round going at record speeds where we couldn't speak the local language to tell the operator to *STOP*.

"Where am I going?" Paul asked, frustration leaking into his voice. I could sense the tension rising. The only times Paul and I really argued were in high-stress driving situations and this was one of them. I was an experienced navigator, but I had never seen such a convoluted map in all my life. So, while my sweet daughters slept in the back seat, I said an actual prayer for our safety and gave directions to Paul, who was already accustomed to driving on the "wrong" side of the road.

"Sorry, the map is so confusing! I'm doing my best," I said. I pinched the screen of my phone to zoom back in. "Okay, stay in this lane."

We rounded the circle one more time and found our exit. I was grateful it was well past midnight and there were few cars on the road. I couldn't imagine what this place was like when it was busy. An aerial view of the roads looked like someone was playing a joke. It would seem that, unless you knew *exactly* where you were going, you took a deep breath before each roundabout and hoped you came out unscathed. And forget reading the signs for directions. Maltese is an Arabic language that has evolved over centuries in the isolation of this Mediterranean island. It was not quickly learned, nor pronounced, nor recognized on a highway sign.

Our introduction to the island's more chaotic side struck us immediately after we left the airport. We'd flown straight from Dublin, landed at midnight and managed to find our car easily enough. According to Google, our hotel was just 35 minutes away. That is, until we took another wrong exit, and with no way to get back to the planned trajectory we added another 15, then 30, minutes to the drive. After a dozen wrong turns and course corrections, we arrived at our apart-hotel feeling like we'd just survived a hurricane.

It was some time around 3:00 a.m. when we were finally settled into our apartment on the sixth floor of the high-rise hotel on the Qawra coastline. Salty air rose up from the sea and indicated a hint of warmth despite a cool December wind. My eyes were dry and bloodshot from the long day of travel all the way from Galway. My sinuses were pulsing with pressure from an oncoming cold. I wanted nothing more than to close my eyes, crawl under the sheets and sleep the day's journey away. But we first needed bottled water from the front desk and to put the girls to bed.

After a short sleep, we arose with the sun, unpacked our belongings and ventured downstairs to take inventory of our surroundings. The lobby area featured a small coffee shop and WiFi. That would be helpful when Paul and I took turns working. But the hotel restaurant is not one we would be visiting much. Based on the continental breakfast, the food was mediocre – and expensive. Fortunately, several good restaurants could be found nearby, tucked away amidst high-rises and busy roads, an incomprehensible amount of them under construction. The newness of our surroundings was both exhilarating and disorienting.

Later, I walked out on my own to buy provisions from a small convenience store nearby and landed on a few staples: Nutella and bread, pasta and tomato sauce. We would figure out most of our meals later. Usually we liked to explore as a way of overcoming fatigue. But, despite the excitement of being somewhere new, Paul and I felt apprehensive about getting in the car. Our introduction to Maltese roads had frightened us. And, for now, we were drifting in a mental fog with the next wave of jet lag settling in.

We were, once again, on a small speck of land standing out from the sea. I felt a bit like Saint Paul, who once washed up on shore not far from where we were staying.

* * *

MALTA IS NOT JUST ANY speck of land. Over the course of time, its location between Europe and Africa has made it a strategic and sought-after naval base. Various layers of history – Phoenician, Greek, Arab and British, to name only a few – have piled up on its shores and forever shaped and reshaped the culture into what it is today. Yet its history of human habitation goes back much further, all the way back to the Stone Age. Archeologists have dated pottery to 5200 BC, and its likely habitation began centuries before that. Ġgantija temples on the Maltese island of Gozo are the world's second-oldest freestanding human-made religious structures, dating back more than 5,500 years.

Scan the present-day landscape of Malta as you drive the brief stretches of countryside between towns and you'll see the steeple of the local parish in the distance, often perched high on a hilltop. It's an apt representation of the dominance of Catholicism today, though the country hasn't always been a Christian state. And then there is the tale of Saint Paul being shipwrecked on "Melite" – believed by Biblical scholars to be Malta – in AD 60. Having learned about it in Sunday school, the child in me could relate to the Catholics' fascination with the incident and the traditions that have formed around it. Christianity permeates much of life on Malta, especially in its capital, Valletta, where various monuments, archways and the famous twin steeples of St. John's Co-Cathedral rise from a criss-crossing of streets and piazzas below.

We explored a number of sites on Malta, braving the roads lined with stacked rubble walls and prickly pear to run our hands through the sand of Golden Bay, hike the coastline to Għajn (pronounced Ahn) Tuffieħa Tower and take a cautious glance over the gaping hole of the Coral Lagoon. We'd be back in Qawra for dinner and usually ate out. We walked the promenade that stretched the coastline from just outside our hotel, grateful we were not sharing the road with cars as the girls skipped around us. We kept our eyes out for new restaurants to try. Seafood, pizza, pasta – Malta had it all.

* * *

"THERE ARE 45 BUS STOPS, Paul," I said.

"What?"

"I'm serious. There are 45 bus stops between here and Valletta." I pointed to my computer screen where I had pulled up the bus schedules. Paul sat down next to me on the sticky surface of the vinyl couch in our hotel living room.

"Geez. That's not gonna work," said Paul, shaking his head.

"No, it won't. It's going to be a disaster trying to hold Léa through all that."

"I agree. She's going to be a wreck and we'll be stuck on board."

It was out of the question to haul a car seat on board so we had somewhere to put her, less so for safety and more to avoid having a squirmy child in our arms. What would we do with the car seat once we got downtown?

"I really don't want to drive down there," Paul said, leaning back into the couch.

We'd been touring less populated parts of Malta and the roads were chaotic – to us, at least. It didn't matter how much experience we had driving on hectic roads all over the world. On Malta, locals knew how to navigate the roads. To us, the way downtown looked like a toddler had taken out a crayon and drawn the map freestyle. Driving anywhere near Valletta would be a nightmare.

"I really don't want to miss Valletta, though," I said. This was the first planned city in Europe, a UNESCO World Heritage Centre and a highlight of the Mediterranean. I had my heart set on seeing it. But if we wanted to get to Valletta with the kids, we were stuck between a rock and a hard place.

"If it was just the two of us, we could take the bus," Paul said. "But driving here with our two children in the back seat just feels so insane, borderline irresponsible."

"Hmm...I'll see if I can find any tips. Or maybe we can ask the front desk. A taxi would be expensive but might be the only way. At least the driver would know how to get us there without any issues."

I did some more research, deep diving into blogs catered to tourists wanting to see the capital.

"Actually, there's a Park and Ride outside Valletta," I said. "You can't actually drive downtown. This will let us park on the outskirts and get a shuttle in."

After more debating, we settled on that as the lesser of two evils.

The next morning we set off. Finding the Park and Ride turned out to be another jigsaw puzzle and reading the map was like reading another language. The locals drove fast and aggressively. We came uncomfortably close to hitting other cars when we needed to change lanes to make a turn.

I wasn't even driving but took deep breaths to stay calm. I could hear Paul muttering swear words in French.

"Can I listen to a podcast?" a sweet voice chirped from the back seat.

"Maya, now is not a good time," Paul said, trying to keep the frustration out of his voice. "We need you to be as quiet as possible so I can concentrate."

"Okay," she said with a kind of singsong. She was old enough to know this really wasn't a time to protest or complain. I couldn't turn around to see what Léa was up to, but she was being quiet.

"If we can't find it easily enough, I'm turning around," Paul said.

"We'll find it, babe. Just stay calm."

"It's hard to stay calm when I'm afraid of destroying this rental car! This is downright dangerous!"

It was true. I didn't blame him for being stressed. But I focused on keeping my voice composed and steady and to give as clear directions as I could. After many wrong turns and vocalized expletives, we were about to turn around when we found the Park and Ride by mistake. It turned out we also accidentally parked in the bus driver's parking lot. No one seemed to care, so we walked to the shuttle.

A kind local sitting on a park bench told us how the shuttles worked. *Thank you, sir.* Figuring things out on our own was tiresome, especially with kids battling for our attention. I didn't say it out loud, but I was worried about how we would manage the drive back to our hotel when our day of exploring was done. About 15 minutes later we boarded a shuttle that took only five minutes to reach the downtown core but saved our sanity.

We quickly forgot our troubles after stepping foot in the pedestrian-only areas of a city so photogenic, if it wasn't for keeping an eye on the kids, I'd be stopping every two seconds to take pictures. If Valletta were on mainland Europe, it would be one of the most famous, most visited cities in the world. Built on a peninsula, the

fortified city is laid out as a grid, sandwiched by two natural har-
bours. Architecturally, its buildings hail from mid-16th-century
baroque to an era of Modernism, with doorways painted in deep
blues and teals and trademark window bays hanging above narrow
cobblestone streets. Knowing I had just one day there, perhaps the
only day in my life I would ever see it, I soaked it in while mind-
ing the needs of the kids, who perhaps weren't as enchanted by the
opportunity to take a step back in history as I was.

As we approached St. John's Co-Cathedral, we decided it was
best if only Maya and I went inside. We'd no doubt be disturbing
the peace and sanctity of the place if we brought Léa in with us. So,
while Maya and I found our way to the entrance, Paul stayed outside
with the little one so she could run around and make all the noises
she wanted.

"Put these on," I whispered, handing Maya an earpiece of a head-
set we were given when we entered the church. I put one end into
my ear closest to her and huddled close to explore.

We plugged into the guided tour and walked along together,
stopping on signs indicated on the floor and listening to narration
about the 16th-century relic. At Maya's age she couldn't have fully
comprehended the meaning of it all. Neither did I, really. But I could
see it had left an imprint on her. She walked slowly, deliberately, her
eyes filled with wonder. The outside of the cathedral wasn't much
to remark, but inside we found one of the finest and best-preserved
(and restored) examples of baroque art and architecture. I didn't
know if Maya would be interested. Then I glanced upwards at the
ornamentation, every surface painted in colours and enhanced
with gold, every surface of even the supporting pillars covered with
detailed carvings. Maya's jaw dropped at the sight of it.

I hadn't grown up Catholic – my family's denomination was
Baptist – but I could feel the sanctity of the place. In my past I
might have felt a connection to the Divine here, but I had since
chosen to find the Divine in the wilderness, in connection, in my
own stillness. It struck me standing in St. John's with Maya, though,
how little she'd even been in churches when my childhood had been

so completely permeated by time spent at church – a second home. I didn't have any regrets about my choice not to raise her in a religion, but I longed to help her understand my past and to understand the beliefs of her extended family.

I was curious about something else too. In a way, I'd had the advantage of having defined boundaries and beliefs, and the awareness of what it was like to feel resistant to them. Would Maya understand what it means to be open-minded without a sense of what it's like to constrain one's thinking?

And when we stopped to listen to the stories of Caravaggio's *The Beheading of Saint John the Baptist*, time stood still. I had a flashback to Sunday school, of scripture, of church plays, and how sincerely I'd clung to Biblical stories, like John the Baptist's, like they were a lifeline. I still felt connected to those stories but now in the same way I reminisce about time spent with my cousins in Muskoka, or leafing through *National Geographic* magazines in my basement. The difference was that I didn't see that little girl in me anymore, the one who marked up her Bible with highlighter. Somewhere along the line, she had disappeared in the grey, messy, middle of things.

Maya and I continued to stand there looking up at Caravaggio's masterpiece, over 400 years after it was painted. The artist's exquisite use of light, or chiaroscuro, took my breath away as I considered each small stroke. I looked down at my 6-year-old, who seemed as enthralled as I was. And I thought: *Each stroke adds up to a painting. Each of our experiences in life adds up to a bigger picture too.*

Later, we exited the cathedral into the blinding sunlight of the day. Paul and Léa were running around the nearby piazza, scaring pigeons that were pecking at breadcrumbs on the ground. As we walked toward them, I asked Maya how she enjoyed the tour.

"You can look at that in a book, Mom, or you can see it in person," she responded. "I loved it."

There it was: Another brush stroke in her life. Perhaps one she'll look back on years or decades later and realize: *I was there.* Some of her childhood memories would stick with her, some would fade. I hoped our travels would stick.

* * *

QUIET. CALM. As we hiked along the top of the Ta' Ċenċ Cliffs near the town of Xlendi, on the Maltese island of Gozo, I had a thought. Walking in the sun and wind by the seaside, the water crashing into the base of the cliffs some 120 metres below, it was apparent from the smiles on our faces and the bounce in our steps that our family was in its happy place.

"Why don't we move over to Gozo for the last few days of the trip?" I said to Paul as we walked along the dirt path that paralleled the deep blue sea. Léa rode along in the soft carrier on my back, while Paul took Maya by the hand. The cliffs were stunning, but the drop was deadly.

The pace of the trip had changed the moment we took the ferry over to Gozo for a day trip. Valletta had left us feeling inspired but reeling with the stress that driving on Malta created for us. The drive back to our apartment had been as hair-raising as our search for the Park and Ride. Gozo, by comparison, was a stark contrast, with a slower tempo and less-developed coastline. I immediately felt at ease when we drove off the ferry after crossing from Malta.

"We could find an apartment right here in Xlendi," I said. I already loved the little village.

"I guess we could," Paul said. He took a few more steps before speaking again. "It feels like a lot of work to pack up our things and get them here, though."

"Yeah, but we could leave most of our stuff back in Qawra. Just bring what we need. We can return to Malta the night before the flights home to repack and get ourselves closer to the airport."

"It would be nice to spend more time on Gozo." Paul had planned to come back to Gozo to photograph on a separate trip while I stayed back on Malta with the kids. By relocating he wouldn't need to brave the chaotic roads and ferry ride after a night of astrophotography. I could spend time with the girls in a more pleasant environment.

"Do you remember how we felt on Rapa Nui when we wanted to change accommodations and couldn't?" I said. A laugh: "Or Dominica?"

Paul laughed too. "Oh gosh, Dominica."

"Well, here's our chance to end things on a good note."

"All right, babe," Paul said. "It's a great idea. Let's look into it when we get back to the car."

I did a quick check on prices when we got back to our rental car and saw that we could afford an apartment in Xlendi. I booked right then and there and emailed our plans to the apartment owner, an Italian who had also fallen in love with Gozo and moved to the island. It would mean taking the ferry back to Malta and driving to our hotel to repack before taking the ferry back to Gozo the next day.

We did it, and we had no regrets.

After we checked in to our new apartment, Paul took off for the rest of the day to take photos at Dwejra Bay, where the sunset illuminated small reflective pools carved out of karst stone sliding into the sea. I took joy knowing he was in his element as he scooted off in our rental car, finally free to do his "thing." Photography was more than a passion and paying the bills. Time away, doing what he loved, was therapy and a much-needed break from the constant barrage of children's needs. He would return feeling happier, lighter and ready to tackle whatever needed to be done. As did I, when he would tell me to go for a run or take my laptop to a cafe for a few hours of uninterrupted writing.

I had been on location with him enough to be able to imagine him at Dwejra Bay, bouncing effortlessly around the rocks as he sprang from location to location to find the composition that excited him most. Then he'd wait for the stars. He'd have that look of determination on his face as he scanned the scene, bent down low, swung side to side and changed angles to help him visualize his shot. He'd walk with purpose as if the clock was ticking, perhaps because he was feeling rushed, but also because he had the same walk doing chores around the house or cleaning the kitchen; time was always of the essence, and the faster he went, the more he could get done.

After I unpacked our bags, set up Léa's travel crib and put food into the refrigerator, I entered the living room area to find my two little girls sitting side by side on the couch, shoving orange pieces into each other's mouths.

I'd been co-parenting on the road for a few weeks now and had almost forgotten what it felt like when all was left on my shoulders. I had a lion's share of experience in solo-parenting to lean on from all of Paul's travels to lead photography workshops the previous six years, but I felt vulnerable as I scanned through my mental check-list of needs to avoid any crises in the near future. *When did they last eat a real meal? Léa should nap soon so she doesn't fall apart at dinner. Maya's got ants in her pants, so she'll need to get back outside soon.* I offered for Maya to play a computer puzzle game while I put Léa to bed. It didn't take long to put the toddler down and soon enough I was able to join Maya and help her unlock the mysteries of the virtual world she was exploring. Mommy/daughter time with her was hard to come by with a 1-year-old around.

An hour later, the baby woke up and I took the girls down to Xlendi Bay to watch the sunset. We strolled down the sloped road before exiting into a stairwell that marched down to a promenade below, following the sun's trajectory toward the water. As the sky turned from blue to mauve and pink, Maya played on the small boulders that lined the path, enjoying the freedom her 6 years war-ranted her without letting on she was proud I didn't need her to stay right by my side. As she scampered around, Léa and I waited below until the sun was about to dip below the horizon, where it would waver and swell as the earth swallowed it. I tried to keep one eye on Maya and one eye on the sun. Meanwhile, a woman walked by with her dog and Léa excitedly called, "Doggie! Doggie!" and begged to get out of the stroller. I was determined to see the sun set, to watch it dip into the sea until it had fully disappeared. And though I'd been trying to hang on to enjoy those sweet moments of bliss, to enjoy them for myself no matter what was happening around me, the noise was too distracting.

"Mom, I'm getting hungry!" Maya said.

"Doggie! Doggie!" Léa exclaimed, her legs swinging so hard she shook the stroller.

"All right," I said, exhaling. "Let's go."

As we left to walk to town, I stole one last glance of the sun as it bid its own farewell.

* * *

BIG DAYS OF EXPLORING often led to big meltdowns at bedtime. That was the trade-off for pushing the kids, both in terms of their energy and adaptability. They were like putty that could be moulded and morphed, but left out too long and they would begin to dry up, lose their softness and malleability. As we wrapped up our day, I expected things would begin to crumble.

It started with the toddler, who was so exhausted after dinner that she got into the "wired and tired" phase of the day. As I worked to unpack our bags and put items in the fridge, I heard her tearing up the place with unruly behaviour: dragging chairs across the floor, emptying drawers, screaming at random intervals. Meanwhile, Maya was on the couch, upset that her stuffed animal had a ripped seam. I knew I'd packed a small sewing kit, but I wouldn't be able to fix the stuffed animal until the baby was in bed. I could sense Maya was about to become flooded with emotion and knew I had a choice to make. Despite my frustration (*Can't she see I've got my hands full?*), I knew this was not the time for a "be a big girl" talk. As Léa whacked the concrete wall with a slotted spoon from the kitchen, I ran to the bathroom to retrieve the sewing kit from my toiletry bag – proof I *would* get to the task, just not right now. That seemed to calm things down, for the time being.

As I was filling the bath for the little one, who was already trying to climb in, I heard a voice from the living room, shouting over the running water: "How do chameleons change their colour?" Feeling exasperated, I offered for Maya to watch a show on the iPad while I bathed her sister. She lit up with an obvious yes and tucked away to her bed. *PAW Patrol*, of all things, is what *she* needed to recalibrate: a little taste of home in a strange Gozitan apartment. Léa moved on to banging the couch cushion with a ladle and I took the opportunity to thread a needle to quickly sew up the seam that had torn open on the multicoloured stuffed poodle (aptly named "Rainbow"). *I wish someone could see this happening right now*, I thought, laughing at myself – sort of. And then I was reminded of how many times this played over in households everywhere; parents pulling out all the stops to bring a sense of comfort and stability to their children. It's the littlest of things that often make the biggest difference.

With Rainbow in hand, I went into Maya's room and the baby scurried by with her latest implement of choice from the kitchen. I was feeling pretty proud of myself as I tossed the dog toward Maya, positive I'd see a smile that her beloved travel companion was no longer oozing cotton. She didn't even look up, prompting me to pause the iPad and point out my handiwork. This was one hero moment I was not letting go unnoticed.

The toddler was in the bath for all of two minutes when she took a step a bit too far back onto the slanted side of the tub and – *swoosh* – went sliding into the water. Though it was shallow, and I was there to scoop her out of the water straight away, the surprise gave her a shock and she burst into tears. The bath, which often bought me at least 15 minutes of peace, was suddenly over and so my attention turned to getting that baby into bed as quickly as possible. I made a deal with Maya: while I put the baby to bed, she could have her bath and brush her teeth and then watch one more *PAW Patrol* while she waited for me to read with her. I'd cut her show short, but she was excited to wash the day's grime away.

"I have no idea how long this will take," I said as I slipped into the bedroom to start what was hopefully a quick process.

Forty-five minutes later I emerged. One down, one to go.

I took a deep cleansing breath before opening the door to the room Maya and Paul were sharing. Two twin beds sat side by side, separated by a small table with a lamp, and Maya was tucked into one of them, reading her chapter book. *My sweet girl*. All the struggles of an hour ago melted away as I gazed upon this sweet child reading quietly in bed, just as she was told to.

"I'll read the first four pages of this chapter and then you read the next four," she suggested. *Eight more pages and then I'm almost done with my parenting duties for today.*

"That sounds great," I said as I slid into the bed next to her, and we took our turns reading.

When we finished, I closed the book and returned it to the bedside table. I could tell that Maya was calm and in a good headspace to listen. Those moments of focus and calm were fleeting, so I knew from experience it was a good time to have meaningful conversation.

"I'm so proud of you," I told her. "The way you tackle each day of our trip. You're always up for an adventure no matter where we take you. Even those crazy roads back on Malta. I didn't travel abroad until I was 16. It's a privilege to travel. And it's really brave of you."

"Mom, I was born ready to be adventurous," she said.

"The older you get, the more we can do," I continued. "And travelling with you is so much fun because of all the exploring we've done together."

She looked into my eyes with her brown eyes, wide as saucers.

"These are the things you can't learn in a classroom," I said. "Watching you soak up everything around you, and getting excited at the things we're seeing…it really means a lot to me. Because we wouldn't want to come all the way here and stay in our apartment and do the things we can do back in Banff."

As we spoke, I took a mental picture of the moment. These heartfelt conversations with Maya, free from distraction, were so rare. I was so aware of it that I stayed a little bit longer, even though I was beyond ready for both kids to be sleeping. We chit-chatted a bit more about our trip before I finally told her it was bedtime. She didn't resist but got a twinkle in her eye as I was sliding out the door.

"Do you think the tooth fairy gives euros or dollars?" she asked.

And suddenly I realized my motherly duties were not over. She'd lost a tooth in the middle of the night on Malta and, though the occasion had slid off my radar, I wouldn't have been surprised if she'd been thinking about it all day.

"We'll have to wait and see," I told her, hoping I had coins of *any* currency somewhere in my purse.

"Does the tooth fairy take the tooth?" I asked her, fishing around for what she might be expecting.

"I don't know," she said, pulling the thin blanket up to her chin. "But you could ask her."

I went along with her. "Yes, I can ask her."

Maya explained how she'd strategically place the tooth under the right-hand side of the pillow and sleep on the left, so she wouldn't crush the tooth fairy when she crawled under it to put the money there.

I kissed her goodnight, closed the door as I left and hoped she would fall asleep swiftly. Now it was a matter of waiting for her to go to sleep so I could slip the money under her pillow.

Back in the kitchen, I hopped on my laptop for a few minutes to edit a magazine article I couldn't ever seem to finish. I was just a few keystrokes into it when I heard a door open. *That was wishful thinking.* I knew there was usually at least one interruption. I took a deep breath to quell the frustration rising within me.

A moment later, Maya was standing in the hallway, blanket in hand.

"What is it, Maya?" I said. Another deep exhale.

"Mom, I've decided. Please don't talk to the tooth fairy," she said.

"You mean you don't want me to ask her if she usually takes the tooth?" I asked.

"Yes. I just want to see what she does."

And in that moment it hit me that she really, truly believed. *Still.* This kid who could solve math equations I couldn't wrap my mind around and read interpretive panels at the museums we were visiting – she was a world traveller with an understanding beyond her years, but she was also just a 6-year-old. Being in Malta or at home made no difference. In her mind, the tooth fairy would find her.

She scampered back to bed. I returned to the kitchen, where I began to rummage through my handbag. I found one euro and two 50-cent coins. Jackpot. I walked out the patio doors and onto the porch overlooking Xlendi Bay. As I rubbed the coins between my fingers, I waited for the apartment to fall into the quiet that only came with two children sleeping. Of total peace and quiet. Of the sign that said, "Your day as 'Mom' is over." Stars twinkled in a dark sky over the bay and I thought of Paul again, out there in his element. *I bet he's stoked to have clear skies.*

A while later, I had finished editing my document and the apartment was silent. I checked on Maya and she was fast asleep, her mouth gently open, revealing the gap where the tiny tooth was once lodged. I fished around under the pillow for the tooth, sliding my hand around as carefully as possible so as not to wake her and ruin the surprise. I couldn't find it. It turned out the tooth fairy *doesn't* take the tooth, in the end. I slid three coins underneath, turned to leave and gently closed the door behind me.

Tomorrow we'd continue our adventures. We'd visit the Gozitan salt pans and the ancient Ġgantija temples. We'd feed the ducks in Xlendi Bay and find the best gelato. But tonight it was childhood as usual. Just a kid, fast asleep, with a tooth tucked somewhere under her pillow.

* * *

OUR LAST BIG DAY OF ADVENTURES on Gozo went seamlessly. It felt like I had been transported back to my pre-kid life. It was a little slice of heaven amidst the wrangling, entertaining and foraging for constant snacks.

And when our day concluded with a sunset at Dwejra Bay, it felt like we'd reached a new milestone as a family. I thought my heart might burst. No one was sacrificing enjoyment or happiness to be there. Tomorrow, we would be getting on a ferry back to Malta, and from there we'd begin the long, long trek home. But for now, we were watching the sun set off the bay. *I* was watching the sun set off the bay. It reflected in the tide pools while mirror images of pink and orange clouds intensified in colour. The salty breeze blew past us, and I stared at the glowing faces of my two girls, their mouths rimmed with hints of ice cream. Paul held Léa up like a tiny airplane and their dark figures cast an adorable silhouette against the sky: father, daughter in a moment of trust, standing on what felt like the edge of the world.

The moment was so sweet I could taste it. I didn't want it to end.

When the sky began to fade to shades of lavender, we walked back to the car. Maya reached out her hand to cross a pool of water and I reflected on how instinctively she'd reached out to me. I was a trusted presence for her and one she assumed she could turn to. But in a deeper sense it reminded me that, amidst all my own way-finding and navigating through life, people can be waypoints too. Constellations. GPS coordinates. I've had many such waypoints in my life, and often they weren't a constant, like a person who came in for a time just when I needed them to help me take the next step.

And so, too, I am that guide for my daughters. While they are young, I am both leading them off the beaten track and guiding them down a bumpy trail. In their eyes, I am the constellations, I am their North Star. I am the wind moving through the landscape pointing the way. I am paddling the canoe safely downstream. I am looking for distant clues that might inform the best way forward.

I am the lighthouse standing in the night, shining a light across the sea, showing my daughters there is a safe way back to shore.

14
The Meaning of Home

CANADA, WINTER-SUMMER 2020

The year 2020 didn't start off with a bang. For me, it started as a tired transition into something new. I had already resolved, prior to the new year, to change what wasn't working in my life. Our trip to Ireland and Malta had confirmed for me that our lives were too hectic. It was mostly good stuff – growing children and growing businesses that were asking more of us each day. But what used to be periods of high-intensity output became a daily experience. And we hit the ground running – no, sprinting – after some massive transit days from Malta through Dublin. We kept the balls in the air on little sleep, rising at 3:00 a.m. with the jet-lagged toddler, later packing a lunch for Maya and sending her off to school, then dividing our days watching Léa when she wasn't at the dayhome. After a week, my adrenals were shot. I woke up one morning and my face had swelled and broken out in blisters – an inflammatory response that would put me on prednisone for a few days. Paul was in better shape physically, but not mentally.

"I don't know what to do," I said to Paul. Tears poured down my cheeks and stung my broken skin. Léa played on the floor of the living room between us, seemingly unaware of what was happening.

"Well, we can't keep doing this," he said. "This isn't living."

It was clear our ability to cope, whether Paul was working abroad or with us in Banff, hinged on how much childcare we could rely on to help us shoulder the load. We didn't have enough of it. I'd previously enjoyed the option of having Maya in part-time care when she was little, but now our lives were 200 times busier. I had been holding onto the idea that I could manage the balance and keep Léa at home a few days a week. The idea of her being in full-time care when she was only 18 months old was a hard pill for me to swallow. It felt like putting a little bird in a cage. And, as her mother, I wanted to be with her. But now I had many more responsibilities weighting the other end of the scale, and it had clearly tipped over.

"I really think we need to start her at the daycare," Paul said.

"I know, I know," I responded, though I still didn't want it. "I'm having a hard time wrapping my mind around it, even though I'm tired of being so strung out all the time trying to make things work."

"But that's just it. This arrangement isn't working. Something's got to give."

Paul spoke with care but also concern. It was clear from my speckled, blotchy, swollen face that I was not in a good place. If I hadn't come to the decision for myself to put Léa in daycare, I think he might have forced me.

"Okay, babe. I'll email the daycare and see where things are at," I said.

The local daycare got back to us straight away. They had a spot opening up in just a few weeks, on February 1.

With that, Paul and I declared that 2020 was the year of "changing what wasn't working." We'd get help with the kids. I could work without leaving a hundred loose ends when my limited work time was up. I could go for a run or sit with a cup of tea, knowing I wasn't sacrificing precious hours. I could make dinner without the laptop open beside me, interrupting my stirring or sautéing to peck away at the keyboard. I could be a better mother and wife because I'd be taking better care of myself.

Paul flew to Iceland for a photo workshop just as Léa started at the daycare. The transition was rocky, with each day starting and ending with Léa in tears. I pushed through my guilt and kept with the routine, hoping she'd soon become more comfortable. By the time Paul had returned three weeks later, things were better; she was finally settling in. And as we peeked around the corner into March, we could see Léa settling into her new environment and our lives returning to a better place. We could even envision a day where we'd drop off the kids and head out for a hike, just the two of us.

I felt like I could breathe again.

So it was with confidence that I faced yet another stretch of solo parenting as Paul was heading back to Easter Island in the last half of March and then to Bhutan in May for more photography workshops. And so it was also with total shock that, in a matter of days, the world, as we knew it, fell apart.

* * *

THE SITUATION IN BHUTAN was the first glimmer that COVID-19 would have a direct impact on our lives in Canada. On March 6, the country announced it would close its borders for two weeks when the first case of the virus was confirmed in the landlocked kingdom. For a few days we considered the possibility that the workshop would still go ahead. But then more and more travel advisories began to surface, first as preventative measures to control the spread of the virus. Soon it was obvious we needed to pull the plug on Easter Island. Our plans for Bhutan followed suit.

Days after Bhutan announced its border closures, we flew in by helicopter to Assiniboine Lodge in nearby British Columbia for an annual backcountry family trip hosted by the proprietors, who had become our friends over the years. For four days, we enjoyed complete disconnection and were largely unaware of what was transpiring in the world. While Paul took photographs for the lodge, I watched the kids and even enjoyed a few hours of quiet reading while Léa napped. It was a stark contrast to my life back home, even in normal times. But the juxtaposition of that blissful state of ignorance in the wilderness and the onslaught of virus-related media, travel restrictions and warnings we returned to will stand as one of the most bizarre experiences of my life.

There was not yet a hint that "social distancing" or "sheltering at home" would be imposed as a measure in Canada. But shortly after we returned to Banff the government began to discourage Canadians from travelling for spring break. It later urged Canadians who were abroad to come home. On March 11, the day we returned home from Assiniboine, the World Health Organization declared COVID-19 a global pandemic. Four days later, the Government of Alberta announced that our schools and daycares would be closed indefinitely. We knew we had made the right call on Easter Island when Chile closed its borders.

And, just like that, within five weeks of starting our "new normal" as a family we were assuming another "new normal" that wasn't normal *at all.*

The changes came quickly, but not all at once. Likewise, the tone of our daily conversations as a couple morphed according to our acceptance of the situation at hand. It began with a trace of panic underlying an adrenaline-fuelled plan that would help us cope with the daily output required to keep our businesses running with two children at home, full-time. In a single broad stroke we wiped our calendar clean of any engagements, travel plans, conferences and events. The schedule was empty, yet life was busier than ever. We gradually adapted and settled into a daily rhythm of taking turns as much as possible: getting up with the kids in the morning, taking care of them for half the day, working for the rest and splitting duties around the house and with bedtime. Thinking beyond the next day, let alone the next hour, was futile. Life as we knew it had screeched to a halt.

If we didn't pivot early and put pieces into place to keep businesses afloat, we risked losing everything we had worked so hard for. So we moved some of Paul's teaching to the web through mentorships, one-on-one critiques and an online community. I began to teach writing and marketing courses online. We plodded away at long-term projects, like books and other passive income. We filled two assistant positions with hopes that their contributions would help propel us forward in this new world.

We didn't want to stop to consider all of the uncertainties, but they were there: *Would we be able to afford our mortgage? Would all of our hard work of growing our businesses be compromised? Which parts of our pre-pandemic world would exist in the post-pandemic version? Would any of our own loved ones succumb to the virus?* And knowing it wasn't just us — that the whole world was living off the beaten track — made us lose track of all sense of orientation.

In the backdrop of our own stressful situation at home, the once bustling, thriving tourist town of Banff faced a devastating situation, as all businesses were shuttered and the national parks were closed to the public. By mid-April 2020, the town had only three cases of COVID-19, which had all been contained (the town would later become a hotspot). Yet 85 per cent of Banff residents lost their employment in a two-week span that spring, and many close personal contacts feared they would lose their businesses. We were living in a town created to welcome people from all over the world, and for months we were imploring people *not* to come. The police set up checkpoints at the town entrances on weekends to prevent any unnecessary visits. Without tourists, the local economy shrivelled and disintegrated before our eyes.

On one of my weekly grocery runs, I stood on Banff Avenue on a Saturday morning, at a time of day that the town usually burst to life with activity. This time, I was alone. Without the constant hum of vehicle traffic, intermittent birdsong filled the air, as did the call of a loon on the Bow River 300 metres away. For several minutes, not a single car rolled down the strip. The sidewalks, normally filled with so many people that locals use the back alleys, had been deserted. The shops were closed.

The peacefulness was both beautiful and dispiriting. The silence, deafening.

* * *

THE FIRST 12 WEEKS OF LOCKDOWN were some of the hardest through the entire pandemic, largely because of the degree of unknowns we were dealing with. It felt like running a marathon for 84 days in a row until we found some help with the kids and the daycare reopened. We didn't yet know what was in store for us, that we'd live for another year, maybe more, with ever-changing restrictions, closures, health orders and rules that would prevent us from hugging our loved ones. Yet if ever there was a silver lining it was being "stuck" in one of the best places on the planet during the pandemic: Banff. Even while the mountain parks were closed to activities, my walks or runs still took me past a glacier-fed river, with mountains standing out against blue sky and sunshine. I could cycle to scenic viewpoints without the added stress of sharing the road with vehicles.

For us, "home" used to mean Banff in general: our house, the town, the national park. When we were flying back from abroad, I didn't think of home as the roof I lived under but rather the natural spaces and wilderness that surrounded it. During COVID-19, "home" actually meant our small plot of land, the physical house standing upon it and the sidewalk out front where our girls could safely ride scooters. This home was one we'd purchased only a year before, when our creative ventures had grown to such a sustainable point that we could spend our savings and take on the mortgage debt. For weeks, the mountains stood around us, unfazed by what was transpiring with the pandemic both in our neighbourhood and around the globe. The trees swayed with the wind, but not the daily news that sent us on a roller coaster, asking questions that had no concrete answers. Having no sense of when the ride would end was the hardest part of all.

But if there is something that travel and adventure had taught me it was that all of life is uncertain. I could try to take comfort in my daily routine, my job and the other things I hold dear, perhaps taking for granted the idea they would always be there for me. Paul and I were accustomed to dealing with the unknowns and discomforts of adventure travel, or even the uncertainties that come with being self-employed creative people. Yet we had also fallen into the trap of thinking we had *anything* we could fully rely on. Without the ability to travel or access to the mountain parks, we were in uncharted territory. Still, the overriding feeling I got when facing COVID-19 was an amplified version of the way I'd felt venturing into the Arctic Circle, waking up for the first time in Kathmandu or when Paul came rushing through the doors on Mo'orea with Maya in his arms. Each day we were in lockdown, I woke up and breathed through the uncertainty. Sometimes I woke up and simply cried. Sometimes it was Paul's turn to feel total despair. We held onto each other and to the hope we'd get used to what was happening. That *this too shall pass*.

Resilience is an incredible thing to witness. I remember our massive travel days, like flying Calgary to Los Angeles to Santiago, then onward to Easter Island. Or the time we miscalculated our distances and Maya pounded out 12 kilometres on the way to Healy Creek. I saw how deep she could dig when I gave her the chance to do it. Had we decided it would all be too much, had we decided not to push her for fear of asking too much of her, we never would have seen just how resilient she was. Nor would she have witnessed that resilience in herself.

COVID-19 was an opportunity to draw from the resiliency bank. It required us to tackle the challenges head-on, every day. One day at a time. I leaned into the coping mechanisms we'd developed as a family during our travels abroad. There were many times we had been forced out of our comfort zones, away from friends and familiarity. Now we just needed to incorporate those learnings in the most unlikely of places: home.

We'd ventured into a foreign land without leaving our own.

"Seeing our lives reduced to the four walls of our homes is enough to confirm for me that life is too short to waste it with *what ifs*," I said to Paul one night. We often worked until 9:00 p.m. before relaxing with a television show. "Honestly, had we waited until our children were old enough, I don't think we would have incorporated travel or even outdoor experiences into our family life. We might have lost that chance for a very long time. Maybe forever."

"It hasn't been easy," he said. "We've worked so hard to get to this point. But I'm glad we did. I'm glad we have memories to look back on." Paul shook his head, bewildered. "It's crazy to think how quickly everything was taken away."

Had we looked at the logistical challenges of hauling a family of four to South America or Europe and decided it was too much to handle, we wouldn't have created these foundational experiences for our family. Had we decided that a creative career was too unpredictable and financially risky, or entailed too much work to build into something fruitful, we might not have been making a living doing something that brought us such joy and fulfillment.

"We'll hit the ground running when this is all over," Paul said.

I nodded. During those months of aggressive social distancing, of cancelling trips, of seeing hopes and dreams slip through our fingers, I felt grateful for our choice to take life by the reins when we had the option to, no matter how hectic it looked or felt. Now faced with the reality it might be years before we stepped onto foreign soil as a family, I looked back with fondness at the memories we had created together. I felt fortunate to have had the chance to travel at all. And I knew deep down that if I ever got the chance to do it again, I wouldn't take it for granted.

* * *

THREE MONTHS into the COVID-19 lockdowns, I returned to writing as a form of therapy. It was the one thing I depended on as solely *mine* between contract work for other companies, including Paul's photo business, and dishing out endless snacks to hungry children. Writing had always been my way of making sense of the world. It let me tap into my ever-questioning nature. So I spent precious hours with my fingers on the keyboard and let my mind drift off to recollection of our travels, digging deeper for the finer details, the learnings, the memories that stayed with me, imprinted on my life like stamps on a suitcase.

In the process of writing, I returned to my memories of Ireland and my stroll down Lower Salthill Road, past Wards Hotel, and to our visit to Menlo Castle where I had wondered about my ancestors. On a whim, I emailed my aunt who had previously looked into our family genealogy. Within a day I had eight emails with digitized items she had on hand, only a small portion of the research that had already been conducted. It was enough to get me started. What began as a slight interest quickly snowballed into a fascination that frequently kept me up past midnight. My well-honed web research skills proved to be an asset as I unlocked more of my family's past and sifted through census reports and marriage certificates, cemetery listings and old photographs. As a Euro-Canadian, I had the fortunate access of a recorded ancestry that went back for many centuries, though it came my way as a massive puzzle with some missing pieces. I joined a website called My Heritage and quickly began to grow my family tree to better organize everything I was learning. I texted questions to my mother, who told me to email her sister. I emailed my dad's cousin, who had already traced a portion of the Ward family line. Within a week my tiny tree had grown and my personal intrigue with my family's past became an obsession.

The driving question in the beginning was to figure out for how long my ancestors had lived on this land we now call Canada. It was a starting point, a mechanism for prying open the entire box of discoveries that would follow. In essence, I was asking a question as existential as it was practical: *How did I get here*? In many ways, my existence seemed random as I thought back to all the factors, circumstances, serendipitous moments and relationships required to end up with my even being born. It was mind-boggling. That context gave me all the more reason to want to make the most of this short life of mine.

It didn't take long to decipher that in most of my family lines it was a great-grandfather or great-great-grandfather who emigrated to Canadian soil from various parts of England, either alone or with his family. But I followed some branches up the family tree, back and back and back through eight or more generations. And there

I found an individual whose story had been more thoroughly documented – a story that resonated with me at this exceptional time in my life.

His name was Johann Heinrich Buchner.

* * *

IT WAS IN THE COMMUNITY OF UNNAU in the Westerwaldkreis region of Prussia (present-day Germany) that Johann Heinrich "Henry" Buchner was born on December 10, 1734. He was one of nine siblings and the youngest born to Johann Martin and Elizabeth Maria Buchner in a family line that had called the Westerwaldkreis region home for generations.

In 1753, a 19-year-old Henry boarded a ship called the *Rowand* near the seaport town of Cowes, England. I am unsure what prompted his interest in leaving his homeland, but he boarded the boat with several other Buchners destined for the American colonies. Today, one can fly from Amsterdam to Philadelphia in half a day. Back then the journey took up to half a year.

We know from other accounts just how brutal the voyage across the ocean could be. Gottlieb Mittelberger crossed the Atlantic to Pennsylvania in 1750, where he worked as a schoolmaster and organist. He returned to Germany four years later, apparently to discourage others from making the trip, with its perils and hardships both on the boat and in life on the other side of the pond. He had sailed to the colonies with a ship filled with poorer immigrants who faced a bleak future as indentured servants.

"There is on board these ships terrible misery, stench, fumes, horror," Mittelberger wrote in *Journey to Pennsylvania*.[1] "The misery reaches the climax when a gale rages for two or three nights and

---

1 The full description can be found in Gottlieb Mittelberger's *Journey to Pennsylvania in the Year 1750 and Return to Germany in the Year 1754*. The section I referenced came from an excerpt posted online by Vancouver Island University. However, numerous reprints exist, including one published in 2018 by Forgotten Books (forgottenbooks.com).

days, so that every one believes that the ship will go to the bottom with all human beings on board."

Mittelberger also described the fighting and frustration amongst the healthy, the suffering of mothers who were confined with their children and the hundreds of bodies – men, women, children – that were thrown overboard when they succumbed to disease. We can't know precisely what Henry's journey entailed, but he likely encountered some of the same discomforts, illnesses and traumas captured in Mittelberger's account. I could hardly fathom what it would take to endure that kind of voyage.

Henry arrived at the Port of Philadelphia on September 29, 1753. Shortly thereafter, he and the other Buchners settled in Amwell, Sussex County, New Jersey. He had numerous children with his wife, Ana Eva Maria Dell, whom he married in 1768. Henry, along with other Buchners, became a Loyalist supporter[2] in the American Revolution in the 1770s and was imprisoned and fined for backing Captain James Moody, a well-known British Loyalist volunteer. The Buchners were stripped of their property and resettled further south in Oldwick, New Jersey.

When the American Revolution ended in 1783, the British had lost the war (and their 13 colonies) and many Loyalists faced resentment and rejection within their communities. Upper Canada became a haven for those fleeing persecution and seeking the security of British law and order. It was also settled to prevent the Americans from expanding northward. In 1784, Henry's younger brother Matthias was the first to relocate his family to Upper Canada. Henry followed suit two years later, trekking with his entire family for 800 gruelling kilometres on foot. His clan included nine children, with the two youngest reportedly balanced in baskets hanging over the backside of a pack horse. They settled in the Crowland Township of

---

2   German colonists were quite divided during the American Revolution and supported both the Patriot and Loyalist causes. It's unclear to me why the Buchners sided with the Loyalists.

Welland,[3] just south of the Welland River in present-day Ontario. Using Google Maps, I was able to find the Buchner land based on historic maps from 1795 and 1862. Today, it's the Rolling Meadows Golf and Country Club, surrounded by farmland.

My great-great-great-great-great-great-great-grandfather, Henry Buchner, and his brother, were some of the first of my direct ancestors, that I knew of, to set foot in Canada. They set down their roots on land that, as it turns out, is only a five-hour drive from the house where I grew up.

* * *

MY FAMILY LINE continued through Henry's granddaughter, Martha. My ancestors remained in various parts of Ontario for another three generations. It was my great-grandparents, Winnifred Evelyn Harris and her husband, Percy Wallace Carter, who moved to Winnipeg. There, my grandmother was born, and so was my father, and it's where he later met my mother.

For most of my life, I had traced my family roots back to Winnipeg because that was all I knew. I realize now how short-sighted that was – like looking at a Caravaggio painting from a centimetre away.

Henry Buchner's story represented only one of hundreds. His was a single branch on a family tree that reached higher the more thoroughly I looked. Yet it also provided the perspective I needed to find my way back to shore. The storm of the pandemic had raged on for months, but slowly, surely, stars began to appear in the sky.

---

3 According to Native-Lands.ca, Welland is in the traditional territory of the Attiwonderonk, Anishinabewaki, Haudenosaunee and the Missisaugas. The 1763 Royal Proclamation (which directed how British colonies should be administered) dictated that Indigenous land needed to be purchased prior to any resettlement, and this could only be done so by the Crown. In 1784, the Mississaugas of the Credit First Nation ceded 3,000,000 acres of traditional land to the Crown, including the land the Buchners settled on. In return for this land, they received £1180 worth of trade goods. In 1792, actual land boundaries were better defined and the Mississaugas signed a treaty with the Crown.

A glimmer of normalcy. Another restriction lifted. A meal at a restaurant. Bike rides with friends. Childcare resuming.

My research told me that Henry had endured the unimaginable. He traversed a sea in appalling conditions with no knowledge of what the other side held in store for him. He struggled through war for a country that wasn't his own. He led his family on an epic journey to Upper Canada, guided by a blind faith that he'd be able to make something out of nothing.

He recreated his life again and again.

Henry's story reminded me that there *is* an after. That the *during* was tough, excruciating at times, but we would get through it. And on the other end of the pandemic, we could recreate our lives. We could make them what we wanted them to be, see what would rise out of the ashes and let the "things that weren't working" lie where they fell.

We had a lot to be grateful for, including a fridge full of food, a roof over our heads, businesses that were still flourishing and a back porch that looked out on a spruce forest and the mountains that encircled the town. And among the good things to come out of COVID-19, we'd made our house a *home*.

* * *

THOSE FIRST FEW MONTHS of pandemic living had nearly broken us. And what we did not know was just how much longer we'd be in it, that for another year we'd be living with more uncertainty, unimaginable disappointments and mental stress we weren't sure we could bear. We would not lose any of our loved ones to the virus itself, but we would see many people struggling, see vitality diminished in nearly everyone. My business partner and I decided to shut down the magazine and I sold my shares in the media company. Paul and I were continually adjusting to a new life at home, to being together nearly every day and to equally dividing parenting duties as long as the world was on pause. For Paul, losing his opportunity to make his livelihood and pursue his passions through international travel was like losing his sight. It was frustrating for me too, but less of a shift in routine.

To manage our mental health, Paul and I spent as much time as we could in nature – by ourselves, with friends, as a family or on a date just the two of us. Fresh air had always soothed our souls, and now we were aware of how it acted as medicine for our broken hearts and tired bodies. We needed it more than ever, and were grateful to have wild spaces so close to home. Paul also coped with the unknowns by planning trips that might not happen. Every month I would get a summary of his research – emails labelled "COVID Escape Plan" or "Revenge Trip" that would slide into my inbox around 2:00 a.m. I coped by doing yoga, going for walks and reading fiction. I also started to write in a journal again, mostly leaning into the timely teachings of various authors: how to set boundaries, how to stop people pleasing, how to let go of relationships and commitments that were no longer serving me. The pandemic had given me a narrower lens with which to view my life and choose what was actually important.

For another year we didn't have the ability to plan (confidently), to gather, to travel, to pursue the experiences we cherished most, to live our best lives. And we were some of the fortunate ones who had entered into the pandemic from a place of privilege, who could pivot to ensure our primary creative enterprises survived, who had a comfortable home to live in and who had a supportive co-parent to help shoulder the load.

* * *

THE SUMMER OF 2020 felt almost as normal as any year. Virus case numbers were low and, apart from a mandatory mask bylaw in town and some capacity restrictions, we could roam freely, drive throughout the park, head into the backcountry and hike every chance we got. On a cool, moody day in late August, we decided it was time to visit Bow Lake with the girls. We'd both been back numerous times, even stayed at Num-Ti-Jah Lodge with Maya when we had friends running the place. Each time it was like a pilgrimage. A coming home. Each time I went back I'd visit my favourite spots – the rock beach, the abandoned corral – and feel emotion swelling up inside me. There is nowhere else on the planet that gives me the same sensation. It is an instantaneous reaction to the power of a single place.

This was the place that changed my life. This was where I chose to change my life.

As I walked with my two girls down the road toward the corral, I recognized just how much my life had continued to change since that first summer I spent at the lodge. My Num-Ti-Jah experience encapsulated what my life looked like free of entanglements, of expectations – mainly ones I had for myself. I allowed myself to be moulded into something new, and that decision forever changed the way I looked at the world.

Life was no longer as simple as putting on my gift shop uniform and selling magnets to tourists, then heading out on a hike. But the life I had stepped into allowed me to explore the world and myself more freely. When I allowed myself to evolve, even if it meant moving away from the comfort of the familiar, my experiences in life became richer, deeper, truer. I was no longer weighing each new choice against what I felt I was expected to do. My inner world and outer world had become more harmonious and the possibilities endless. And for all my searching and wayfinding, I had come back home to *me*.

The good girl in me wished I could be more honest with my family about my beliefs – be accepted fully, no matter what. Perhaps those conversations would come. Yet I chose to hold on to something wonderful, something so abundantly clear: that they hadn't stood in the way of my chosen path – the life I had built, the man I had married, the woman I was. Their support might not have been explicit, but it was there. Any shame I felt was mine to let go of. Not only for me but for my children. It didn't matter anymore what they thought of me. *I* needed to accept who I was.

I strolled past some fireweed, showcasing purple-pink petals. Come autumn, the flowers would dry and detach; the leaves would transform into vibrant reds and oranges. A thought crossed my mind: perhaps now my loved ones actually expected me to do the unexpected.

I watched as the girls scurried toward the old corral, Léa zigzagging across the empty road yelling, "I go!" I hoped above all else that they, too, would embrace a life of their own creation. Inevitably, that meant that one day I'd need to step off the path, relinquish my desire to guide them and let them wander for themselves into the great unknown. Would I be able to keep an open mind about where their journeys took them? About which version of themselves they encountered at the other end?

Maybe they'd choose the mountain life, maybe not. No matter what path they chose, I at least hoped they'd retain the lesson that "off the beaten track" looked different for everyone. I would need to embrace that for myself when they stepped off the path I had blazed.

As we approached the corral, I slowed my pace. Returning here with our children reminded me how fleeting life can be. Our girls were growing up quickly. That summer, my life was less busy than it had been years before, but I wanted to be a better observer, to be more present to those around me. Pandemic or not, I wondered: *How can I take that sense of wonderment I feel while I'm on an adventure and inject it into my daily life? How can I make magic out of the mundane and live life to the fullest, no matter where our family might be?*

I still dreamed of travelling, of exploring and seeing what was around the next corner. But I also saw value in stillness, looking at the little things, learning to be content with what was right in front of me. I reflected back to my hike back down Diamond Hill in Ireland, about Léa and how, at her age, she was only concerned with the very present. How I found it easier to adapt or accept my circumstances the more "knowns" I had available to me. But now the pandemic had taught me to live each day more fully, to keep the unknowns on the periphery. On one hand, I had feelings of gratitude that seemed that much sweeter amidst all the disappointments and hardships of the pandemic. On the other, I refused to accept my circumstances as a valiant act of hopefulness. My mantra became: Keep expectations low, hopes high.

We approached a large clearing where the skeleton of the corral was still standing: some fences, the gate, a hitching post. In the distance, more peaks – my old friends – showed their faces. Mountains we'd climbed by daylight, moonlight and under dancing aurora. But the old Corral cabin, as we called it, and the Tack Shack, were no longer standing. The Corral lay on the ground, dismantled, like a pile of bones. In the place of the Tack Shack there was an empty space. The undergrowth had taken over quickly, mostly with grasses and dandelions, but I could still see the dirt where the cabin had packed it down. I stood on it and breathed deeply, remembering, then wandered over to inspect the remains of the Corral.

While I sifted through planks of wood, Maya remained where the Tack Shack once stood. After a few minutes, she suddenly exclaimed, "I found something sitting in the grass!"

Indeed she had. We all wandered over to look at her discovery. Undoubtedly, it was an old piece of the Tack Shack, a small fragment of wood with red paint chipping off one side of it. To almost anyone else it would be garbage. For Paul and me, it was a treasure.

We took it home with us that day and I perched it on the frame of a picture of the Tack Shack that hangs on the wall in our room.

It is now my reminder that life goes on and it will *always* be full of surprises. I may have more experiences ahead that will change the course of my life as dramatically as they did at Bow Lake. The pandemic was proving to be one such experience. But life is too short to cling to what I know myself to be. Whatever happens, I have permission to reinvent myself, again and again.

I can choose a path less travelled, knowing it will eventually lead me *somewhere*. And when I feel lost, I can close my eyes and see the stars. I can track the waypoints, feel the wind and find my way back home.

Epilogue

Light was dancing on the tent when I opened my eyes, casting shadows of tree branches and speckles of sunshine across the rainfly. The world was quiet, except for the birdsong, revealing something other than me was awake in this forest. It took me a moment to realize what that meant: that not only had I slept in but my entire family was still snoozing.

I checked my watch. Seven o'clock! These days, Léa had been rising early, sometimes at 5:00 a.m. She usually announced her presence by gently placing a clammy hand on my shoulder to wake me. A few seconds later, she'd be chatting and scampering around the room and either Paul or I would usher her back to her room to rest a little bit longer.

This morning, I sat up, careful not to rustle my sleeping mat too loudly. I turned my head toward Léa, who was cocooned in her sleeping bag at the other end of the tent. Paul lay between us. Her tiny nostrils flared from just below the brim of a knit cap that was pulled over her eyes. The temperatures had dropped overnight and her sleeping bag was pulled right up to her chin. I listened more closely and heard her nose whistling as she breathed in and out. Beside me, Maya was out cold, mouth open. I looked to the other side and could tell from Paul's expressionless face that he, too, was in a deep slumber.

I lay back down with my head on my pillow and felt the corners of my lips lifting into a smile. *What just happened?* Only yesterday Paul left the campsite with Léa at 5:30 a.m. so she wouldn't wake up the rest of the family – or the campers nearby. They drove back to Banff, where he found breakfast at a coffee shop and even dropped by the house to pass the time.

This was the advantage of staying close to home for our two-day trial camping trip with all four of us out at Two Jack Lake. It gave us the option to bail, if needed. So far, we hadn't needed it. Apart from the early start, Léa had largely passed the test – the real benchmark being that we *actually* enjoyed ourselves. It had not been total rainbows and sunshine, but we were still here, right?

This morning, it was my turn to get up with the kids and I felt like I had won the lottery. After a deep sleep in the cool mountain air, I felt rested – more rested than I had in weeks. More than that, it was around this age that with Maya we had given up on camping, at least for a few years. The success of this night meant we had reached a new milestone. I had plenty to be smiling about.

* * *

I HAD NOW BEEN A MOTHER for eight years and had learned not to make a big deal of any one, particularly challenging, phase. I had seen how quickly children changed, sometimes within a few hours. Yet, despite my previous experience, going through the boundary-pushing, independence-seeking phase that Léa was in at age 3 felt like it was still a test of my strength and patience.

When we first arrived at Two Jack, two days before, I could tell Léa felt insecure. She wasn't sure what to expect or what was expected of her. We had camped with her when she was a baby, but she didn't remember that anymore. As we unpacked the car, she wandered off into the forest, which impeded our progress in setting up our campsite. I could see her attempting to hide behind a skinny lodgepole pine about 15 metres away – her black and white striped dress gave her away.

"Léa, that's too far! We need to be able to see you, sweetie!" I called.

She looked out, her round eyes and long lashes staring back at me with a look that told me she was thinking about her next move. She darted to the next tree.

"Léa, come closer, please."

"Nnnnno!" said the voice from behind the tree.

"It's not safe to be alone in the forest," I said. There had been a sow and three cubs roaming the campground and I wasn't about to let her out of my sight. "Once we're set up, we can make some hot chocolate!"

That got her attention. She sauntered toward me, dragging her feet. I didn't take my eyes off her until she was a few metres away.

"Here's a bucket," I said, pulling it out from the bag of sand toys we planned to bring to Johnson Lake the next day. "Why don't you pick up some pine cones?"

She perked up at that idea and ran toward me. "Okay, Mama!"

It was an activity that would last five minutes, but it gave me enough time to set up our camp kitchen.

Once the site was set up, Maya curled up in a camp chair to read a book and it struck me as I prepared our dinner just how little she needed from me now. All those years of struggle with her spiritedness felt like a distant memory. She'd grown so tall she barely had room to sit with her legs perched up on the camp chair. She was reading chapter books now and sparkled with a keenness to learn. She reminded me of me at that age. But with Léa in the mix, we had wound the clock back and re-entered the young years that made me feel like I had prematurely aged. Where Maya had been spirited, Léa had sass. For the rest of that day, it felt like Léa was going against our flow and our desire to relax at the campsite. She whined and cried when she didn't get what she wanted. Away from our campfire the mosquitoes were bad, but off she wandered, out into the woods, and Paul and I took our turns wrangling her.

Later, she wouldn't settle in the tent when it was time for her to go to sleep. I tried for an hour and was about to give up when Paul said, "I'll give it a try."

"Sure," I said, "but I feel like it's a lost cause."

He must have had the magic touch because half an hour later the tent was quiet. The only sounds around me were the crackling fire and Maya turning her pages. I heard the tent unzip and out came Paul. He looked at me, astonished, and shrugged with a silent, "We'll see how this goes."

The next day I asked Paul if he could put her to bed again. Bingo.

* * *

BESIDE ME, Paul suddenly took a deep breath. I had picked up a book and was enjoying some quiet reading but promptly laid it across my torso to look at him. He blinked his eyes open and took in the silence. Then he turned toward Léa and her tiny flaring nostrils before looking back at me, his eyebrows raised in disbelief.

I grinned at him as if to say, "I know!" Paul, content not to be driving to town this morning to keep a noisy kid from disrupting the campground, closed his eyes to squeeze in a few more precious minutes of sleep.

Stillness descended once more and I was left with my thoughts. I had learned to take these rare occasions of quiet to contemplate and reflect. And for the first time in over a year, I felt like I could also *dream* again. The pandemic was still wreaking havoc and, just a few months before, we had returned to severe restrictions and weeks with the girls home when the school or daycare was closed. But by July, with the vaccine rollout and numbers falling once more, we were feeling like a return to "normalcy" was within reach. The idea of travelling abroad and resuming the photography workshops was becoming more promising each day. I was feeling cautiously optimistic that, by the end of the year, our lives might resemble the pre-pandemic version, at least to some degree.

Planning a trip was painful knowing that new restrictions or travel bans might be enforced again at a moment's notice. Yet Paul and I were starting to toss some destinations around; we wanted to be ready when we finally got the green light. Costa Rica came up. I was excited about the prospect of introducing my family to this country that had been so transformative for me all those years ago. We discussed the prospect of going to Eastern Europe, maybe back to the Caribbean. By this point in the pandemic, I was happy to be going *anywhere*.

Staying close to home, anchored to the same environment nearly every day, had given me the opportunity to do some deep soul-searching. I had redefined my boundaries so I could live more purposefully with positive influences in my life, and live more in the present moment. In recent weeks, however, I felt a deep longing rising within me, an impulse to get out of my bubble, to see the world again. Of course, it wasn't as simple as buying a plane ticket, not while the whole world was still figuring out how to manage the virus and roll out vaccines.

But would anything ever feel certain again? In the future, pursuing our passions might require us to make decisions that seemed risky to others. What were we willing to put on the line to live the life of our dreams? To leave the shore amid swirling clouds and white-capped waves?

At this moment, I didn't have any answers. As I watched the sun creep higher and felt our tent grow warmer with each passing minute, I landed on the truth of this longing rising within me: I was ready, more than ready, to head back out to sea.

* * *

"HAVE WE GOT IT ALL?" Paul asked. We scanned the campsite to make sure we hadn't left any tent pegs or garbage behind.

"Yes, I think that's it!" I said.

I looked over at Léa, who had hunkered down in a camp chair and stuffed her dollies, blankets and books so tightly around her she couldn't have stood up if she wanted to. I smiled with a sigh as I took in the sight of her, sitting alone under a tree. I hadn't realized until this moment that the whole time we had been packing she was sitting there, sucking her thumb, watching the fire from a distance.

In fact, the whole morning after her sleep-in, she'd been mellow at the campsite. It would seem she had found our flow, slid into our slipstream. Instead of scurrying off into the woods, she engaged with the process. She found sticks for the fire and helped me stir the hot chocolate. She looked for ants and collected pine cones. And, at some point along the way, she found her camp chair and settled in.

"Léa, sweetie, it's time to go," I said.

"I don't want to go," she said, twisting her doll's hair around her fingers.

"The car is all packed up and we need to leave now. See?" I pointed to Paul pouring water over the firepit. "Daddy is putting out the fire too."

"But, Mama, I like camping!" Her bottom lip curled down. "I'm not leaving!"

"I love that you love camping," I said. "We'll come again, I promise!"

Reluctantly, she began to remove objects from her chair. I helped her get out of it, then lifted her up. Together, we scanned the campsite one more time before I clipped her into her car seat. Maya and Paul were already in the car waiting. And as I loaded her dolls and blankets and books into the car, it struck me just how quickly she'd learned to settle in to camp life – that in a matter of hours she had adapted to something new.

When we drove off, I looked back at our campsite in the rearview mirror. It was as though we were never there. The tents were gone. The picnic table was bare. The fire had been extinguished. Yet the memories we created there burned brightly within me.

As we turned onto the main road, back toward Banff, the mountains stretched out before us. I looked out the window to the deep blue sky of a summer morning. Then I turned my head and found my children in the back seat, their cheeks streaked with dirt. They smiled at me and in that moment I knew the memories were burning in them too.

ACKNOWLEDGEMENTS

I first started to type the sentences of this book, some of which made it to the final manuscript, while sitting on the beach on Motu Tiapaa in French Polynesia. That was in April 2014. Since then, I've been on a journey with this book that has taken me to places I never imagined. I have many people to thank for being waypoints along the way.

The team at Rocky Mountain Books has been steadfastly supportive. A special thanks to Don Gorman, for officially setting me off on this journey, and to Jillian van der Geest, Chyla Cardinal, Grace Gorman, Kirsten Craven and Lara Minja for your parts in bringing this book to life.

A component of Chapter 7 was first published in the anthology *You Won't Remember This: Travel with Babies* (Flamingo Rover, 2016), and was rewritten for this book. Editor Sandy Bennett-Haber was gracious to include me in such a wonderful group of writers.

Thank you to my fellow adventurers featured in this book for the wonderful memories and for graciously agreeing to have me tell my version of our trips together: Rachel Slater, David Paynter, Adam Zier-Vogel, Carolyn Withey, Dee and Anthony Larosa and Doug and Karen Urquhart.

I set off on this journey without much by way of a writing community. Just as I've met people on my travels that seemed to come in my life at just the right time, some key people have played a role in the development of my writing career and this book. Drs. Jennifer Stephenson and Natalie Rewa at Queen's University planted the idea that maybe writing was in my future. Erik Lambert helped me to lift that anchor and set sail early in my writing career. A special thank you to Bruce Kirkby, Jim Davidson and Lynn Martel for your support and encouragement over the years. To Sonya Lea, Emily Gindlesparger and the Scribe Tell Your Story community, thank you for standing in your own stories and encouraging me to do the same. To Ryan Correy and Carlyle Norman, my kindred spirits in all things writing who no longer walk this planet, thank you for your inspiration.

Writing can be a lonely venture, especially when you head out onto the open water. In addition to my writing community, my beta readers helped me point the compass when I wasn't sure which direction to go. An enormous thanks to Trixie Pacis, SE Quinn, Tyler Dixon and Sky England for using your valuable time to read early drafts and give me your feedback. The book wouldn't be the same without you asking me to go deeper.

Some acknowledgements can't be easily categorized, but each of these people provided me with support and guidance that has been invaluable to me. Thank you to R. Robert Mutrie and the Niagara Settlers website, which provided me with a starting point for my research into the Buchner family origins; to Evelyn Ward de Roo for walking with me on this journey in a way no one else could; to the online community of outdoor adventurers and parents who inspire me to keep exploring and expanding; to Jeff Hemstreet and Riaz Mohammed for making me feel like I was seen and heard; to the many creatives and entrepreneurs, particularly Dave Brosha, Erin Boyle and Dee Larosa, with whom I've collaborated on meaningful projects and business ventures; to Sithara Fernando for her insights into matters of privilege and cultural sensitivity; to Caroline Van Hemert for contributing her words to the front of the book; and, finally, to Claire Gagnon, Jacques Zizka and Étienne Zizka for your loving support.

Jim Risk, you put the compass in my hand, both literally and figuratively, when I didn't know that the guidance you were providing would shape me forever. Between your OAC Creative Writing class and various years taking Outdoor Education, I built the foundation of my eventual career. And I can still hear your voice calling to me from the sidelines of the rugby field – another avenue that proved to me I could really take the bull by the horns when I wanted to. Thank you for being such a positive force during those formative years.

It's not lost on me that the land I set off from was that of a stable, loving household and a family that has been supportive as I've meandered my way off the beaten track. To my parents, Doug and Meredith Ward, and my sisters, Lydia Brown and Laura Lee, just knowing you are there has been like a beacon in the dark, even if I was sailing away from it sometimes. Thank you for letting me drift and explore. I love you all, as I do your families: Kevin Brown, Peter John Lee and all my nephews.

To Léa Claire and Mistaya (Maya) Joy: I don't think I'll ever have words to express how much I love you and how much it means to me that I get to share these adventures with you. Thank you for teaching me in your own special way. I certainly appreciate things more when you're around me, encouraging me to slow down and look at things through your eyes.

The first gift you ever gave me, Paul Zizka, was Ben Gadd's *Handbook of the Canadian Rockies*. In it, you wrote: "To a girl who understands and feels the passion those mountains can create." You saw this in me before I did. As a fellow adventurer, creative collaborator and one of my early beta readers, you have been on many aspects of this journey with me. I am beyond grateful to have found a partner – in life, creativity, business and parenting – and someone who supports me, inspires me and ignites my own adventurous spirit. I can't wait to see where our journeys take us from here.

SELECT READING

The navigational and wayfinding references throughout this book were inspired by a number of sources. The research is, in itself, fascinating and what I included in this book is only a drop in the ocean. These are the texts I leaned on most heavily.

Aporta, Claudio. "Inuit Orienting: Traveling Along Familiar Horizons." *Sensory Studies.* https://www.sensorystudies.org/inuit-orienting-traveling-along-familiar-horizons/.

Lewis, David. *We, the Navigators: The Ancient Art of Landfinding in the Pacific.* 2nd Edition. Honolulu: University of Hawaii Press, 1994.

O'Connor, M.R. *Wayfinding: The Science and Mystery of How Humans Navigate the World.* New York: St. Martin's Press, 2019.

Pike, Dag. *The History of Navigation.* South Yorkshire, England: Pen and Sword Maritime, 2018.

ABOUT THE AUTHOR

Meghan J. Ward is an outdoor, travel and adventure writer based in Banff, Canada. A Fellow of the Royal Canadian Geographical Society, Meghan has written several books, as well as content for anthologies, films, travel agencies and some of North America's top outdoor, fitness and adventure publications. She and her husband Paul Zizka love to explore the wilderness and the world together, and take their two daughters along for the ride whenever they can.

meghanjoyward.com
Instagram: @meghanjward